THE
TEN ROADS
TO
RICHES

FISHER INVESTMENTS PRESS

Fisher Investments Press brings the research, analysis, and market intelligence of Fisher Investments' research team, headed by CEO and *New York Times* best-selling author Ken Fisher, to all investors. The Press will cover a range of investing and market-related topics for a wide audience—from novices to enthusiasts to professionals.

Books by Ken Fisher

The Ten Roads to Riches
The Only Three Questions That Count
100 Minds That Made the Market
The Wall Street Waltz
Super Stocks

Fisher Investments Series

Own The World
Aaron Anderson

Fisher Investments On Series

Fisher Investments on Energy
Fisher Investments on Materials

FISHER
INVESTMENTS
PRESS

THE
TEN ROADS
TO
RICHES

THE WAYS THE WEALTHY
GOT THERE
(AND HOW YOU CAN TOO!)

KEN FISHER
WITH LARA HOFFMANS

WILEY

John Wiley & Sons, Inc.

For general information on our other products and services or for technical support, please contact our Customer Care Department within the United States at (800) 762-2974, outside the United States at (317) 572-3993 or fax (317) 572-4002.

Wiley also publishes its books in a variety of electronic formats. Some content that appears in print may not be available in electronic books. For more information about Wiley products, visit our web site at www.wiley.com.

ISBN-13 978-0-470-28536-7

Printed in the United States of America

10 9 8 7 6 5 4 3 2 1

CONTENTS

PREFACE

WHY TEN ROADS?

Before reading this book further, please read this preface.

Wouldn't it be wonderful if everyone were rich and no one poor? If poverty didn't exist? If the only wealth disparities were whether she had $20 million, he had $7 million, and another one had $7 billion? Feel free to disagree, but I don't see much merit in poverty. Sadly, I can't see poverty being eliminated in your lifetime or mine. Still, I believe you can do your little part toward that goal by making yourself wealthy in a way that creates wealth for society as well. If you get yourself rich in one of a handful of appropriate ways, you make the world a better place. Others benefit as you get rich, as you will read later. I, for one, would like you to do that.

But how? Well, that's what this book is about. There are really only ten ways to get rich. This book details them and shows you the good and bad qualities of each so you can pick among them and decide which is right for you. Then, the book teaches and guides you on the basics of each.

It's true not everyone can become rich. But it's clear to me that most people can—they just don't know how. If more people knew how, we would have more rich people and the world would be a better place. I'm asking you to read this book and then do your part.

Now, if you know me from past books or my long-running *Forbes* "Portfolio Strategy" column, you may not know I'm a roads scholar. Not a Rhodes Scholar who got money to study at Oxford, but the more important kind—that studies the various roads leading to financial success and failure.

It started as a kid in the 1950s, dreaming of becoming a professional baseball catcher and simply adoring Yogi Berra who famously said, "When you come to a fork in the road, take it." For decades I've kept a large version of that quote on a note board within three feet of me at my desk, collaged with photos and notes of people that are and have been important to me. Takes decades of wisdom to get life down that simply. Pretty much sums up how to get super wealthy, once you understand the roads.

Berra later decried most all his most famous Yogisms. He claimed this particular quote was simply driving directions to his home, and when you got to the fork it didn't matter which way you went because they reconnected later and either fork got you there. If so, it's kind of a Zen-like statement about continuing—like the command, "Further"—and we can use that too. But growing up I assumed Berra's was a comment about making quick, fundamental, timely decisions without great road signs. Maybe I was wrong all this time. But I still prefer my interpretation of the great American Yogi. In life there are roads leading to riches and roads not. There's nothing wrong with ones that don't, but if you travel them you'll go where they take you. Don't be surprised.

To methodically get rich there are only ten basic roads. Find one making sense for you, get to that fork in the road, take it, and stick to it. But ten roads can be confusing. Ten! Hence the need for this book. Reading it may not make you a roads scholar, but you'll know enough to get the rest of the way down your chosen road (or roads) on your own.

One point: If you've read any of my prior books, this isn't like them. They were largely about capital markets, primarily stocks and bonds. That is my main background as founder and CEO of a global money management firm running over $45 billion in stock and bond money for institutions and wealthy individuals. But this isn't a capital markets book at all. It's a detailed micro and macro inspection of how very wealthy people get that way—and how you can too!

Why ten roads? Why not five? Or 100? It's just the observation of this roads scholar from studying wealthy people all my 36-year investment career. I've got over 25,000 wealthy clients I've studied carefully—some for decades. As a 24-year *Forbes* columnist I've studied and written about the annual *Forbes* 400 list of richest Americans for decades—and been on it and the *Forbes* global billionaire list myself since 2005—and know people on both lists in and out of America, and interacted with many more very wealthy people. From all my observation, I can tell you they all fit into ten basic categories.

But this book isn't about "what most rich folks have in common." There are plenty of those books and they're perfectly fine. They're usually about one road—"live frugal and save." Like *The Millionaire Next Door, Rich Dad Poor Dad, The Automatic Millionaire*, on and on. They tell stories from a traditional American Calvinist, Christian background—about down-to-earth, frugal folks with a great work ethic who own gas stations and trailer parks and sock away a few million. Or your typical, middle-class, modest homeowner in a modest neighborhood driving a modest, used car, working 70-hour weeks, saving and investing well. These books admonish you to be like them. That's a fine road, to be sure. It's the most common way people get wealthy, though it doesn't generate the biggest fortunes. I call it "The Road More Traveled," and it's this book's last chapter. It's a perfectly valid road—the preferred road for many and the only for some. While fine, it's just one road and generally not how the mega-rich did it. The richest can be frugal or not—it doesn't much matter because they create so much wealth mastering one of the other nine roads. Frugality is a virtue but isn't necessary to becoming super wealthy, as you'll see.

A ROADMAP TO THE TEN ROADS

No one tells you how to get mega-rich—which is why you need this book. But you may not want to be mega-rich. Well, the good news is the same roadmap to these ten roads applies if you want to be worth $3 million, $10 million, or $300 million.

One convenient feature—this book is modular—one chapter for each road. You needn't read them in order if you don't want. If you want, after this preface, skip to the middle of the book—doesn't matter where. Start a chapter. If you decide that road isn't for you, skip to another one more suitable. Throughout the book I reference the other roads—as in, "No, that isn't this road, that's that road in Chapter 9"—sometimes earlier in the book and sometimes later. Think of it like a collection of ten little mini-books.

Now, all these roads aren't for everyone. Can't be! But at least one is right for everyone who wants to be wealthy. What are these roads? To acquire big wealth, you can:

1. Start a successful business—the richest road!
2. Become CEO of an existing firm and juice it—a very mechanical function.
3. Hitch to a successful visionary's wagon and ride along—it's high value-added.
4. Turn celebrity into wealth—or wealth into celebrity and then more wealth!
5. Marry well—really, really well.
6. Steal it, legally—no guns necessary!
7. Capitalize on other people's money (OPM)—where most of the mega-rich are.
8. Invent an endless future revenue stream—even if you're not an inventor!
9. Trump the land barons by monetizing unrealized real estate wealth!
10. Go down the Road More Traveled—save hard, invest well—forever!

Follow one of these ten roads. Or a combination. We'll see some people who went down one road successfully and switched to another. For example, become CEO of a firm you didn't start (Chapter 2), build it up, sell it off, and use the proceeds to start your own firm, which ends up even more successful (Chapter 1). Or be a media mogul (Chapter 4) and a successful CEO. Some people do two roads at once. I'm a founder and CEO of a firm (Chapter 1), but it's a firm capitalizing on other people's money (Chapter 7). If you can do two at once it's faster. Harder, but faster. But most wealthy folks travel one road their whole lives. That works. It's more than enough.

Warning: Some Parts May Be Offensive to Some People!

You may see some roads as ill-advised, squawking, "That's ridiculous. Starting your own business is too risky." Or, "Who'd want to own real estate today? It's a bubble." Others may say, "That's both terrible and tacky! You shouldn't suggest everyone marry for

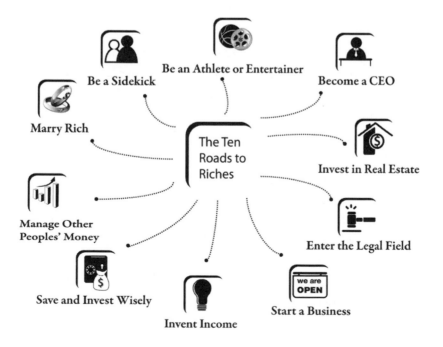

money like **Anna Nicole Smith** or **John Kerry**." I'm not suggesting any of that. Or, if you disagree with me and don't think you should be rich, that's fine with me, too—totally up to you—not my business that you get rich or how. Life has many rewarding roads not about wealth. You should find that right path for you, whether it's about money or not.

Note: I guarantee some roads, or parts of some roads, may offend you—and will definitely offend some people. There will be offended Amazon.com reviewers decrying what they see as the terribly offensive things I suggest people do. Why? I don't know—but since forever, people getting rich in certain ways have always been offensive to some other people. But that's ok—again, ten roads. Every one of these roads is valid for someone—although offensive to someone else and that someone else may be you. Sorry! Don't shoot the messenger.

If a particular chapter seems frivolous or offensive, that's not your road. Read through or skip it—up to you. My intent in writing this book is not to offend. For example, I talk about myself in several of the chapters as an example, because I have a lot of first-hand information about me. Some of you may think me talking about me is offensive. I'm just trying to show you the roads and not trying to offend. If you get steamed up while reading, have a glass of wine, take a walk, kick the dog, do whatever you do—and then come back and start in on another chapter.

And of course, there are some who simply find the whole concept of "getting rich" offensive. If that's you, I have no further advice for you and you won't like the book for obvious reasons.

Actually, becoming rich usually means doing good (as you will see) and often living an exciting life. Where would humans be today had Bob Noyce not co-invented the integrated circuit? He chose a path to riches and benefited the world immensely—rich, poor, in between, everyone. We'll see that beneficent effect repeatedly in people who changed the world for the better, doing good, getting rich, and enjoying their lives. That's a beyond-great thing for everyone. And feels great to those who do it.

The good news is—and few will tell you this—making $30 million or so in your lifetime isn't that hard. Example: Build a not-so huge business (Chapter 1) that in 10 years grows to $15 million in revenue. If it has a 10 percent profit margin, you have $1.5 million in profits. If it's worth 20 times earnings—not extraordinary—there's your $30 million. After a few years, you'll know if your firm is further scalable or not—if it can grow much larger. If so, you could be very wealthy. If not, sell, collect $30 million, and go be happy. Or maybe start something else. Or retire! Up to you.

Is it impossible? No! Is it trivial? No—but if you fail, you can start over. Start young enough and you have maybe three to five stabs at it. If you fail, you can try being an entrepreneur again or try another road. Nine more!

WHAT IS RICH ANYWAY?

Well, what does "rich" mean to you? A million? Five million? Fifty? Ten billion? What's plenty to some falls far short for others. An example: A married couple, two schoolteachers, makes $60,000 a year. One spouse works part time and stays home with their two kids. A modest lifestyle, but they fully fund their IRAs each year and invest wisely. At 65, they conceivably could have $4 million saved. Or more, if they take advantage of their school's 403(b). That $4 million, if managed well, could kick off $160,000 in annual income after taxes and inflation (distributions of 4 percent). That couple may feel rich—their income increased over two and a half times in retirement. If your income increased over two and a half times, you might feel rich, too.

Conversely, a surgeon makes $600,000 a year with a big house, new cars, annual face lifts for his wife, expensive vacations, and a high-society lifestyle. He believes he can afford it. Why not? It's his money. When he retires, he's socked away $4 million too. But will *he* feel rich on $160,000 a year? No—it's a mere 27 percent of what he used to make. Four million makes some feel rich, others poverty-stricken. "Rich" is relative—truly in the eyes of the portfolio holder.

What can we know about being rich? Well, generally wealth must last longer than it used to because people live longer. Our surgeon may be 60 with a 45-year-old trophy wife. He may live 20 more years and she may live another 55—until she's 100. Their $4 million must cover her life. A few excess inflation hiccups along her 55 years and that $4 million may make her feel a lot more pinched and very unrich.

It used to be a millionaire was considered rich. That's pretty much never true now. Financial planners will tell you to withdraw no more than about 4 percent per year from your assets, depending on circumstances. For some, much less. But a millionaire taking 4 percent with 30 years to live would be getting below median income where I live, near pricey San Francisco. Not poverty—but not rich. So it still comes back to you deciding what's rich for you. Feeling rich is being rich.

Yet if you think of these roads correctly, it's possible to simply forget all that because you can create so much more wealth that issues of what is or isn't enough can simply fade away. As you read, you'll see examples of people creating mega-wealth that makes frugality become unimportant by any standard. It's just a matter of making one of the roads that leads to big wealth work for you.

CELEBRITY OR NO?

This book isn't about celebrities—though I use many famous people as examples of success (and sometimes failure). The book is about the roads, not the people. Basically there are two types of celebrities. One got famous and subsequently rich from the celebrity. For example, boxer George Foreman retired penniless but famous, so he leveraged that into an enterprise based on his fame (Chapter 4). Merv Griffin got fabulously rich, even appearing briefly on the *Forbes* 400, building a media empire from his relatively modest fame as an entertainer (also Chapter 4). The second celebrity type made money first, and then got famous. Warren Buffett comes to mind. Or Ron Perelman. Famed for their wealth.

The topic of getting rich through celebrity leads me to harsh advice. Acting, singing, sports, or other entertainment done with the explicit goal of becoming rich is the wrong motivation and terribly tough—as shown in Chapter 4. It's a legitimate road, but be warned: Other roads have much higher success rates. This is not a comment on the nature of celebrity, which is neither good nor bad by itself. The right motivation to be a singer or actor is wanting to sing and act. Overwhelmingly, most starve. I'll take you through the stats, but they're scary. Almost none get rich. Celebrity is not a goal. In this book I won't be able to avoid some discussion of celebrities. But the focus is on the roads.

For example, of the money-first-then-fame crowd, it's hard to avoid mentioning Bill Gates. He's the pinnacle of success of a particular road to riches. I can't really cover that road or any other without at least citing those who've traveled it most successfully. But I focus more on the less famous or nonfamous wealthy who used that road—right on down to those using the same road for nonfamous amounts of wealth. For your purposes they may be more useful examples. If you want salacious stories about Bill Gates or other celebrities, there are plenty on the Internet. This book simply identifies which road or roads these celebrities took, and how you can navigate those roads to success—to whatever degree you choose.

WHAT ABOUT OTHER ROADS?

Are there really just ten roads? Yes and no. There are more ways to get wealthy, but none you can plan for. For example, I can't write a book on how to inherit $50 million. Either you're closely related to the rich or you're not. There could be a book on how not to squander a fat inheritance or not to tick off your grandpa so he leaves it to charity instead of you—as **Paris Hilton's** grandfather did. Or **Leona Helmsley**: When dying in 2007 she left $12 million to her Maltese dog, "Trouble," and more to Trouble's custodian—Leona's brother. Half her grandchildren got nothing—not even Trouble-visitation rights.[1] The rest of her estate (anywhere from $5 billion to $8 billion) is intended to go to "dog welfare"—the Humane Society should make out huge.[2] There's no strategizing for how to be an heir or heiress. Or for how to be a pampered pet pooch.

Nor is there a strategy for how to be a super-rich lottery winner. But this is a fate you shouldn't hope for because of the well-known and documented lottery curse. Tragedy doesn't promptly damn every huge lottery winner, but it does more often than not. And it will damn you, too.

For example, Jeffrey Dampier Jr. was by all accounts a nice guy. Had a tough upbringing on Chicago's West Side. As luck had it, he won an Illinois lottery—$20 million. He left cold, snowy Chicago for Florida, but didn't forget his family—showering his parents and nine siblings with gifts, trips, cars, and homes. He even treated his wife's family. But it wasn't enough for his wife's sister, Victoria. She and her boyfriend kidnapped Jeffrey and shot him dead. No more Caribbean cruises after that.[3]

Jack Whittaker won a 2002 $315 million Powerball jackpot. Soon his wife left him (money can't buy love either), his much-loved granddaughter died from a drug overdose, and his daughter was diagnosed with cancer. One may sympathize with his need to self-medicate, but there's no excuse for his DUIs. His habitual frequenting of strip clubs also proved painful. On one visit, his car was burgled. Thieves almost got $600,000. (The money was reclaimed later. His reputation was not—stripped of it at the strip club.) His money was hard to keep track of too. Whittaker repeatedly wrote bad checks—was even sued by an Atlantic City casino for check-kiting. In all, he estimates he's been involved in over 460 court actions.[4] Admittedly, he's still got money and is alive and kicking—so he made out better than Mr. Dampier. But 460 court actions? That's misery, not rich. It reminds me of the famous Mexican curse, "May your life be full of lawyers." Besides, you can't plan to be rich that way—and you don't want to be miserable that way.

I believe from studying it, people who create their wealth on these ten roads end up more happy than the few who get lucky getting wealth in ways that can't be planned for. The people who made their own wealth earned it and are confident about themselves relative to their money. Reading about these ten roads, you're going to see lots of happy people. Yes, you'll see a few who aren't and I use them as examples of what not to do. For example, in Chapter 6 I show you how to steal money legally. It's a kind of touchy issue that may be offensive to some—maybe to you! But I show you that the folks who go down this road feel great about themselves. Then I give you some examples of people who forgot the legal part. They did almost the exact same thing but broke the law and are in jail. They don't feel so great about themselves.

Every chapter has its successes and failures—and lessons from both. But going down these ten roads successfully is also about being happy in your life. Chapter 5 isn't called "Marry Rich," which might imply marriage for money without love—leading to a future that might have money but also misery. It's called "Marry Well," which includes the whole package of all good things. But that chapter also covers mistakes to avoid that can otherwise lead to failure and misery. Every road has blind side-alleys to avoid.

A Sidetrack Off the Road

There are plenty of ways not to get rich that may work one time out of a million. Someone goes boating. Boat sinks. He dives to find said boat—finds sunken treasure instead. Doesn't mean you should take up boating. That isn't a road to riches; it's pure luck. That someone did something and succeeded doesn't make it something you should try. For example, writing is perfectly honorable but doesn't make many rich, as I detail in Chapter 8. I'll also show you what to do instead if you're a writer and want to be rich. But for the most part, writing is a labor of love, not money. Yes, some few do succeed at it like JK Rowling and Stephen King. And we cover them and show you how they went down one of the roads—and how you as a writer can emulate their success. But Chapter 8 is about the twist they apply. Otherwise, getting wealthy as a writer is extremely rare. Normal writing is more a wealth rut than a road.

And book writing is a lot of work. So if it isn't a good road to riches, why do I bother, and particularly for this book? Two reasons! First, writing is a labor of love and I enjoy it and have for a long time. I have a great time writing. Second, being already rich, this book is a way to give back and show others how to get rich, so someone like you can if you want. I'm 58 and late in my career. I like what I do but I don't have that many more career years ahead of me relative to behind. My wife and I have three grown sons. I get to live where I want, do what I want. I have hobbies I like. My version of giving back is not giving money to opera. Nothing wrong with opera; it's just not me. My charitable output has been completely defined through the grave for a long time. The overwhelming bulk of my wealth goes to Johns Hopkins Medicine—which in my view helps people after my life through medical research. In effect, for a long time now, in a financial sense, I simply work for the benefit of that fine institution. But giving back for me isn't about being a Boy Scout leader—again, nothing wrong with it—just not me. For me this book is a logical way to give back so someone, maybe many, maybe *you*, can see for the first time how you can become rich to your satisfaction in a logical, methodical manner.

THE RIGHT ROAD

Now you have your roadmap in hand and we're ready to embark. Consider each chapter a trial run. Maybe the road appeals to you, maybe not. But there's a right road here for everyone who desires riches, if you can navigate the common pitfalls. The beauty of these roads is they work in good times and bad. Doesn't matter what's happening to others on other roads—it only matters that you find and pursue your road.

Some of the folks profiled here you'll want to emulate. Others are (sometimes comical) examples of what not to do. But even the more comical folks profiled here have made big wealth. Who's to say who is right and who is satire? If you want to be rich, who's to say someone's road wasn't the right one as long as they got down it happily without breaking the law and with their mortal soul intact? If they did it by dancing in a chicken suit as I detail in Chapter 4, who are you or I to judge?

May your own journey start now! At the end of this book if you've decided none of these ten roads is right for you, and you have no interest in being a *roads* scholar, at least by reading about the ten roads you'll have saved yourself the trouble of going through life and finding yourself at the end of a dead-end road. And that's not so bad, either.

Enjoy the tour and learn what you can from these folks who've already found their roads.

ACKNOWLEDGMENTS

The notion for this book stemmed from conversations between literary agent Jeff Herman, me, and David Pugh, the John Wiley & Sons editor of my 2006 *New York Times* best seller, *The Only Three Questions That Count*. Before that book, Jeff wanted me to write a broad wealth book—an all encompassing ultra-wide spectrum book covering the waterfront. I hadn't written a book in a long, long time and didn't feel like taking on that project, but ultimately evolved to do *Three Questions* which was a much more narrow capital markets book—and where I felt confident I could offer unique insights. Still, after that, Jeff wanted me to do a wealth book. And David wanted another book (and broader spectrum to him meant it might sell even better). It was really only when we started talking about focusing on only the mega-wealthy as a road map for everyone else that I saw something I wanted to do—and knew I could do. For that, I thank them both for their patience with me.

So then I went back to Lara Hoffmans who worked with me in crafting my prior Wiley book. Prior to that book she had been an investment counselor in my firm's client services group but since then had become a manager in our content group. It produces all our written client communications including client reviews, marketing materials, and our daily webzine, www.marketminder.com. The content group is also responsible for, and Lara as been instrumental in, the origins of our new, first-ever for a money management firm, partnership with John Wiley & Sons—doing a whole series of specialty investment books under the *Fisher Investments Press* imprint.

That operation in fact debuts soon with three guides on energy stocks, material stocks, and global investing, all coming out in February and March of 2009, and then dozens more over the next few years, all written by Fisher Investments research staff—and having nothing really to do with me except it's my firm. So, I crowbarred Lara away from most of that and made her principally involved in working with me to craft this book. She was still involved with the content group to where she returns now—but temporarily this book became her principal focus. We would meet weekly and discuss structure, topics, content, and what was to be done. Then Lara would set out to do the research and render rough drafts of each chapter tailored to what I'd envisioned as a goal. Her work gave me the freedom to do what I otherwise must do on a daily basis, which is focus on my day job at my firm.

Along the way Lara pulled in Carolyn Feng who works in the firm's content group to do further research and fact checking. Evelyn Chea and Dina Ezzat, also from the content group, did fact checking, copy editing, and tactical manuscript details like footnotes, which overflow the book as you will see.

Then, I'd edit/rewrite on nights and weekends and Lara would clean it up and fix my mistakes with her crew and then I'd edit/rewrite again, and we went on and on like this through five to seven rounds on every chapter. She and they put in tremendous work on this, but in the end the book is mine from conception to final words including any omissions or errors. If you find fault in the book it is my fault, not theirs. But without them I'd never have had the patience or time to get this book started or completed. Particularly Lara, which is why her name is on the cover with mine.

Others from my firm also contributed in varying ways including Molly Lienesch, our branding manager; Marc Haberman, our Chief Innovation Officer; Tommy Romero, our group vice president of marketing; and Fab Ornani, who is our web maestro and much more. The book is what it is in material ways because of suggestions they made.

Despite this being a book on people, it would have been impossible to do it without the generous help of a variety of data sources. It would be remiss of me not to thank them including Bryan Taylor of *Global Financial Data* and Rob Carr of *Thomson Datastream* for their permissions. The ability to use data has exploded in recent years and you will see documentation supported by footnotes from these sources scattered throughout the book. Some of my more bizarre claims can only be made by putting the statement in scaled context which can only be done with the fine data these firms allow me to use.

I've also, and for obvious reasons, made extensive use of both the most current *Forbes* 400 List of Richest Americans and its predecessors going back to the origin of the "Rich List" in 1982, as well as more recently the *Forbes* annual, "Global Billionaires" list. And why not? After all, these lists are the gold standard measuring America's and the world's mega-wealthy and without them this exercise wouldn't have had the metric-based foundation used to show how these folks got where they are. The *Forbes* 400, which started as a lark by Malcolm Forbes, has evolved into an institution with universal acceptance establishing the basis for how we determine quantified wealth. That is just one more major contribution *Forbes* as a publication has made to the world.

I must thank Jeff Silk, vice chairman at my firm and someone who has been my ride-along for 25 years and who I write about extensively in Chapter 3 as a ride-along role model. Jeff read through parts of the book, made comments, and in that way improved it as he improves everything he ever touches.

Grover Wickersham, a long-time friend and associate, securities lawyer, money manager, Chairman of the Purisima Funds and former executive with the Securities and Exchange Commission read most of the book, making highly detailed editing suggestions all along the way, page by page, line by line, probably 75 percent of which I ultimately incorporated into the book. His contribution to this book, as with my last book, was simply over the top. He edited on planes, on two continents, in three countries, faxing me material in the middle of the night and arguing with me when I didn't accept his suggestions. With friends like Grover I need fear no enemy. I only wish his handwriting were easier to read because I sure read a lot of it. Actually, I mention Grover briefly in Chapter 1 and Chapter 9. The book would be better if I mentioned him more.

Speaking of lawyers, Fred Harring read the whole book for libel to make sure I wouldn't get my rear-end sued off. I still may well be sued for some things I've said, but at least I have confidence I'll prevail in court. San Diego hot-shot plaintiff's lawyer Scott Metzger did another libel read on Chapter 6 just to make sure, and I appreciate the parallel views between Scott and Fred, providing me double reassurance.

Oh, and friends. I've written about a lot of them in the book. Whenever you do, you run the risk you depict them in ways they don't care for and maybe you lose the friend. There are dozens herein, too many too list, and I thank them all as a group, hopefully, for remaining friends after they read these words.

And, of course, I thank those who offered pre-publication praise for this book on its back cover. They read fast in a premature draft, thought hard, and offered lavishly.

Finally, one more time, as so often in the past, this book has been an excuse to engage in the spousal abuse of neglect. My wife of now 38 years has evolved over the decades to be exceptional at letting me go as I become temporarily insular, focusing almost solely on the cranking out part of doing a book. The nights and weekends I owe her for this book can never be repaid in full. A book like this is a labor of love and much of it from the author's spouse. It is good to be loved.

My career is getting old now. Much more of it is behind me than the few years I have left ahead. It has been and still will be tremendous fun. Doing a book like this, which is really a tangent from my day-to-day work is also a lot of fun, more so than pretty much any hobby anyone can do—or any that I can imagine. And, so, I also thank you, my reader, without whom my publisher, nor any other, would indulge me in such fun. Thanks to you all.

Ken Fisher
Woodside, CA

1

THE RICHEST ROAD

Have a compelling vision?
Leadership skills?
An understanding spouse?
You just might be a visionary founder.

This is the richest road. Founding your own firm can create astounding wealth. Half of the 10 richest Americans did this, including **Bill Gates** (net worth $59 billion), gambling mogul **Sheldon Adelson** ($28 billion), Oracle CEO **Larry Ellison** ($26 billion), and Google wunderkinds **Sergey Brin** and **Larry Page** ($18.5 billion each).[1] Close behind are info magnate and now NYC Mayor **Michael Bloomberg** ($11.5 billion), Nike's **Phil Knight** ($9.8 billion), finance's **Stephen Schwarzman** ($7.8 billion), discount broker **Charles Schwab** ($5.5 billion), and many of the richest Americans from nearly every industry and angle.[2] Even better? These folks get wealthy and spawn rich ride-alongs too. (See Chapter 3.)

And this road works with scant restriction by industry, education, or pedigree—PhDs and college dropouts are equally welcome.

Be warned: This road's not for the faint-hearted. It requires courage, discipline, Teflon skin, strategic vision, a talented supporting cast, and maybe luck. Those lacking entrepreneurial spirit needn't apply—nor folks who are fear-driven.

No mistake, it's tough. Few new businesses survive more than four years.[3] But starting a business *is* the American Dream. Succeeding is the realm of supermen and superwomen. The key to success is a novel twist making what you do different—the difference that works.

Are you a person who can't be stopped? Can you, as Phil Knight would say, "Just do it"? You must be great at your core business and the *business* of business. Vision alone won't do! You need acumen, charisma, tactical thinking, and leadership skills. I've never met a successful founder folks didn't want to follow. They're just super. They know their product cold. They're skilled at sales and marketing. They become great delegators. They also build a common culture into repeated waves of new employees so their firm takes on a life of its own beyond the CEO. This is a tall order.

Before you start down this road, you must answer five critical questions:

1. What part of the world can you change?
2. Will you create a new product or innovate an existing one?
3. Will you build a firm to sell or one to last?
4. Will you need outside funding or can you bootstrap?
5. Will you stay private or go IPO?

PICKING A PATH

First question—what part of the world can you change? Make no mistake, founders create change, be it little or big. Ideally, you can create change where you're passionate. Change creates value even in lousy industries. Changing lousy to not-lousy is huge! Or if you're not really passionate about something, it might be ok just to follow the money—focus on high-value areas. For this, flip to our Chapter 7 exercise on how to determine what fields are most valuable.

You can also focus on sectors likely to become more relevant—in America and globally. For example, service industries have grown tremendously—indeed, America's economy is almost 80 percent services.[4] Technology will become more critical, not less—count on it. Same with health care—good or bad economy—we still want ever more medication. Financials took it on the chin lately, but folks always need to invest and borrow—particularly entrepreneurs starting firms. These are all areas likely to become more relevant.

Or flip this concept a bit and focus on industries likely to become less relevant. Now, I'm not forecasting what happens to any industry in the next few years, but long-term, firms in unionized fields (like autos and airlines) die a slow and painful death, have lousy stock returns, and ultimately get replaced by something—somehow, some way—that sidesteps unions. Maybe you want to start the firm that creates the change and does the replacement.

Pick a field that will only become more relevant.

Start Small, Get Bigger—Always Think Scalability

Starting small is best. Few set out to found the next Microsoft—they start tinkering with computers in Mom's garage. When I started my business, I started small. If you had asked me then if I'd be running a firm as big as it is today, I'd laugh. Start small, get bigger—always thinking scalability.

For example, a dry cleaning facility is small. Demand is fairly inelastic—folks always need clean clothes even in bad times. And it's easy entry. But for these same reasons, it's unlikely to grow into a massive, national business—it lacks scalability. Dry cleaning chains basically don't exist. How rich can you get owning one or a handful of local stores? Then again, maybe you become the person who cracks the scalability issue and figures how to create a huge dry cleaning chain—sort of the Sam Walton of dry cleaning.

Start small— think huge.

Taco stands are tiny like dry cleaners. Easy entry too—just tortillas and a cart—but massively scalable. You wouldn't pull off the highway to visit your favorite dry cleaner, but you would to grab lunch at your favorite taco joint. For example, Chipotle was a tiny regional burrito joint in Denver. McDonald's invested and Chipotle went national, then public in 2006. They did this by focusing on scalability and taking every advantage they could from centralized buying, mass advertising, and, yes, technology. Tiny into huge.

NEWER OR BETTER?

Next question. Entrepreneurs change the world two basic ways: Creating something entirely new—filling a product or service hole—or making existing products better, more efficient. Which is for you? The entirely new crowd is like **Bill Gates** and Apple CEO **Steve Jobs** (net worth $5.7 billion).[5] Or **Will Keith Kellogg**— creator of corn flakes and the cold breakfast cereal genre. Or **John Deere**, an ironsmith who invented the steel plow and one of America's oldest firms. Entirely new!

Your initial motivation can be more personal—maybe changing a small slice of your world. That can pay big. My friend Mike Wood was an intellectual property lawyer frustrated by the lack of good electronic games to help his son learn phonics. Inspired by this product hole, he founded Leapfrog in 1995. When he stepped down nine years later, his stake was worth about $53.4 million.[6] When Mike isn't serious, he shows his creative side doing a heck of a job playing guitar and singing cowboy songs. You may think you need an MIT degree to discern the next great product. The truth is sometimes all it takes is having a need you believe others have too—and maybe some creativity and cowboy songs.

You must choose—fill a product hole or innovate on an older theme?

If you can't visualize new products, try improving existing ones. Many of today's wealthiest entrepreneurs simply took a fresh take on something existing—improving performance, productivity, or profit margins—making it better.

Charles Schwab ($5.5 billion)[7] didn't create discount brokerage, but he made it widely accessible. Bose CEO **Amar Bose** ($1.8 billion)[8] didn't invent stereo speakers. He made them sound awesome. The Crocs cofounders didn't invent boating shoes—they made them insanely ugly and inexplicably popular. With a market cap over $1.5 billion,[9] the Crocs founders are laughing all the way to the bank (wearing ugly shoes). These folks found new, more profitable ways to deliver old functions—which generated wealth, created jobs, and aided our nation's growth. Simply stupendous.

Efficiency and lower costs through building proprietary distribution are another way to innovate. That was Wal-Mart founder **Sam Walton's** way—the low-cost provider. His vision left his four surviving children (including one daughter-in-law) a legacy of over $16 billion each.[10]

Or try the reverse of Walton's way—intentionally make something simple really, really expensive. Like **Ralph Lauren** (net worth $4.7 billion),[11] founder and CEO of Polo, with his pricey, profitable eponymous clothing line. He's branched into outdoor wear (he designed the 2008 US Olympic gear and at one point outfitted Aspen Skiing Company's ski patrol[12]—how upscale can you get?), as well as home furnishings, fragrance, and even something as simple as house paint. Lauren discovered a great branding strategy could persuade rational people to pay huge premiums for the most basic men's pants. Go figure! **Vera Wang** is another fashion innovator who built a fortune taking traditional white wedding dresses to extremes. One gown can run $20,000 and up, with huge profit margins. This takes a convincing, innovative brand—tough to do!

BUILT TO SELL OR BUILT TO LAST?

Third key question—what are your future plans? Is this firm one you'd like to make last for generations? Or is it one you want to build, grow, sell, and walk away from? Either is fine. There's nothing wrong with building a business you don't want to run forever. Some folks want a legacy. Others just want to cash in. The average founder won't want to do what it takes to create a legacy. But lots of founders have the stuff to build a business and sell it for $5 million, $20 million, even $500 million, and move on. Up to you!

Built to Sell

Building to sell is easier. Succession management is less of an issue. You find some enticing product hole or improvement. Then you think like a buyer—"What would make someone want to buy me out?" Answer: profits or profit potential. Also, your business must be transferable—which means you must be replaceable. Building to sell may make you wealthy but generally doesn't create mega-wealth—and that's fine. Remember those Nantucket Nectars commercials? "Hi, I'm Tom. And I'm Tom. We're juice guys." The "two Toms" started serving homemade juice to tourists from their little boat in Nantucket in 1989. In 2002, Cadbury Schweppes envisioned huge profit potential, selling a burgeoning brand through their already-huge existing distribution channels—they bought them for $100 million.[13] Neither Tom is on the *Forbes* 400, but they're likely satisfied with their lot.

Build a firm to sell or to endure. Both are lucrative.

Californians recall H. Salt Fish & Chips—a British-style fish-and-chips joint that was huge in the 1960s. H. Salt was and is a guy—Haddon Salt. He and his wife moved to California from Britain and brought their fondness and recipe for deep-fried cod with them. This small, deep-fried firm was eventually built into something regionally huge. When Salt sold to Kentucky Fried Chicken in 1969, there were 93 franchises.[14] Today, only 26 remain.[15] What does Salt care? He took his money and retired long before that. Now he spends his spare time playing the most wickedly wonderful electric violin you'll ever hear. Founder CEOs tend to blend creativity and passion. (The violin Salt plays comes from Chapter 9's Grover Wickersham, who runs Zeta Music.)

Businesses often get sold and then implode. That doesn't diminish the founder's accomplishments. If the buyers blow it up, that's their fault—not the founder's. If you build a business to sell, don't fret afterward. (Speaking of afterward, many start, build, sell, and retire only to discover—too late—it was the challenge of working that kept them happy.)

Built to Last

If you'll forever fret your business's fate and want a lasting legacy, build it to last—the very pinnacle of success. Problem is, you may never live to see it. Herbert H. Dow was long dead by the time Dow Chemical became America's third, second, and finally largest chemical company. But his legacy enriched generations of his family, Dow employees, and their families.

When I was a kid my father idolized Herbert Dow. I grew up hearing Dow quoted endlessly. To me, Dow was bigger than life. Early on, Dow made inorganic chemicals, originally bleach— efficiently making basic commodity building blocks cheaper than others, underpricing, and gaining market share year-to-year. Dow's focus was still alive when I was young. Dow was number one in inorganics and number five in US chemicals. Today, Dow is number one in America and number two in the world. If you can be satisfied in your grave, surely Herbert Dow must be. That's legacy!

I've tried to build much of what I learned from my father about Dow into my own firm, despite my firm not being in commodities or manufacturing. If I were writing a book solely on how to build an enduring firm, Dow's philosophy and life lessons would be central to it. For example, Dow emphasized investing heavily during your industry's down-cycle because he knew his competitors didn't have the courage to do it. The benefit? On the next up-cycle, Dow had new, modern, low-cost, efficient capacity to take business away from the less courageous.

Another Dow-ism was hiring young people, straight from school, and leading them to become part of Dow's culture permanently by building lifelong career paths. The benefit? Loyalty, commitment, and corporate culture you can't otherwise have. One of his great quotes was (and my father repeated this endlessly), "Never promote a man who hasn't made some bad mistakes; you would be promoting someone who hasn't done much."

> To build to sell, think like a buyer. To build to last, think like an owner.

In an era before today's social nonsense (where "ideal" boards of directors are dictated by government agencies and law), Dow was committed to a board of former insiders. Share-owning, retired Dow executives who could no longer be fired were fiercely loyal yet free from the power of the CEO. They also knew where the bodies were buried and who had buried them so they could find out anything fast. That basic board structure was still mostly intact when I was young four decades ago. The benefit? No future CEO could pull the wool over the board's eyes. Internal problems couldn't be hidden. If Enron had been like that, it wouldn't have rotted as it did. Dow knew 80 years ago that an outside board (today's required norm for a public stock) is largely useless.

If our society had the sense Dow had, we'd all be better off. Skip outside directors if you can. It's better. Outside board members like it but the value they add is really zero. You can hire or befriend all the advisers you may ever need—you don't need them on your board.

Culture or Cult-sure

Among the most important tasks you as a founder have in building to last is creating an enduring culture that maintains your strategic vision long after you're gone. Fail and your successor may fold and sell to the first viable buyer or morph your firm into some bastardization.

My firm's based in the woods where few would suspect—on a mountaintop above San Francisco's peninsula. I've lived my life in forests and see them as a benign and peaceful work environment. Years back, as we started growing into a larger firm with more employees, industry locals would refer to us derogatorily as "the cult on the hill." I don't know if I'll get my way or not, but if I do, long after I'm dead they'll refer to us as "the cult-sure," because if you're trying to build something lasting you must have a culture so "sure" that no person, event, economic cycle, or social trend can knock it off course. That's what Dow did.

BOOTSTRAP OR FINANCE?

Fourth question: Capital intensive or not? Another way to think about that: Will you require equity financing from outsiders that dilutes your ownership, or will you largely be able to bootstrap—financing growth from recycled profits plus bank borrowing?

Capital-intensive businesses tend to be in categories like industrials, manufacturing, materials, mining, pharmaceuticals technology, and biotech. Noncapital-intensive ones tend toward providing services—financial firms, Chapter 7's money managers, consulting, and maybe software. But even noncapital-intensive industries may want to start with big bucks. The advantage is that you start bigger, faster. Bootstrapping requires patience and can be a long game, starting small and pouring profits back into the firm to self-finance growth—requiring patience plus.

Don't be beholden to venture capitalists. Bootstrap all you can.

It sounds grand to "start big," but be warned: Venture capitalists know the start-up game far better than you ever will. They fund endless deals. You'll do one or a few in your life. They're not funding your firm for charity, but for ownership and more than their share of profits. They can create a game plan, so by your firm's second or third financing round, they own much more of your firm than you ever imagined possible. But bootstrappers can do whatever they wish with cash flow and needn't kowtow to outsiders' wishes. If you can avoid venture capitalists, do it. (Should you decide to go the VC route, I needn't waste your time telling you how. There are myriad books on it already available.)

PUBLIC OR PRIVATE?

Finally, do you want to build a publicly traded firm or a private one? When folks think of a CEO, they usually think of heads of public firms like Bill Gates or Steve Jobs—mega names, mondo firms. But the vast majority of firms are private. That's better in my view. This is like choosing between outside funding or bootstrapping. Generally, firms go public to raise capital—selling their souls to the public. But like getting VC funding, you must wrangle with owners besides yourself—now maybe millions of them!

Folks idealize the initial public offering (IPO), imagining endless riches. While a tiny percent of IPOs have been spectacular—like Google, Microsoft, and Oracle—overwhelmingly most are losers. As detailed in my recently updated 1987 book *The Wall Street Waltz*, IPO usually stands for "It's Probably Overpriced." Most IPOs disappoint afterward. And as the founder-CEO, for you, headaches have just begun. From then on as a public stock, you are beholden to strangers and public rules, forever and ever, amen. You share control with them, regulators and courts—all sometimes fickle mistresses.

Less so if you're private! **Fred Koch** founded Koch Industries in 1940. Huge and awesomely successful, Koch is possibly the world's largest private company with estimated annual sales of $90 billion.[16] Besides smarts and acute business acumen, Koch loathed commies—another trait making him dear to my heart. Before founding his firm, Koch built refineries in the Soviet Union, where he fired most all Soviet engineers, replacing them with non-commies.[17] Love it!

Despite a terribly tough industry with global competitors of massive scale and clout and annoying governments everywhere, Koch thrived. Koch's sons David and Charles now run Koch—each worth $17 billion.[18] They are successes in their own rights. Surprisingly, they're about the nicest guys you could ever meet. And they have no need to go public. Fact is, **Charles Koch** has said Koch will go public, "literally over my dead body."[19] Hopefully his son Chase, who stands to inherit significant ownership, feels likewise.

I share Charles's views. Shopping in my local supermarket, sometimes I'll see local clients. They expect I'll give them time—and should. I'll chat as long as they want because we both willingly entered and remain in a business relationship—a 50/50 deal. They didn't have to hire us, and my firm never had to accept them as clients. It was a mutual choice. We made a deal. They get my time.

Not so with public shareholders. As CEO of a publicly traded firm, you have no control over who owns your stock. Anyone—the nastiest little snark from Rip-offsville with an online brokerage account and an urge to pester you in the frozen food section before suing (see Chapter 6 on pirates)—becomes your owner. You can't

Who runs your firm? You or John Q. Public, courts, and regulators?

talk to them. Their interests are often harmful to your longer-term vision and your firm's health. They may only care about the stock next week.

Sometimes to do the right thing for your firm's future, you must make costly decisions that could hurt earnings and stock prices in the here and now. Today's public is often short-term oriented. And you can't tell anyone anything in the supermarket you don't tell everyone, or you and your firm are in legal trouble. So in the dairy aisle you smile, shake hands, shut up, run like hell, and hide.

If you can, it's best to remain private and see only customers and vendors at the supermarket. That doesn't mean I don't like public stocks. I do—my business is built on investing in them—I just never want to run one. You shouldn't either.

THE BIG BULL'S-EYE

There's great satisfaction in building an empire and employing others. But there are downsides—the bigger you get, the more people attack you. The truly successful develop sharkskin and an ego requiring scant maintenance.

You're ridiculed from the start. Since your novelty is new or different, it isn't from the established order. Most folks can't envision it as you do, and will think you're a bit crazy—until after your firm is seen as a success. Then you'll be hailed as a visionary. This is true of almost every radically successful founder. The bigger the success, the more they were ridiculed early on.

On this road, you will be seen as crazy, too. When my firm started doing direct-mail marketing (which I prefer to call *Junk Mail*) for high-net-worth investors, industry experts said we were nuts. Ditto when we started Internet direct marketing—wouldn't, couldn't work! No one would respond to advertising like that and become clients! Next came radio, print ads, and TV. They all worked, which is a part of how we built my firm. But most everyone "in the know" thought we were daft. When we started doing it in other countries, their pundits said, "Maybe it will work in America, but never here." Just examples. Whatever you do, if it really works, everyone will think you're crazy until you're a proven success.

Later, success attracts attackers who are increasingly vicious and often dishonest for their own self-interested reasons. This starts for you somewhere between 100 and 600 employees, depending on what you're doing—but long before you have mega-wealth. And you must be tough in response, taking on your attackers and beating them into submission. I promise—guarantee—the bigger your firm, the more you succeed, the more you'll be attacked by petty, snarky parasites. Some want money. (Why not? They can't create their own.) Some sue for slights, real or imagined, personal or social. Others attack to steal customers.

This isn't the Coke versus Pepsi wars, or those cute Apple computer ads where the Mac is a young, energetic kid and the PC is bespectacled and portly (like me). That's normal competition. No, this is ill-intended, slanderous, and duplicitous lies aimed at siphoning a sliver of customers and keeping you from getting more. A different kind of normal! They're small and petty, so to make it pay, they need only convince a gullible few who can't see they're being duped with lies. You must deal with it. Or you lose. Real founder-CEOs don't lose.

Hackers, Mobsters, and Embezzlers

My firm, like everyone else's, has had to thwart covert attacks from every slimy angle—I've seen it firsthand, including small-scale competitors and rogue operators at large firms, wannabe embezzlers, securities criminals, and even the Russian mafia—all normal and all wanting to get our clients' money. Former employees, too! And they all work with the media, trying to create stories that slam your firm's reputation to shake some of your fruit off your tree.

Then, too, every major firm today suffers dozens to hundreds of daily attempts by computer hackers trying to break through the firm's external computer firewalls to snatch customer information for the purpose of account or identity theft or embezzlement. These aren't nice guys. You, as founder-CEO, must be tougher than they are.

You will be sued, attacked, and sued again. It comes with the territory.

Employee and customer class-action lawsuits are standard. Any firm, once big enough (more than $30 million in payroll), will start getting these. The plaintiff's lawyer usually is just a pirate—a shakedown artist—wanting to be paid to go away (see Chapter 6). The lawyers are the big beneficiaries, not the employees or customers. They never accept that your employees didn't have to come work for you—but did by choice, relative to less favorable alternatives. They never accept that customers didn't have to buy your product, but did so because they found it the best alternative. The parasites always—always—act self-righteously. A founder-CEO must harden him or herself to simultaneously keep focused on customers, employees, and product superiority while finding some good bug spray. For this, I recommend hiring plaintiff's lawyers for legal defense work. They know the tricks of the pirate trade better than non-pirates. I'd hire the very best pirates around, make it worth their while, and buy them endless rum. Arg, matey!

Keep "Just Doing It"

Nike's **Phil Knight** is a perfect example. First, no one believed he could do it. He built a huge, successful multinational firm and offered great, cutting-edge products—creating thousands of jobs globally.

In the 1960s, Japan was to America what China is now—a source of cheaper goods. (Then, we griped about Japanese outsourcing like we do now about China.) Then, American running shoes were heavy and uncomfortable. Germans had light, comfortable, but expensive designs—about $30 a pair (which, with inflation, would be $215 today).[20]

A garden-variety track runner with a passion for Japanese culture, Knight wrote a business school paper titled "Can Japanese Sports Shoes Do to German Sports Shoes What Japanese Cameras Did to German Cameras?" Or, could Japan produce a superior design far cheaper?[21]

Knight cut a deal to import Japanese knock-offs of great German shoes, selling them from the back of his run-down car.[22] That valiant little firm (start small, dream big—and scale it up) became Nike. No one believed his cheap shoes were any good, except customers, who are all that really matter. If others in the industry could have figured this out, they would have already done it. But since they didn't, they didn't see why it would work for Nike.

Early on, Nike targeted serious athletes. But few of us are serious athletes. We just have feet. Millions of weekend-warrior feet! Millions more couch surfers—all potential Nike feet. How to get them to want Nikes? Knight got a talented young Michael Jordan to agree to wear Nikes. Suddenly, everyone wanted to "be like Mike." Celebrity marketing hadn't really caught on yet on a big scale—taking an athlete's personality and making it the face of a brand. From there, Nike became a branding machine. Suddenly, it was cool to sport the Swoosh.

But, naturally, with success, Knight was attacked. To keep Nike's designs inexpensive, Knight used factories in emerging markets. Classic Adam Smith! Classic target of anti-capitalist **Michael Moore**. In his crockumentary *Downsize This!*, Moore complained conditions were harsh in Nike's overseas factories. Journalists piled on, calling for a Nike boycott for "outsourcing" and its alleged factory worker abuse. His attackers wanted a sensational story—plus they had a social agenda to advance.

They had their viewpoint. Knight had his. His was: Though working conditions in his overseas plants might not be up to middle-class American standards, those workers didn't have to take those jobs. They did so out of free will. And, in general, Nike's factory workers earned far more than their compatriots[23] and had better benefits—onsite clinics, schooling for employees' children, etc. They took those jobs because they were better than alternatives. None of that, of course, slowed the attackers. He got attacked from myriad sources, including his alma mater. Knight remained resolute that he was right—that the overseas plants were necessary to deliver good quality, inexpensive shoes.

Here's my point: Knight could have fatigued and sold out—tiring from getting attacked. After signing Jordan, he could have stayed solely in sneakers and been an attractive takeover target. Selling out then, he wouldn't have hit the *Forbes* 400, but he'd be plenty wealthy and wouldn't get annoyingly attacked anymore. He wouldn't have shareholders to answer to. He could shop in peace. But he didn't cave—luckily for Nike's employees, shareholders, and anyone who likes buying competitively-priced sneakers. He toughed it out and kept building, adding products beyond sneakers, overcoming his attackers eventually. Knight built Nike to last. Few have his grit and enduring quality. Do you?

FOUNDERS ARE QUITTERS—JUST DO IT

So you want to be a founder. Then don't be stopped. Quit everything else. Founders are quitters first. If you've got a job, quit. Find a way to sustain yourself and just do it. If you're in college, drop out. If you're president of the United States, resign to make something useful of yourself and hand the front door key to that little VP twit you picked because you had to pick someone. Just do it. Quit. Founders quit before they found.

Once you quit, it's quiet. No one to bug you but your spouse and kids. Find a quiet place to work. If you live in a studio apartment, wall off a corner with blankets to keep your spouse at bay. Find space—doesn't matter where. You'll work more out of your briefcase and laptop than anywhere else at first.

I only offer certain suggestions about how to be a founder because lots have been written on entrepreneurialism. My first suggestion, if you haven't done so, is read a few books. Good ones to start with are:

- *Innovation and Entrepreneurship* by Peter Drucker. A great overview of what every entrepreneur needs to know to succeed.

- *Entrepreneurship for Dummies* by Kathleen Allen. A good introductory how-to on everything tactical you must know to start a business, particularly when and where you need a lawyer.

- *Beyond Entrepreneurship* by James C. Collins and William C. Lazier. This covers how to take your relatively new business to the next level and move toward building a great firm.

Take your books and go to your blanketed-off quiet space. I assume—if you haven't been stagnating in the upper Amazon basin, rapidly fleeing humanity—you've got, and are comfortable with, a laptop. Get a boxy, functional, non-fancy briefcase. Now sit in your quiet space a while. Notice how quiet it is? That's because there's nothing going on there. So put the laptop in the briefcase with one of those books. Now get out of your quiet space. Go.

Gene Watson was a founder of myriad laser companies including, in the 1960s, industry pioneers Coherent Radiation and Spectra-Physics. During a laser deal we did together in the 1970s, he drummed into my head: "The problems are in here; the opportunities are out there." Get out of your quiet space and go where you think the opportunities are. If you don't know where to go, stop at a park somewhere. Get out your laptop and figure out 20 likely customers. Rank them in order of importance. If you can't fathom 20 likely customers, something is off and you need to go back and start this chapter over again—or take another road.

Now take the three lowest-ranked of your 20—not the highest—and go talk to them about your idea. While you're there, ask them for money in exchange for some future interest in using the results of your idea. Why will they see you? Because you're *Just You*, founder and CEO of *Whatever-You-Call-It*, which has novel ideas that could help *Whoever-They-Are*—because those ideas will change their world.

Don't see your most important prospects first. You're not ready—don't have your strategy down enough yet. Better still to think up prospects number 21 through 40 and see them first, rather than blow up with your most important prospects. But go. Talk. Ask. Listen. Do it. The next steps of your initial business plan will come to you as you keep making such calls. Don't register with your state business licensing officer yet. Don't hire a lawyer or incorporate *Whatever-You-Call-It* yet. Don't rent office space. Or raise money—yet. Get customer interest first.

Why did I tell you to put one of the books in the briefcase? Because you can't fill all your time with customer appointments, so spend the time in between booking more appointments and reading the book. Reading the book will make you think more and more about what you're doing—founding a company. The appointments will tell you what to do next. If you can get a customer to commit money in exchange for a future interest in the results of your idea, you can fathom what's next.

Once a Quitter, Always a Quitter

Now is the time to remember, once again, you're a founder and hence a quitter. So quit again. Since your basic idea is novel and useful, the customer interest you discovered is just an indication of greater interest for your novel approach to solving their problem. So quit calling prospects and delegate. Hire a salesperson to approach your prospects. Doing so makes huge sense. First, you need someone to generate sales. Second, you pay your sales rep a commission, which means no up-front cash (which you don't have). Third, if he or she sells, you can focus on other things (all of which you want to quit, except being CEO).

Many salespeople want base pay. Forget it—and them. You want someone who gets your enthusiasm, vision, and hopes to be ground-flooring onto something big, so someday, he or she is national sales manager of a vast enterprise. The right salesperson is only a little less entrepreneurial than you are and is otherwise a ride-along (see Chapter 3), hoping to get wealthy on your coattails.

Remember, "The problems are in here; the opportunities are out there." Now that you have a sales rep, go back to your quiet space and notice . . . still not much is happening there. So quit that and hire someone to sit in your quiet space in case anything does happen there. Someday you hope lots will, and you'll call your quiet space "headquarters" and it won't be quiet anymore. Hire someone to be there. It shouldn't be you. Stay out where the opportunities are. Keep seeing prospects and customers. That keeps you close to your market.

Just a Walk in the Park

There's lots to do out there. Go back to that park bench and pull out your laptop. Make a list of all the functions you think you'll need to have back at headquarters once it's not quiet anymore. *The Entrepreneurship for Dummies* book helps you with this list if it's in your briefcase. Think of one person who can handle maybe half those functions, even if imperfectly—hire that person with a title like Operations VP. It's ideal if this person has skills that might regularly crank out your novelty (whatever it is). This person's job is to take orders your sales rep gets and turn them into noise so your quiet space isn't quiet.

When you wake up in the morning, ask, "How do I get out of my not-so-quiet space?" Then turn to your sales rep and operations VP and say, "What can I do to help you today?" Then call 15 prospects and say, "What can I do to help you today?" This is all so simple, it's hardly justifiable to put in a book.

One day you wake up and do everything from the previous paragraph. Then you turn to your sales rep and say, "It's time we hire another sales rep—one you could train and manage so we could have more noise for our operations VP." So do it. Of course, that day you also call 15 prospects, as always, just to do it.

Maybe you're a faster quitter. If so, hire folks to do all the other functions on the list you made that second day on the park bench. Marketing, post-sales service, product development, recruiting—whatever—every function on your list. And each time you hire someone, you quit that function. Then ask those people every morning, "What can I do to help you today?" If they actually want you to do something, fine, do it. But the next day, quit and hire someone to do that thing.

This is what an entrepreneur does. It isn't rocket science. If you do what I've described, you're a founder-CEO—just one of a small firm. If you want to become a bigger company CEO read Chapter 2—the road to riches as a CEO—which is about building a company into more than what it was—because as founder, that's where this road ends. So quit this chapter and on to the next.

 ## The Guide to **Being a Founder**

Starting a business is the American dream. But most new firms fail within four years. How do you succeed instead? Follow this guide.

1. *Pick the right road.* Which part of the world can you change? Select an area that will remain relevant or one you can fathom steering out of irrelevancy.

2. *Start small, dream big.* Don't dream of being like Nike. Find an area that needs changing or improving, no matter how small. But think in terms of scalability.

3. *Innovate or improve.* Create something novel or improve something, or do both. Novel is a marvel but it's ok just to be a better, faster, cheaper, more profitable version of an old version.

4. *Build to sell or build to last.* These are two different mindsets and done differently, so decide early if you can. Each option has separate considerations. And you can build an empire and later decide to sell. But building to last means thinking like an owner. To sell, think like a buyer.

5. *Bootstrap or find financing.* If your business is capital-intensive, you need outside funding, but if not, you have a choice. Venture capital is for "building to sell," because your investors like liquidity. Bootstrapping is better if you want to build to last and allows more freedom. But you can go either way.

6. *Go public or stay private.* Going public has prestige but is a pain. Try to stay private. Again, more freedom, control, and free time at the deli counter.

7. *Ignore naysayers.* The bigger you are, the more you'll be attacked. So build your toughness.

8. *Be a quitter.* Founders are quitters, so just quit. Find a quiet space and notice there's nothing going on there and quit it. Keep quitting until it isn't quiet in your quiet space. Find a vital function and quit it.

9. *But never quit your clients.* Stay with your prospects and customers even when you have great sales representatives. You never, ever get to quit clients or potential clients, or your business goes poof.

2

PARDON ME, THAT'S MY THRONE

Responsibility and running things come easy? But you're no visionary founder? Maybe the corner office is in your future.

Some of our finest CEOs didn't found the firms they lead—like GE's Jack Welch. Non-founder CEOs can take firms to unthought-of heights. Sometimes reinventing is easier than creating from whole cloth, so while founder-CEOs usually rank higher in mega-wealth, just becoming CEO pays big. And it is a rich road indeed—even if you don't aspire to billionaire status. Fully half of America's largest firm CEOs make in excess of $8.3 million.[1]

Warning: Heavy is the head wearing the CEO crown. Firm successes are rarely wholly, directly attributed to CEOs—as in, "success has a thousand fathers but failure is a bastard." The bastard is the CEO, always. So a big failure can kill your future. CEOs must be tough—more now than ever. Failed CEOs don't just lose their jobs—they frequently end up vilified by the media, even indicted! And CEOs are often demonized just for their big pay—which they get precisely because of the career risk they face.

On this road, you need leadership and executive qualities to rise, be anointed, and keep the throne. The world loves successful CEOs—heroes! But the difference between a hero, a zero, and a weirdo often isn't much, as we'll see.

GRAY HAIR AND DUES-PAYING

Where to start? Like Chapter 1, start where you're passionate. Most CEOs, except for some very few founders, aren't young. It takes time, so you better enjoy the ride. Working for a firm you love, in a field you have passion for, is critical—and the more profitable the better (see our exercises in Chapter 7), but to endure long enough to become CEO, passion trumps profitability. Enjoy it.

Though there are shortcuts to being CEO (covered later), you toil long and pay your dues. But there's good news: If successful, you can keep your seat a long time—like **Hank Greenberg** (worth $2.8 billion).[2] Former AIG CEO founder Cornelius Vander Starr tapped him as CEO in 1968—a post he held until 2005. Microsoft CEO **Steve Ballmer** (worth $15.2 billion)[3] was a long-time ride-along (Chapter 3) to Bill Gates and got the throne in 2000. As a ride-along-turned-CEO he rode two roads well. Non-founder CEOs are often a ride-along variation who switched to the hot seat. To do this, study Chapter 3 on how to be a ride-along.

It takes a while, so find a field you love.

But if you aren't successful, you can be booted fast—even though you had paid your dues. Consider **Stan O'Neal**, who joined Merrill Lynch in 1986. Long seen as **David Komansky**'s heir-apparent, he became president in 2001 and CEO in 2003. His stint ended in 2007.[4] Booted, basically! Still, by my count, including severance, his pay totaled about $307 million during his short CEO tenure.[5] Not bad.

A CEO-VOLUTION (THROUGH MY FATHER'S EYES)

The single most important CEO trait is leadership. If you can't lead, you can't be CEO. It's not something you must be born with, though some are. You can develop it. But it's necessary. You don't need charisma, but you must lead.

How can you learn to lead? Well, I assure you I wasn't born to be a leader—very far from it—so let me take you through my personal evolution to show you what I did, because yours can be similar. For me it began with my father, Philip Fisher. He was hella smart but suffered a then-undiagnosed condition now widely known as Asperger's Syndrome—a form of near-autism often called "Geek's Syndrome" because sufferers often seem "geeky." They have ultra-high IQs, are great with math, verbal, and written skills, but have poor social skills. Typically, they're physically twitchy, pace the floor, and can't keep their hands from tapping. They have almost no ability to fathom how others feel. That is the defining feature of someone with Asperger's. My father was classic. He could say the cruelest things, yet wasn't cruel. He simply didn't know you would react that way when anyone else would've—like a vacuum in the feelings department.

Like most Asperger's sufferers, my father spent lots of time alone thinking. He was a great thinker—just didn't feel much. He loved sitting alone thinking—hours on end in solitude! But he was generous with his time with me. He may have been the world's best bedtime storyteller. Every night he told the most marvelous stories until I fell asleep. Action stories he invented with vivid protagonists—superheroes, natural leaders. At the time I couldn't see how they applied to me or why he was telling them.

His career was in OPM (Chapter 7) as a sole practitioner. Alone! He was an amazing analyst of business managers and CEOs in particular. He analyzed their actions. He knew little about their feelings. I recall as a young man watching him interact with executives.

When conversation turned toward feelings, my father steered them back to actions. He was right about emotions relative to business functions. For 40 years our society has focused too much on feelings—too touchy-feely for its own good! Bernesian psychology taught me why our feelings follow our actions and not the other way around. Act certain ways and your feelings follow. Trying to adjust your emotions otherwise simply goes nowhere—no matter what you do. Do the right things, you feel better. Do the wrong things, you feel worse. Your actions determine how your feelings trend. Early motivationalists like Dale Carnegie and Napoleon Hill got this. Freudian psychoanalysts didn't.

Un Poco

As a child I didn't get it either. The youngest of three, my family nickname was *Poco*, from Spanish meaning "little" or, as I thought it applied to me as a youngster, "of little significance." Both my brothers were bigger, older, smarter. I was a sleepy school kid—bad grades, lazy, the dog ate my homework, daydreaming—generally going nowhere fast. My eldest brother was the opposite: six years older, perfect grades, star athlete, perennial teacher's pet, popular, handsome, articulate. He was student body president of his elementary, intermediate, and high schools before becoming valedictorian, winning a Rockefeller scholarship, and going off to Stanford. I was Poco!

In sixth grade—don't know what happened—the dog stopped eating my homework and I studied, got good grades, joined the Boy Scouts. I read a lot. However, studying and good grades aren't really too tough for a child of someone with Asperger's. You think through what's needed and do it. Skip the feelings.

Since my brother had been student body president, I decided I should too—youngest brothers are great copycats. But to win, I had to run against a really popular kid, Robert Westphal. No one else would—only I was that stupid.

The school president was elected by fourth-, fifth-, and sixth-graders. I knew I couldn't win sixth-graders who knew us well—no chance. But I figured sixth-graders would be generally snotty toward younger kids, and fourth- and fifth-graders couldn't tell one sixth-grader from the next. So I spent my time with younger kids while Robert spent his time with sixth-graders, assuming the younger kids would follow. It worked. I lost the sixth-grade vote big but won the election.

And it dawned on me: You get out of life what you put into it. I put time into the younger kids so I got their vote. It worked so well, I repeated my success in seventh and eighth grade, winning by appealing to those who didn't really know the candidates. So I had these leadership positions where I should have been a leader, but I wasn't. Like any politician I didn't really care about my fourth- and fifth-grade constituents; I only cared about what it took to get elected. Leaders care about those they lead, even if they're only fifth-graders. I knew what I was doing politically, but didn't have a clue what a leader was until I discovered JC.

> *Any fifth-grader can tell you—you get out of life what you put in.*

Follow Caesar's Lead—From the Front

In California public high school, I needed a foreign language for college and picked Latin. Howard Leddy, my Latin teacher, had the class read from the text. Every day, someone would query him about the story and he would launch into storytelling mode—particularly about Julius Caesar. We liked that better than reading Latin so we baited him whenever we could.

One aspect boosting Caesar's success was he led from the front of his troops, whereas Roman officers otherwise marched behind. You can't lead from the back and Caesar knew it. The Roman model assumed if the general was killed, the troops were vulnerable, so he remained behind—win or lose. This is the chess model—protect the king. Problem: Front line soldiers are vulnerable moving forward—a wrong move can lead troops to battle, have them decimated, retreat, and the "leader" is still personally safe. Soldiers knew that. When Caesar led from the front, his troops knew he wasn't asking them to take a risk he wouldn't take himself, so they were more confident, fought harder, and won always. Latin put Caesar in my bones.

The Drifter's Decade

After finishing a confusing college stint (it was 1968 to 1972—Northern California was crazy), I had no particular direction. Beyond my sole-practitioner father, I had no real-life business leader role models. Caesar led soldiers, but what else would you lead? So I worked for my father. No better ideas. If that didn't work, there was always graduate school. And after a year, I didn't want to stay. My father couldn't identify my feelings and I wasn't feeling too good. I'd either kill him or he me. Not good. So I quit—started my own firm. I didn't know I was too young to be able to do that, so I could. There I was, alone, the sole-practitioner son of an Asperger's sole practitioner spending lots of time alone thinking.

The Other People's Money (OPM) world (Chapter 7) was vastly different then—more primitive, less specialized. Brokers were still on pre-May-Day monopoly commission rates but also dominated asset management. Financial planners existed but weren't what they are now. They were tax shelter salespeople who vanished with the 1986 Tax Reform Act. Independent registered investment advisers, my ticket, existed, but were few and could have been doing any darned thing in terms of fees and activities. I basically drifted for a decade, getting and losing a very few clients, while getting paid for some crazy things.

I got paid for library research projects—a lot like school. In those pre-Internet days you could get paid for library capability because information wasn't otherwise easily available. I got paid to provide information on stocks, industries, and various oddities.

For example, I did a study of over-the-counter drug side effects and which drug firms were affected. I got paid for specific stock ideas. I had clients paying for investment advice—I think they thought they were secretly getting my father's views. I built portfolios and financial plans for folks. I helped several tiny firms get bought.

I took side jobs in construction to make ends meet. For a year I got paid every Wednesday night to play slide guitar in a Bay Area bar. Anything for a buck! And no employees—never thought of that! I had a part-time secretary once, briefly, about nine months. She quit—said I was a lousy, imperious boss. Probably was. Besides, who would work for me? I was no leader.

But I read a lot. Books about management and business—and maybe 30 trade magazines a month for years. Like *Chemical Week* and *American Glass*. I studied companies. At various times I studied steel making, glass making, fiberglass, fertilizers, shoes, farm implements, cranes, coal mining, machine tools, surface mining, chemicals of all kinds, and electronics. During this decade I did my original studies of price-to sales-ratios, which later largely launched my career. I was drifting, but learning lots.

Around 1976 I drifted toward packaging venture capital deals. There were very few real VC firms then, maybe 30 nationally. I met occasional entrepreneurs who had a novel idea but couldn't raise money to fund it. I helped them. I didn't see that if they couldn't raise their own money, it was a bad reflection on them. Still, I helped put together prospectuses and tried to raise equity capital from the existing VC firms and wealthy Bay Area individuals.

I really tried hard on four deals: a laser maker, a restaurant, an airport limo service, and an electronic materials maker. I got paid cash and/or equity for done deals. Fortunately, the restaurant never got funded. I'm sure it would have flopped. The laser company was great in all ways and motivated me to do more. The limo firm funded but failed almost instantly. But the most important on my path toward leadership was the electronic materials maker.

Making Material Progress

The company was called Material Progress Corporation (MPC) and was funded with mostly East Coast venture money and some Bay Area rich individual money. It had leading-edge scientists and was to grow an array of exotic garnet crystals used in electronics. It had proprietary technology in crystal growing and polishing. It got funded, yet wasn't going well.

Eventually the board demanded a new CEO. They still loved the concept and technology so they ran a search for a top-tier CEO and put up more money to expand. Meanwhile, MPC was rudderless and bleeding money. To stanch that, I got to play part-time, interim CEO. My charter was simple. I was to cut costs as much as possible to reduce losses without losing the key scientific or operational people. It was 1982. Things were tough everywhere. The world was in recession. Poco was starving and pretty recessed himself. I needed income. This was it.

On Mondays I worked from my normal office doing my work and theirs. Tuesdays at 3:00 AM I'd drive two hours to Santa Rosa where MPC was located. I'd stay through Thursday evening, drive home, and work Friday in my office again. I got paid by MPC by the day, like a consultant. There were about 30 employees in one facility. I'd never managed anyone. Now I had to. And I did ok—much, much better than I expected. And do you know what I learned?

I learned the most important part of leadership is showing up. Could have fooled me! That wasn't in the books I read. Turns out eagerness is infectious. I moved the CEO's office to an open glass conference room where everyone could see it and me. You couldn't get in or out without seeing me and me seeing you. I made a point to be the first there every day and the last to leave. I took employees to lunch every day and dinner every night— at cheesy cheapo diners—but I gave them my time and interest.

Learning to lead is easy. Just show up and try.

I wandered around endlessly talking to them, focusing on every single one and what they thought.

I brought them all together regularly to talk them up. The effect amazed me. And them! That I cared made them care. This is a basic truism of management and leadership—straight from Julius Caesar. Suddenly I felt what it was to lead from the front. They worked harder and smarter, innovated, and just generally gave a darn whereas they hadn't before. I did this for nine months. We cut costs and boosted sales—got to cash-flow positive and break-even on the income statement. We even developed new products for the next CEO's arsenal. I felt needed and was sad when they found their new CEO. My time was done.

Meanwhile, a "normal life" client hired me for a consulting project. I took a week from MPC to travel with him, interviewing leading investment names for a mutual fund venture of his. He was young himself and I acted like his sidekick—helping him think through what he was doing real-time.

We interviewed the legendary John Templeton and Arnold Bernhard, Valueline's founder and CEO—a big name back then. And John Train—then a *Forbes* columnist who ran a money management firm and had just written a bestselling book, *The Money Masters*, with a section on my father. And we interviewed many more. Most of these folks didn't know any more about running a real business than I did. Guys running real money with real employees—and they didn't know the leadership basics I was just learning but feeling in my bones at MPC. That was an amazing eye-opener. If they could, I could.

Maybe I could get a few employees who would work for me, just like at MPC, and do as well as these guys at building a business, or better. Templeton's investment prowess impressed, but none of these guys' business and leadership acumen wowed. Templeton was super rich and successful, but none of them were what Ken Iverson of Nucor (covered later this chapter) was. None were what I considered a role model CEO.

Back at MPC I had to pay for my own hotel rooms and was starving. The cheaper the hotel the more alone you feel. One night, alone in my $18 flop-house hotel room, I sat thinking. Alone, alone! No TV. No phone. No air conditioning. Son of Asperger's before Asperger's was known. Dots started connecting. My father had written a book and it had been good for him in the 1950s. I had the price–sales ratio thing. Even my childhood political foray made sense—you get out what you put in. I could manage and lead at least a few folks. Maybe I could learn to write. Maybe about price–sales ratios. Maybe I could build a firm that just did money management. So after MPC, I started building my firm. (That's the founder-CEO route in Chapter 1, not this one.) But for any CEO there are two major issues: How to get the job and how to lead.

HOW TO LEAD

Hey, I just told you how to lead—from the front. Show up, care, focus on people, be there—early and late. Focus on every rung of the ladder separately and together. Spend time with managers. Spend time with line soldiers. Give your time—from the front. Don't ask them to do anything you wouldn't do. Make them know you care. Go with sales folks to see their customers—your customers. Go with your folks to see your vendors—their vendors. If you travel and they fly coach, you must also. Stay in the same hotel and class of room they do. You're with them. If you don't put yourself above them, they will put you above them in their hearts, which is where it matters. If you care, they will. If they care, they will do as well as they can.

That's leadership—getting them to care so they do as well as they can. People often ask why I don't have a private jet. It would demoralize my people if I did. I fly commercial. They love that.

When I'm with them I fly coach. Amazes clients who see me on board! If you crave CEO bucks, don't be a big jerk. Focus on your people. Skip the perks that may bug your people. That's leading from the front.

Show them you care— by leading from the front.

You can't lead from the back, really. Ask yourself what Ken Iverson would do. Or Julius Caesar. Ok, maybe *he* should have gotten a few bodyguards.

I've read lots of books on CEOing. Some are listed at this chapter's end. But the most important things I ever learned about leadership and being a CEO, I learned from Julius Caesar and at Material Progress. Whether you're a founder-CEO as I am or a replacement CEO as I was at Material Progress, it's all about how you get it in your employees' bones that you care—about them, the firm, the customers, the outcome. They need to believe you aren't just in it for the bucks. They need to believe. You need to make them believe. The best way to make them believe is to believe yourself. The more time you put into people, the more fun it becomes. Staying in lousy hotels and flying coach aren't fun. But it works.

HOW TO GET THE JOB

There are four best paths to becoming a non-founder CEO. You can:

1. Ride along to the throne.
2. Pay for it, literally.
3. Be the go-to.
4. Get recruited.

Riding along (Chapter 3) then switching paths is fairly common for CEOs—the technique used by Jack Welch, Steve Ballmer, Stan O'Neal, Lee Raymond, and so many more. This is the rise-through-the-ranks model. It's lower risk, but it's still hard to get started. It requires ride-along skills, yet has no certainty.

Paying for It—Literally

Or just buy a small firm (if you have the money). It's basically a one-man private equity transaction. This can be easier than being a founder. Buy it, fix it, make it huge—like Warren Buffett did with a tiny textile firm he built into Berkshire Hathaway. Or like Jack Kahl when he bought a tiny plumbing products firm, Manco, in 1972 for $192,000. One product they had was an unassuming, silver industrial tape that was versatile. He rebranded it "Duck Tape" and gave it a duck mascot. Kahl sold Manco to the Henkel Group nearly three decades later when sales topped $180 million.[6] Not bad!

Be the Go-To

Many CEOs come from VC, private equity, and major consulting firms. Just as I got the job when Material Progress faltered—because I knew the VC people—you can too. Had I not been too young and inexperienced, I might have kept that job permanently. One VC firm that invested in Material Progress was Boston-based Ampersand Ventures. Among their young associates assigned to MPC was a chap named Steve Walske. Steve and I spent lots of time together then and were pretty good friends. Great guy. Smart. Savvy. He knew their holdings well.

One holding, Parametric Technology Corporation, a Boston-based enterprise software firm, was struggling. Steve quit VC to run it. When he became CEO in the early 1990s, it was a public stock with a total market value of about $100 million. By then, he had the chops to step in as a full-fledged CEO. Before he bailed out, it grew to a market value of more than $10 billion in the late 1990s.

Coming from a VC background, Steve had a great CEO career, prospered, and split. One reason to work for a VC firm out of school isn't to do VC but to bide your time until one of their wobbling portfolio companies becomes an opportunity for you to be a CEO like Steve Walske. You can do the same thing from a major consulting or private equity firm.

Get Recruited

The final path I propose sounds strange and is perverse, but it works:

1. Take some acting classes, and
2. Study recruiting firms (aka headhunters).

Not low-end firms, but top-tier executive search firms like Spencer Stuart (www.spencerstuart.com) or Russell Reynolds and Associates (www.russellreynolds.com). When boards need new outside CEOs, this is where they go. Recruiters and board members will disagree with me completely about this, but the process is pretty simple and superficial. It starts with resumes, goes to telephone interviews, in-person interviews, background and reference checks, and then interviews with the board.

As such, it's more about interviewing skill and the *appearance* of management skill than real leadership skills. I've seen blokes I wouldn't hire as a dog catcher get hired repeatedly as CEO this way without ever really doing much in real life because they're dynamite interviewers. This is where acting comes in. Acting helps you make a great first impression and bowl someone over briefly.

CEO recruitment isn't pretty. Recruiters think they can see through a gilded-lily resume. Some may, but many can't. If you haven't been CEO yet, those that can't are your market. You can gild your resume by packaging it well. It isn't lying—it's packaging. I'll bet two-thirds of you reading this book not only know a lot more about packaging a resume than I do, but have done it multiple times. If you haven't, there are books on this trivial part of job searches.

Aim Small . . . at First

You aren't trying to start as IBM's CEO. You want a tiny private firm with an external board needing someone to come fix it. You needn't be any better than I was when I was at Material Progress to make your own material progress.

Folks who do this well never stop interviewing or marketing themselves to executive search firms—never ever. Once you're CEO of one tiny private firm, immediately start interviewing at firms twice the size. You can't do that through the search firm that got you the first position. They can't and wouldn't want to take you away from where they just put you. But you can market yourself everywhere else. Right after becoming CEO of a 20-person firm, take to lunch every recruiter you can find. Keep updating them on your firm's progress. You want to be off to a bigger CEO job within two years so you're not too associated with the lousy little firm you're actually running and its faults. Keep moving. Never stop. Don't worry about leaving the smaller firm behind. You can make a lot of progress there in two years, just like I did at Material Progress in nine months.

I saw one guy—great at this—who to my certain knowledge was a former securities criminal (whose name I leave out so he won't sue my sorry arse). He used this process to get four CEO jobs of increasing size in eight years—all through headhunters—one he used twice. He did ok at these jobs and never broke the law again as far as I know. Once he made it past the first job, he never really got background checked in a way that would have uncovered his past. My point is, for this, interviewing skills are more critical than any other skill.

Another guy—I like him, nice guy—but he's a rotten leader. He used this process to go from running a company division that was no good before, during, and after he was there, to running a string of progressively bigger firms until he was selected to run a Fortune 100 firm which he promptly led to be taken over—giving him a great golden parachute. I love the guy, but he couldn't manage his way out of a paper bag—no leadership skills at all, tries to lead from the back. Couldn't analyze a pair of dice for their dots! Never kept a job more than two years from when I met him. But he got progressively bigger CEO jobs and pay because he interviewed so well and was so personable, charming, engaging, and made you believe him—at least long enough. He was also great onstage as an actor. Take a few acting classes. They help. You can do this.

THE BIG PAYDAY

Your goal? Big firm CEOs (and some smaller ones) collect big pay, stock options, deferred comp (salary set aside in tax advantaged ways), and other perks. Smart CEOs negotiate great terms and their potential exit package—up front.

Who makes the most? Table 2.1 shows America's ten best-paid CEOs in 2007. Note: The top ten names change, sometimes radically, year-to-year, based on which industries flew high, who personally blew up, or who negotiated the best terms. Morgan Stanley's John Mack will fall in 2008 tied to his firm's mortgage woes. Glenn Murphy's new to the list—appointed Gap's CEO in 2007. Lots of flux here—well-paid career risk. Some of 2006's top ten are not only off the list, but lost their jobs, like Merrill Lynch's Stan O'Neal and Yahoo's Terry Semel.

> *Negotiate great terms up front—including your exit package.*

Table 2.1 Top Paid CEOs in 2007

CEO	Firm	Total Compensation
John Thain	Merrill Lynch	$83.1 million
Leslie Moonves	CBS Corp	$67.6 million
Richard Adkerson	Freeport-McMoran	$65.3 million
Bob Simpson	XTO Energy Inc.	$56.6 million
Lloyd Blankfein	Goldman Sachs	$53.9 million
Kenneth Chenault	American Express	$51.7 million
Eugene Isenberg	Nabors Industries	$44.6 million
John Mack	Morgan Stanley	$41.7 million
Glenn Murphy	Gap Inc.	$39.1 million
Ray Irani	Occidental Petroleum	$34.2 million

Source: The Associated Press, "List of Highest-Paid CEOs in 2007."

Many of these aren't household names. Ironically, top pay doesn't always link to which firms did best. It often reflects who had great career prospects and could have been CEO at any of many firms, but took a huge career risk to live for a few years in head-on-chopping-block status—betting his career on what happens in a short time span. Semel and O'Neal gambled their futures and lost. Probably no one will pay them again to be big-time CEOs, but they negotiated terms up front paying them for that risk.

Media Whining

Beware: CEO pay often leads to media harping, "They aren't worth it." Maybe, maybe not. But it's up to their board, so complaining won't help. If you don't like it, don't buy the stock. If you like it—great! Maybe this is your road. The media was apoplectic when **Lee Raymond**, former ExxonMobil CEO, retired in 2005 with a $351 million exit package.[7] Did he deserve it? I don't know. I'm sure most, if not all, was part of a contract negotiated beforehand. It works like this: I make a deal where if I do this, the stock does that, sales and profit do the other, then I get paid X, Y, and Z. The formula says what I get if you fire me or I quit. Both sides think the deal favors them. It usually works better for one side than the other.

Timing helps. In 2005, Exxon recorded the largest single-year profit of any firm, ever—$36 billion.[8] Effectively, Raymond got 1 percent of that. He oversaw the big Exxon-Mobil merger—no small feat. During his 11-year reign, the stock rose about 400 percent.[9] Put simply, $1,000 in the S&P 500 over the period became $3,323, but $1,000 in Exxon became $5,000.[10] Millions of Exxon stockholders—individuals, institutions, pension funds—benefited. Don't forget about Exxon's 80,000+ employees[11] and their pay and retirement assets received. If most big firms could guarantee their stocks and firms would do so well for so long, they would eagerly pay Raymond's compensation or more. The problem is there's never certainty.

Big pay seems "obscene" to some. If that's you, this isn't your road. Most observers aren't so upset at big pay for successes, but they really hate failed CEOs (perceived or otherwise) getting a huge check going out the door. Crucify them! Still, if you become CEO, fail, and get crucified publicly—you still almost always end up well-off financially.

CEOS AND SUPERHEROES

It's tough becoming CEO, and tougher lasting long-term. One way to boost your odds is: Think hero. Be a swashbuckling risk taker. The one with vision, fearlessness to pursue it, and fortitude to recognize mistakes, alter course, and plunge fearlessly ahead again. Good heroes make exceedingly lonely decisions, but sell the board, employees, and shareholders on why the road less taken is better. Those unpopular decisions can flop, but real heroes usually bounce back.

One former superhero CEO was GE's **Jack Welch** (net worth $720 million).[12] Welch became CEO in 1981 when GE was a great company, turned it upside down (read: layoffs), and made it greater. Welch didn't just trim payrolls—he decimated whole business lines. To him, if GE wasn't a world leader or a close second at anything, they shouldn't be doing it. Throughout his career, he fired the bottom 10 percent of managers yearly.[13] While those fired managers likely weren't pleased, there are few CEOs in modern history as well regarded as Welch.

Non-heroes shy from massive restructuring, viewing major overhauls as risky. They fear backlash. Employees and the media hate terminations. Welch wasn't frightened. Now, many emulate Welch's style, which fared well

> *Being a hero is a good path to the CEO chair.*

for GE—$1,000 invested in GE during his 21-year reign became $56,947, whereas in the S&P 500 it became $16,266.[14]

Ken Iverson, former CEO of Nucor, was among the all-time greatest CEO heroes ever. People adored him. Heck, I adored him. Iverson brought Nucor back from bankruptcy's brink in the 1960s and built Nucor in an otherwise unprofitable world of steel. Nucor is today America's largest steel firm. He did it the old-fashioned way. He developed technology, low-cost production, and novel management techniques. He challenged conventional steel head on, underpricing them—eating their lunch. He built a lean, mean machine and a model of superior management—a model now globally emulated.

American steel was dying for decades from bloated bureaucracy, union strangulation, and government protectionism. Iverson decentralized decision making, axed executive perks, and mandated only four management layers between factory workers and him. He demanded innovation—from everyone. His employees loved him and would have marched off a cliff for him. His story is in a truly great 1991 book *American Steel* by my friend, Richard Preston.

I first met Iverson in 1976. Few could then see Nucor's future. But Iverson simply bowled me over, and I'm not that easily impressed. He was bigger than life. Within minutes he made you a believer. He was more comfortable in the mill with his crew than in fancy office buildings—but he was comfortable there, too.

And that quality is key to being a hero-CEO. You must make your employees adore you while also being seen as a tough son-of-a-bitch. You must be fair and even-handed, though heavy-handed when needed—but always without a hot temper. Willing to take the big risk but also shrewdly calculating, not scheming. A man of the common people who is as happy or happier with his smallest customer or lowest-level employee as with the board! Usually a hero-CEO sets his compensation up in advance so he trades off base compensation for big upside. Then when he gets rich, few complain. Most wannabe hero-CEOs fall down on one or more of these qualities.

Carly Fiorina, ousted from Hewlett-Packard in 2005, fell short as a hero-CEO. She adorned TV and magazine covers—widely seen as a glamorous hero. She led HP through its merger with rival Compaq. Initial results were rocky, as mergers often are. At first she seemed bigger than life. But HP's culture was built on the "management by wandering around" style of cofounder David Packard. She seemed aloof. If employees don't adore you, a wannabe hero-CEO won't endure. She seemed more comfy with media and her board than her smallest customers and lowest employees. It's here, in my view, she fell short and lacked support from underneath when things got tough—so she got axed. Of course, she made out ok with a $21 million parting gift.[15] But in my opinion no one will ever make her CEO of a top-tier firm again. Done.

This leads to a basic rule: Every CEO, every month, must spend time with normal bread-and-butter customers and bottom-of–the-org-structure employees. Forget this and you're lost. Ivory tower CEOs get by with it briefly, easing their own lives—but eventually fail. Top CEOs never forget what makes the firm tick. It's why employees adore hero-CEOs—he or she isn't aloof, seems like one of them, is comfortable with and interested in them—but is bigger than life.

> *To be a hero-CEO, spend time with your smallest customers and lowest employees.*

Mind you—Fiorina, O'Neal, Semel, Countrywide's Mozilo, and so many others who tumbled from their thrones—still traveled this road well. Even if you don't turn out to be a lasting hero-CEO like Welch or Iverson, you can still make huge bucks, bank it, and retire. Or get a paid board position! Lots of firms will hire former CEOs for their boards.

THE BEST PART

The big pay isn't the reason to travel this road. The greatest part about being CEO is helping build people to be more than they were when you met them and more than they thought they could or would be—very rewarding. Money aside, once you get the feeling real leadership imbues (that I got at Material Progress Corporation), you become of the people—your people. You can't get that out of your system. Once you become that kind of CEO, it takes you over.

This is a road I encourage anyone to aspire to because if you're a real success, you help people and build something of social value beyond the firm's financials. A GE or Microsoft provides huge social benefits to our world. Were they run badly, it would be terrible. Ditto for smaller firms—where you may start on this road. It's a terrible waste when a CEO manages badly. You see that happen and you know it's bad. You can do better than that gal or fellow. She or he wasn't leading from the front. Remember my experience—you don't need to have tremendous training to manage, just focus first on showing up, caring, and leading from the front. It's a caring position if done right.

Executive Education

To continue your journey on this road, these books can help:

■ *Your Inner CEO: Unleash the Executive Within* by Allan Cox. The author provides case studies and practical tools helping you see yourself and reinforcing the traits necessary to run businesses from tiny to huge.

■ *What the Best CEOs Know* by Jeffrey Krames. This is a great tutorial on how to be a hero-CEO—lots of examples from past celebrity CEOs.

■ *From Day One: CEO Advice to Launch an Extraordinary Career* by William White. A guide for ride-alongs (Chapter 3) seeking a switch to CEO. It covers creating great first impressions, managing above and below you, and networking.

■ *How to Think Like a CEO: The 22 Vital Traits You Need to Be the Person at the Top* by D. A. Benton. Built from more than 100

CEO interviews, Benton takes you through the personal qualities, like humor, helping you on your way and at the top.

■ *The Five Temptations of a CEO: A Leadership Fable* by Patrick Lencioni. This new, single-sitting read is impossible to put down and exposes the traps awaiting you, like putting yourself first or confusing being liked with leadership.

 ## The Guide to **Becoming the Chief**

Even if you don't found your own firm, you can still lead it to new heights. Meanwhile, you can earn a big paycheck and other profitable perks. It's not easy and takes a long time (usually) to get there. Once you're crowned, the media can skewer you mercilessly. You may get blamed for any mishap! That's the risk you take—but it's well-paid career risk. Failed CEOs can do just fine, but a long career is preferable. So how can you last a long time on this profitable path?

1. *Enjoy what you do.* It usually requires a long career before landing the corner office. It's easier to put in the years if you have a passion for what you do and love—yes, love—your firm.

2. *Don't start as CEO of IBM.* At first aim small—better odds of getting the job and less likely to screw up in ways preventing you from getting the next CEO job at a bigger firm. Or you can just do a great job and grow from tiny to huge.

3. *Get the job.* Beyond founding your own firm, there are several ways to claw your way to the top.

   a. Ride-along. The rise-through-the-ranks method is tried, true, and profitable. Many of our finest CEOs were one-time ride-alongs.

   b. Buy it. If you have the cash—your own or other people's—you can do a one-man private-equity transaction and just buy a firm you like.

   c. Be the go-to. If you're in a VC, consulting, or private equity firm, you can get tapped to step in to lead a troubled portfolio company. You can even go that route specifically looking to be the go-to guy (or gal).

(Continued)

(*Continued*)

    d. Get recruited. Take acting classes, practice interviewing, and wine and dine recruiters. Once you get a job, start selling yourself for the next, bigger one. Repeat this and you can leap-frog your way to CEO of a big firm.

4. *Lead. Just do it . . .* The key to leadership is showing up and doing it. You can read about it, but the best way to learn is by doing it. Show up and care. Talk to your employees and make them feel you're putting them first. Do that enough, and you'll discover you *do* care and you *are* putting them first and you *do* want them to be the best they can be.

5. *. . . but only from the front.* Learn from Julius Caesar. Your employees will respect, follow, and love you more if you lead the charge, every time, and don't hide in the back. Talk, spend time, and travel with them. Stay in the same dingy hotels on the road they do.

6. *Spend time with your lowest employees and smallest clients.* Once you're Big Time, keep leading from the front. It's more important to be comfy with your lowest-level employees and smallest customers than in the boardroom. It breeds trust and loyalty and keeps you connected with your firm's culture.

3

ALONG FOR
THE RIDE:
RIDE-ALONGS

Good at picking winning horses?
Think being boss is tough?
Your destiny could be to ride along.

S ome big-buck cravers don't want the buck to stop with them.
Ride-alongs rise high, play critical roles, are well-respected
leaders, and get rich—but never bear a CEO's ultimate
pressure. Ride-alongs don't point the way. They find the right
horse, hitch their wagon to it, and help the horse. Though they
may never wear a CEO's crown, some famous ride-alongs ride high
on the *Forbes* 400—Buffett's sidekick, **Charlie Munger,** for one,
with $2 billion.[1]

This is no cakewalk! It's devilish divining whether the CEO you
follow is leading you to new heights or off a cliff. Real ride-alongs
aren't lemmings or stooping yes-men (though bad ones can be). No!

Ride-alongs have the board's, the employees', the shareholders', and the CEO's respect—and are paid for it. And, they can say and do things CEO's can't. The CEO is too public! Too visible! When it's time to play good cop–bad cop, guess who plays bad cop? Maybe they don't make founder-CEO mega-wealth, but great ride-alongs get big pay, firm ownership, and big net worth.

WHY RIDE ALONG?

Sound worse than being Dr. Evil's cat, Mr. Bigglesworth? No! Don't equate ride-alongs with "toady" or "groveling sycophant." Toadies aren't powerful—ride-alongs are. This isn't just being a top corporate officer—it is being a partner the CEO won't do without.

Big Backseat Bucks

Top ride-alongs make bucks rivaling other roads. They don't quite keep up with the Richest Road (Chapter 1) or the OPM Road (Chapter 7), but do as well or better than other roads. Munger's $2 billion is far from Buffett's $52 bills. But still! eBay's first employee **Jeffrey Skoll** was a **Jerry Yang** ride-along, now with a $3.6 billion net worth.[2] **Peter Chernin,** a **Rupert Murdoch** ride-along since 1989 and News Corp COO, collected $62 million in total 2007 pay.[3]

Another advantage? There are many more opportunities to ride-along than to be CEO. A single CEO can have multiple ride-alongs—big firms can have many senior VPs, directors, and other senior managers. You may not reach Bill Gates-style wealth or even Jeffrey Skoll-style, but you can get mega-wealthy here.

Make no mistake—these guys (and gals) aren't just riding coat-tails. This is no free ride. They are legitimate leaders with awe-inspiring accomplishments. For example Chernin launched *The Simpsons* and *Beverly Hills 90210*—huge hits for Fox. He was key in Murdoch's DirecTV negotiation and responsible for making Fox a hit-movie machine. And his name was oft suggested as potential CEO for Disney.[4]

Heavy Is the Head

Many just don't set out to be CEO. It's tough! Huge risk, tensions, personal sacrifices—not good for bad hearts. It can be much easier to follow. **Steve Ballmer,** Microsoft's CEO, was with founder **Bill Gates** since almost day one—an ultimate ride-along. He evolved later to be CEO in 2000, but first he ran numerous areas (a typical ride-along trait). Our pal **Hank Greenberg** (net worth $2.8 billion)[5] from Chapter 2 is another long-time ride-along, longer-time CEO. And **Dr. Eric Schmidt** ($6.5 billion)[6] wouldn't now be Google's CEO if he hadn't first rode along with founders **Larry Page** and **Sergey Brin.**

But the ride-along road to CEO-dom isn't easy, smooth, nor for everyone. Recall Stan O'Neal from Chapter 2 was long a loyal, respected Dave Komansky ride-along, but was run out as Merrill Lynch's CEO. David Pottruck, too, was a Chuck Schwab ride-along who failed fast as CEO.[7] Riding along is one path to CEO! But riding along forever is a legitimate road on its own, with no detours.

Another risk and benefit trade-off: Shareholder lawsuits are huge business (see Chapter 6). CEOs are personal and media targets. Maybe you don't want that—or your kids' friends reading about it. You'll be impacted as a ride-along, but not like the CEO—the face of the firm—who bears the brunt of the ill will, the depositions, and stress.

> *A major ride-along benefit: You're less of a target.*

CEOs are often portrayed as heroes or villains—it's that stark! And even if monstrously successful, they're skewered for their big payday (like Chapter 2's Lee Raymond). Being a ride-along doesn't make you immune, but it takes the bull's-eye off your back. It can be a better lifestyle.

The Right Stuff

Some ride along forever because they know they don't have the stuff to be CEO. Big-time successful CEOs are usually charismatic leaders. Not everyone inspires. Maybe you just don't want your employees' and shareholders' fates ultimately on your skinny shoulders. Many folks don't!

In basketball, the fabled players are those who—in the game's last four seconds, when they're down two points and their team is inbounding the ball—think, "I hope I get the ball!" That's a freaky way to feel! Many don't want it. What if you get the ball and don't hit the three-pointer to win? Infinite pressure! Guys who really want the ball right then, right there, are CEO types. But the guy inbounding with the lightning fast pass to the guy who really does want the ball—*he's* the ride-along.

> *Ride-alongs don't score the most points, but they're usually team MVP.*

Under the Radar

In some ways, being a ride-along is harder. You get few accolades. Ride-alongs usually aren't on TV or profiled in *Forbes* (until you become Charlie Munger). But ride-alongs get huge perks—big pay, respect (at least within the firm)—without the giant bull's-eye. And they get a private family life. Aspiring ride-alongs often write their own tickets. Want to run Sales? The CEO sees it as a broadening feature that's good for you. Want to open the London office? Just tell the big man (or lady) and it can happen. And you can have a great life. Sold? Great—but how do you get there?

PICK THE RIGHT FIRM

Finding the right CEO-leader and firm is vital. Ride-alongs remain with the same firm a long time. Even if hired as a high-ranking guy, they subsequently stick with the firm. Ballmer rode along 20 years before becoming CEO. And Munger's been with Buffett over 46 years.

To be taken seriously, you want a long history with whomever you're riding along with—and an image from all sides of complete loyalty. CEOs get hired in from outside, but ride-alongs rarely do—unless hired in with a new CEO. But even when brought in, like Munger and Buffett, they often already long knew each other.

Starting Your Ride

If you're young, start now. But, if you're further into your career, you needn't make drastic changes—unless you're in a shrinking or dying industry. Then you should change regardless. For this, all of Chapter 10's rules on picking a profession apply. But do even more research to ensure you're in a field you want to stick with. As always, pick a relevant field likely to become more so.

Or not! Maybe you want to work for a visionary who will revolutionize American autos. Forever, American autos have been irrevocably doomed. All my adult life, Ford and GM have been trying to go bankrupt, but they're just not very capable so it takes them a long time. I have abundant confidence they will get there eventually. Maybe you will ride along with a visionary who will help speed them toward their goal.

Take once-upon-a-time heavily unionized Caterpillar Tractor. It hadn't done well for a long time. In 1994, then-CEO Donald Fites had a vision, but to implement it, he would need to free his firm from the union's shackles. So he did what few unionized CEOs have the courage for—he took on his union and won. They were picketed for 18 months. Fites refused to cave. He called the union's bluff! Thirty percent of his workforce walked off the job, so Fites hired temp workers. Even his white-collar executives pitched in—his lawyers learned to weld. After that, his union lost power and Caterpillar boomed—and continues to boom.[8] You want to ride with a guy like that. Visionary, tough, single-minded, and futurist.

Pick your firm carefully. You'll be there awhile.

But how do you find him or her? Take Ken Iverson (from Chapter 2). His two initial key ride-alongs, Dave Aycock (operations) and Sam Siegel (finance), did well in life, believing in Iverson and loyally playing help-the-leader. They both told me essentially the same thing about how they chose to ride-along with Iverson—they didn't—it wasn't really a choice.

In the last chapter I told you from the moment I met Iverson he simply bowled me over, and I'm not that easy to impress. He did the same thing with Aycock and Siegel, and they weren't that easy to impress either. You're looking for someone who is everything you aren't and a visionary to boot. You're looking for a leader. You're looking for someone with a certain magic about them, charisma or not. And you keep looking until you find that one person. It's a lot like seeking a spouse.

Leader or Newbie?

You can pick an established firm with an established leader to start your ride, or an entirely new venture—both have ride-along pros and cons.

On the established route, you needn't pick the field's number one firm, though you can. Becoming a high-ranking ride-along in any S&P 500 firm would be profitable. You can find compensation for any large- or medium-sized public firm by checking proxy statements posted on their website. Ever heard of Moe Nozari? No? He's Division Executive VP at 3M and made $7.6 million in 2007.[9] How about Dr. Joan Miller? How can you not know Joan? She made $1.4 million last year as a Senior VP at Quest Diagnostics,[10] a much smaller firm. You don't know these people; I don't either. But someone high up in their established firms knows and likes them. You can be like that.

What you want more than anything is a leader-CEO. One person! Your Ken Iverson. Bigger bucks come from riding with a visionary CEO in a small firm doing a product revolution and helping grow it to a massive size.

But risk here is great. Will you end up at Google? eBay? Or will you pick wrong, joining WebVan, Petopia, or SweetLobster. com, thinking Internet lobster shipping is the future? Sometimes it's obvious. TootsieRollsForEver.com may be an obvious loser, but rewind 10 years. How would you know which search engine would be tops? That's when you need serious private

> *Pick an established or brand-new firm. Brand new is riskier but has bigger rewards.*

equity–style analysis chops. Whether a wholly new field or product or an existing one, you must analyze the business strategy *and* management team. You may have the world's best strategy but a dumbo management. The real key is the leader.

Picking the Winning Horse

The horse you hitch to is what matters. Some say, "Find someone with a fancy pedigree." Wrong! Pedigrees are fine but don't predict CEO or ride-along success. Steve Jobs dropped out of Reed College—not a top 20 school. Don't get me wrong—Reed doesn't produce dopes. My great friend Stephen Sillett, a brilliant guy doing revolutionary research on redwoods, graduated from Reed. But either Steve could have gone anywhere—Podunk-ville Junior College—and been huge. My point is, Harvard, Reed, Podunk-ville—whether you finish or no—doesn't matter! (Bill Gates is perhaps Harvard's most famous dropout.) I went to community college and Humboldt State University (where Sillett researches), but that never stopped me an iota, and a pedigree or lack of it won't make or break you.

> *Pick a horse who's lost a few races, as long as they don't lose the same way twice.*

So what made early Apple-ites choose Jobs? Or Gates? Or Buffett? Or any of the wildly or even modestly successful CEOs who inspired ride-alongs to join them? Charisma and vision. They have it—you have to figure out if it's real or not.

Plenty of people with charisma and vision still flame out. Again, think like a private equity guy and review that section in Chapter 7. Then answer the following questions:

- Does your potential horse have an exciting business vision? One you believe in so much, you'd put your own money into it? (You don't have to, but would you?)

- Does your horse do a good job of firing himself from jobs and delegating? This is vital. Review Chapters 1 and 2 on founders and CEOs and make sure your guy (or gal) is exhibiting most if not all of the required attributes.

- Has your horse failed before? Failure is ok! If your horse has failed, tried again, and failed again (but differently from the first failure), it shows diligence and a learning curve. Don't hitch to someone who keeps failing in similar ways. Learning from his failures (like Herbert Dow from Chapter 1) may bone up your horse for victory. Even Sam Walton flamed out his first time out the chute.

Once you've found the right person to drag you along through his or her success, go with your gut. Either you trust and completely admire this person or you don't. If you do, be endlessly loyal. That's what a CEO demands from a ride-along as a quid pro quo for being the one the CEO can't do without. If you can't find it within you to trust your future success to the fate of one leader, you may be better off taking the established firm route. That works! But the bigger bucks are definitely in being a ground-floor ride-along.

BE THE RIGHT GUY

So you found the firm and horse. How do you become the one who gets to ride along? How do you become the one who catches the visionary's eye? The one he can't do without? Again, it's loyalty!

Loyalty today is more valuable than it has ever been because it's scarcer. Ever since the 1960s our society has extolled the virtues of whistleblowers, activists, he who quits and goes out on his own, protesters, radicals, someone who is no patsy, someone who tells the big guy to blow—you get the point. From movies like *Wall Street* on, there has been an endless tendency to fantasize that the boss is bad and he who upends him is good. That aims square at the CEO, who in turn, more than ever, values loyalty.

Loyalty Goes a Long Way

Successful ride-alongs live and breathe the firm's vision—and not just superficially or for show (which is why you need a firm you love in a field that excites you). Your colleagues should point to you and say, "That guy is *on board*," but not think you're witlessly drinking the Kool-Aid. CEOs and other senior managers (if you're not one yet) want to know for certain you're beyond "in it for the long haul."

Loyalty implies trustworthiness—what's most important. If early on you can't be trusted not to spill the beans on the impending Christmas party's details, no one will trust you later with details for a top-secret product launch. Be loyal, but give feedback honestly. Successful CEOs rarely hear "No" much. Hence, many super successes, not just CEOs, go a bit bonkers. Take Michael Jackson and Madonna—for a long time no one told them, "You know, I think what you're doing is a really bad idea." This happens to CEOs surrounded by fearful yes-men. You must be brave enough to say, "No," but loyally.

> Be loyal, but give feedback honestly. Don't be afraid to say, "That's a bad idea."

One of the legendary things that made Ballmer so invaluable to Bill Gates was his ability to politely tell Gates when he was wrong while still being and seeming ever-loyal.

Munger is known at Berkshire as "The Abominable No-Man."[11] But don't just say "No" to be contrary! Say "No" and bring new insight. If you're loyal and trustworthy with a good track record of unique insight, the CEO will listen and love you.

You must truly feel, in your heart, that your firm is right and just and holy, otherwise you won't make a good ride-along. You must believe your firm is making the world better. That you're making your CEO perform better. That any shortcomings can be overcome—no obstacle is too great. And that while the firm isn't perfect, its benefits overwhelm its shortcomings, and those shortcomings can be fixed.

Ride-alongs can't grouse or complain. All you can do is present a strategy to fix what irks you. Ride-alongs aren't bitter—they're rational but enthusiastic firm cheerleaders. If you don't think you can feel that way about your CEO and firm and you want this road, it's time to find another firm or horse—or both. If you're sarcastic, take a different road.

Be Flexible

If you're an engineer who only wants to write code, it's tough to ride along. The CEO's sidekick must know or learn sales, marketing, branding, manufacturing, supply-chain management, you name it. Jack Welch made this management style the one to emulate. His managers ran one division, then rotated elsewhere. He had depth guys (and gals) who never rotated but had deep, unmatched knowledge in their area. But he also had breadth guys and fostered that. In essence, he was creating an army of ride-alongs and a stable of potential future CEOs—not only for his firm, but for any major American firm. Who wouldn't want a Jack Welch School of Management ride-along leading their firm?

Will Do . . . Not Can Do

Which raises another point—one huge at my firm. I want people with a *will do* attitude. Note I said *will do* not *can do*. There's a difference. *Can do* means capacity and capability. That's nice—cuts it at some places. Not with me and not at GE. When Jack Welch said, "Bob, love your work on microwaves and appliances. Kudos!

But I really need you in water now, particularly emerging markets purification plants. You'll be stationed in Djibouti City. Okey dokey?" Bob doesn't say, "Ok, Jack. I can do that." Bob knows nothing about water purification and couldn't find Djibouti with both hands and an army-issued GPS. But Bob happily says, "Great, Jack. Yes, I *will* do that."

> *Have a* will do *attitude, not a* can do *attitude.*

Can do is what's on your resume. *Will do* means you eagerly stretch beyond—outside your comfort zone. You jump. You will "get 'er done." You will do what's important for the firm, whatever it is. You will take relevant skills and talent and get on the learning curve, fast. You will hire people, perhaps smarter than you, who know more than you and can make Djibouti a success. It's not about *you*—it's about the firm and the CEO's success. His or her success is yours. It's a little about you because you get to go on a roller-coaster ride that, should you survive, makes you better and ready for the next will-do task. But in essence, it's about doing what you will for the firm and CEO, not what you know you can. Huge difference.

Good ride-alongs live the *will do*. They don't whine about shipping to Djibouti. They say, "Done." They volunteer for the ickiest and most unglamorous tasks. You may think this jeopardizes your standing, but believe me, the guy you want to ride along with notices when you will happily do otherwise nasty tasks. That's a guy (or girl) loyal and wanting to go above and beyond and do what's best for the firm and CEO.

At My Firm

More than 25 employees at my firm have become millionaires, several who retired under age 40 to never work again. One of those got bored, returning to work here. Some are much wealthier.

Above them all is Jeff Silk, an archetypal ride-along.

Fifteen years my junior, Jeff was referred via Mike Brusin, a professor and lifelong friend of mine, later a professor of Jeff's.

(Continued)

At My Firm (*Continued*)

(Your past professors can be good reference sources to seek someone to ride with.) Early on, Jeff could barely get his socks to match on a daily basis (seriously). But he never stopped improving, moving forward, and trying while demonstrating loyalty. He checked his ego at the door every morning. He did it all: entry-level research, computer hardware, trading, managing trading, managing service, running our institutional division, and being president and chief operating officer. Now he is vice-chairman and can do whatever he wants in the firm. He has never worked harder than he does now—mostly doing just what he wants, likes, and thinks adds the most value—and he's never been happier. But if I ask, he'll do anything.

I've never had to worry about where Jeff is coming from. If I asked him to do anything, it would be done. Never once have I sensed any envy on his part toward my relatively much greater wealth and notoriety. And he says he has never felt any. Jeff has been here 25 years and is worth somewhere upside of $150 million, which makes him richer than all but a tiny handful of the most famous entertainers. He has an adoring wife (his teenage sweetheart), three great kids, a spectacular home—a great, balanced family life that CEOs rarely can have. He lives a version of the American dream. He feels great about his life. We just had a little 25-year anniversary party for him. He can be very tough, but there were tears in his eyes then. You should go where you will have tears in your eyes 25 years from now, feel good about yourself, and be as rich as Jeff is. It's hard to do better.

'Til Death

Being a good ride-along really is like being a good spouse. A good spouse or ride-along does what's right, first and foremost, and is loyal. She knows when her partner is being an idiot and isn't scared to tell him. (I say "her" because I know which side my bread is buttered on.) He or she has a *will do* attitude (e.g., "Yes dear. I will clean the gutters"; "I will go with you to see the new Harrison Ford flick where he isn't an action hero blowing up bad guys and everything is exciting, but the one where he plays a romantic lead and nothing explodes for three dreadful hours"). A good ride-along or spouse sees the other for all his (or her) faults and still loves him (or her). Being a good ride-along is like getting married—only these relationships often last longer and pay better!

Ride-Along Reading

I've just given you the basics. There's plenty more you can do to research and prepare for this road. The following books provide guidance as you plan your ride-along route.

1. *Good to Great* by Jim Collins. You need to understand what makes a good company versus a great one—it's better if you ride along at a great one. Collins tells you what to look for in a firm that's likelier to become great.

2. *The Five Dysfunctions of a Team* by Patrick M. Lencioni. Is the management team you're riding along with likely to make it? Or are they circus clowns? Read this book to avoid the clowns and figure out how to find and join the right team.

3. *What Got You Here Won't Get You There* by Marshall Goldsmith. A must! This book teaches how to evolve over time into an ever more valuable (and well-paid) ride-along. And if you want to ride-along to CEO-dom, this book helps too.

4. *How to Win Friends & Influence People* by Dale Carnegie. I recommend this for salespeople too, but it's a must for ride-alongs. It's simply the best guide to learn how to positively assert yourself, ask the right questions, negotiate, and deliver more than your boss, clients, and employees expect.

The Guide to **Riding Along**

Just because you're riding along doesn't mean you're just skating by or riding coattails. Good (i.e., rich) ride-alongs are accomplished in their own right. Like becoming CEO, this takes time, grit, determination, and a well-enforced ego. Ride-alongs frequently do dirty work, but don't get CEO-like accolades. Don't fret—ride along well and you'll be more than compensated. Follow these steps:

1. *Pick the right horse to hitch to.* More important than the right field or firm is finding the right guy or gal to ride along with. It's like marriage! Make sure your horse has vision and skill, and you can trust and live with him/her most of your adult life.

2. *Pick the right firm.* More than any other road, picking the right industry, field, and firm is vital here, because ride-alongs are there a long time. You may get carried to a new firm, but you'd still likely be in the same field. Do your research and you'll stick where you land.

3. *Choose—established or new.* You needn't be a ground-floor ride-along like Google's Schmidt, Yahoo's Skoll, or Microsoft's Ballmer—though it's lucrative. If you fear the added risk of a new venture, you can ride along at an established firm—making not billions, but potentially very many millions.

4. *Be loyal.* Be loyal and trustworthy above all. But learn how and when to say "no." Ride-alongs are picked for loyalty, capability, plus honest feedback and criticism. Be a reasonable and rational firm cheerleader.

5. *Have a* will do *attitude.* Go beyond *can do.* Stretch yourself. Do what's right for the firm. Volunteer! Anyone can do what their ability allows. Do more than that.

4

RICH . . . AND FAMOUS

Seeking fame and fortune?
Don't mind abdicating privacy?
Try cruising the rich-and-famous road.

*R**ich and famous* is a popular dream. But most rich folks aren't famous. They own trailer parks or small businesses. They're accountants or doctors, not living fantasy lifestyles. We think big limos, Superbowl rings, Oscars, owning sports teams, or making movies. This road is the stuff of grade-school career aspirations—baseball player, actress, Oprah, Tiger. This road's riches can be planned for, though realistically it's closed to most by the time we're adults. It requires a young start. Kids dream of stardom. Such kid dreamers kid themselves. Be warned—though this road's riches are legitimate, it's hard work and odds of success here are super slim.

Or not. This road has two forks. One is talent—**Derek Jeter, Whitney Houston,** and **Cameron Diaz.** The other is mogul—**Ted Turner, Rupert Murdoch**—who own and run media empires.

The media mogul road is more attainable—you needn't throw a tight spiral or look like Cameron Diaz. You just need what any successful businessperson needs—perseverance, smarts, and luck. It happens later in life, too. But that doesn't make the talent road less tempting.

There's an occasional crossover here—talents who become moguls and vice versa, though it's rare. **Oprah** (worth $2.5 billion)[1] is the richest talent-mogul crossover. She parlayed a newscaster career (talent) into a talk show she produces (talent and mogul). En route, she starred in movies (notably *The Color Purple*, as a talent) and as Broadway producer (also *The Color Purple*, now as a mogul). Such blending is rare. Martha Stewart (worth $638 million)[2] is a talent in her own mogul world. Talent/moguls tend toward bigger wealth than pure talents. And don't forget those diminutive twins—Mary Kate and Ashley Olsen. I'm too big a fuddy-duddy to know which is which but their production firm and clothing lines make them crossovers—worth $100 million each.[3]

Another recent crossover, but this one initiating from mogul land, is pop-culture phenomena **Mark Cuban** (net worth $2.6 billion).[4] In addition to his other fine crossover qualities, Cuban is tough—cares not one whit what his critics say—even has a beyond-great sense of humor about it. In this sense, he's a textbook founder-CEO (Chapter 1). The former bartender began building wealth as a dot-com cowboy, founding Broadcast.com, a web radio station, with a college pal in 1995. Just before 2000's dot-com crash, he made a timely sale to Yahoo for $5.7 billion in stock.

Not only was his firm's sale well timed, but he didn't wait for Yahoo to tank in the tech crash. He swapped a huge chunk of change with Ross Perot for the Dallas Mavericks, and he's been annoying NBA officials ever since. By mid-2006, Mark had already been fined in excess of $1.6 million by NBA officials for his courtside antics and quick temper.[5] And for claiming the league was as poorly run as a Dairy Queen, Mark paid penance by donning a paper hat and serving soft serve for a day from a franchise in Coppell, Texas.[6]

In 2000, he cofounded 2929 Entertainment—a media holding company—and he's chairman of HDNet, a high-definition cable station. In 2007, he joined the cast of *Dancing with the Stars*—a reality show pairing D-list celebrities with professional ballroom dancers for a weekly dance battle. This qualifies him as talent as much as other celebrities who've appeared on the show. (Though he's a bit of a cheater. At one point, he made a living as a disco-dance instructor.)[7]

My editor feared I sounded too mean-spirited in describing Cuban—particularly my last few sentences that don't make him sound like a great talent—and that you wouldn't like that. And it's true—I really haven't said anything really laudatory about him. Well, I'm pretty sure it's the other way around and that I haven't said anything sufficiently nasty about Cuban to make him really like it. For him to love it, I'd have to rag on him pretty heavily. And I like him. Ok, Mark, this is just for you: You're a dirty rotten blah, blah, blah. Feel better? For the rest of you readers, my point is that if you've made a bundle as a mogul and you know how, you can go from the *rich* to the *famous* as a celebrity, just like Mark Cuban did.

THE TALENT SHOW

So how do you become a rock star, NFL pro, or Cameron Diaz? This road's journey starts young. If you're past age 15 and starting football, you won't ever go pro. Sorry. For acting maybe you can start a bit later—age 18—though many start much younger. Any road requires industry and perseverance. Think of a 50-year-old, financially successful CEO—he's likely been at it since he left college, maybe 30 years! But a 35-year-old pro athlete has been at it almost as long. **Tiger Woods** famously started golf at age two.[8] His dad probably enjoyed that more than two-year-old Tiger did. But for winning the Masters at age 22—starting at age two seems right. As Michael Jordan said, "Being a pro is practicing when you don't want to."

Getting Started

Getting rich as a talent requires youth or a youthful decision. A 35-year-old newbie aspirant won't make it in Hollywood, the NFL, golf, or pretty much anything—no matter what. That doesn't mean older folks aren't talents. **Katharine Hepburn** still starred at age 87. But she also starred young. Can miracles happen? Yes, but almost never. **Glenn Close** didn't land her first movie role until she was 35. **Wynonna Judd**, offspring of country superstar Naomi, didn't have a hit until she was 38. The key? Recall the "almost never" part. Most celebs start very young. If you aren't and haven't, the cost of this book will have been worth it, because now is the time to stop wasting time considering this road and seek another.

If you're young and determined with grit—now what? Practice. All day, every day. Successful stars start young but are also freakishly single-minded. Britney Spears and Justin Timberlake worked far harder as children than probably anyone you ever met. Pro athletes generally led monastic childhoods, rising pre-dawn, practicing before, during, and after school. So start waking at 5 AM now for wind sprints.

Want to be a rock star? Join a church choir, play guitar at the old folks' home on weekends, play county fairs. Never decline a gig, no matter how mortifying. Have you seen *American Idol*? Pretty much all of them have been singing for crowds since age nine.

If you want to act, do it. Take classes at your local community college. Big cities have lots of choices. Classes are really just another excuse for practice. To self-teach, pick up *Respect for Acting* by Uta Hagen and *An Actor Prepares* by Constantin Stanislavski—*the* book on method acting. But find a local theater or summer stock and just do it.

Sell Yourself

To succeed, you must sell yourself or you miss gigs. If you make it, you'll have an agent selling you. (Entertainment and athletics are highly unionized. You must play by union rules.) But how can you get to needing an agent? *Back Stage* magazine lists casting calls in every major city for TV, films, voiceover, radio, you name it. They even have listings for non-pros like you! You can search and post your resume (skinny though it is) online at Backstage.com. You need a headshot (8 × 10 black-and-white photograph—have a pro do it, or a very skilled friend) and a phone number. The listings tell you just what you need for the audition—a prepared monologue, an accent, eight bars of a Broadway tune. With *Back Stage*, a stack of headshots, and some postage, you're ready. Getting the job—that's up to you. It's selling.

Eventually you'll need an agent. They'll find you higher-profile work but also take a cut of profits. Agents are also listed in *Back Stage* magazine. Note: Never pay to audition or have an agent look at you. Real agents won't ask for money until you get paid. If they want money up front, it's a scam. Always. Run.

One day, like Brad Pitt, you can be picky. But at first, if someone offers you seven bucks an hour to wear a chicken suit and dance, start dancing. For more on getting started, *Back Stage* is a great source overall. (Read the section on "Avoiding Scams" first.) Also, pick up *Breaking Into Acting for Dummies* by Larry Garrison and Wallace Wang, which covers acting's business side, from resume building to finding every kind of job and dealing with unions.

Eventually, you must join a union. You can't get certain jobs unless you do, but then you're bound by draconian union rules. Remember the 2008 Hollywood writer's strike? Many writers probably didn't want an unpaid four-month vacation, but if the union strikes, them's the breaks.

Rock On

The same rules apply for would-be rock stars: Sell yourself and take whatever work you can. Walk into every bar and offer to play—for free! (Once you get a following you can demand money.) Create a press kit—a picture, some reviews (have your mom write them—if you're too old to have your mom write them, then you're too old), newspaper clippings, and a CD. Hit as many venues and booking agents as you can. It's a numbers game! The more people you contact, the better your odds.

Once upon a time it was all about the studio album. Not anymore! With a decent computer, pretty much anyone can make a CD, and anyone can buy most any single song through iTunes. These days, to make it big you either have to be a songwriter (see Chapter 8) or tour. Even big names like **Madonna, U2,** and rapper **Jay-Z** (more on him later) have abandoned traditional record labels and signed huge contracts—$120 million for Madge and $150 million for Jay-Z—with Live Nation.[9] Live Nation, a spin-off from radio conglomerate Clear Channel, owns and operates hundreds of music venues internationally.

But before you can negotiate a $150 million deal, you must log hours on the road. So how do you find a "booking" agent? Same as actors! Again, don't pay up front. Second . . . sell! Booking agents are listed in yellow pages or with your local union. Send them a press kit and invite them to gigs. Required reading: *All You Need to Know About the Music Business* by Donald S. Passman walks you through finding an agent and negotiating a contract. And for a clear-eyed look at the industry, read *So You Wanna Be a Rock & Roll Star* by Jacob Slichter. You may not want to anymore after reading it.

The Sporting Life

Athlete's paths are better defined. High-school sports star. Recruited for college. College stand-out. Recruited for pro team. If you don't make it as a high-school sports star, take another road. It's very rare to go pro direct from high school. Some have, like Kobe Bryant, but don't try it. If you suffer a career-ending injury, you'll at least have a college degree. Tennis champs generally don't go the college route. Nor do Olympic gymnasts—at least not until after the Olympics—but gymnasts' careers are over by age 19 and they generally aren't "rich and famous." But Tiger went to college! Sure, he dropped out (like Steve Jobs and Bill Gates), but first Stanford wanted him.

Pro athletes require an agent. IMG is perhaps the best-known sports agency and manages many huge names. For others, check the Sports Agent Directory (www.prosportsgroup .com). Again, *don't pay up front!* They get paid when you do—always. Your agent helps negotiate better contracts and lands sponsorships and Wheaties boxes. That's where the

> *To make big bucks on this road, you must sell yourself.*

big bucks are (like lunch boxes and action figures for writers—see Chapter 8). So, to become a pro athlete: 1. Practice 2. Finish high school. 3. Get recruited to college. 4. Find an agent. 5. Become the face of Nike. Easy as that. Now go do more wind sprints.

POTHOLES AHEAD NO ONE SEES!

The talent road is youthful, but unreliable. Persistence has no high correlation with financial success. Nor does talent alone. No matter how talented an actor you are, odds are seriously against you ever being employed in acting. The numbers are scary. According to the Bureau of Labor Statistics (BLS), in any year there are only about 157,000 acting jobs. Not 157,000 actors—157,000 jobs (some as dancing chickens). No way to know how many wannabes are waiting tables instead. The Screen Actors Guild (SAG—the TV and movie actors union) has about 100,000 members, but even SAG admits only about 50 earn, say, in excess of $1 million per picture. Only a tiny elite make much more. The rest, according to BLS, make a median salary of $11.28 per hour—*when* they're working![10] Recall those Dell computer commercials with the floppy-haired kid yelling, "Dude, you're getting a Dell!"? He did countless Dell commercials for three years or so—likely earned quite a bit. Despite that success, he's recently been a bartender at a popular Manhattan Mexican restaurant, Tortilla Flats.[11] And he's an acting success!

Let's assume 100 unemployed actors for every acting job (probably a low estimate). That means about a million and a half claim to be "actors" when their tax returns don't so indicate. (Most don't earn enough to *pay* income taxes.) So if there are 1.5 million of you and 50 big earners, you have about 0.003 percent odds of hitting it big. You may scrape out a living, but that median hourly rate means you're likelier making $25,000 a year than anything close to Cameron Diaz status.

Musicians face similar daunting odds. There are no numbers for out-of-work musicians, but very few become the Rolling Stones. Or athletes! Odds are best for baseball players. If you play high school varsity, the NCAA says you have about a 0.45 percent shot at making the major leagues.[12] Terrible! And you still must be a superstar to make superstar salary. Minimum salary for pro baseball players is about $300,000.[13] Not bad, but you don't get super rich on that because you don't last long enough. If you can't hit a fastball, try hockey—the odds are 0.32 percent you'll play professionally—but the top pay isn't so high. Pay is high for top football stars but the odds are worse (0.08 percent chance you'll go pro). Basketball? Only 0.03 percent. Women have it worse. Varsity female high school basketball players have a 0.02 percent chance of going pro.[14] They have fewer teams. It's an unfair world. Still, overall those odds beat the odds of being Cameron Diaz.

Start very young. Stick with it. But make sure you have other marketable skills.

You may say, "But Cameron Diaz makes $20 million a movie!" With that, you don't need a life-long career. One $20 million movie—pay your manager, accountant, trainer, chef, Kabbalah coach, and yoga instructor, take the $7 million left over and retire. Fine, but to make the $20 million, you still actually need to *be*

Cameron Diaz—and that requires having started young or possibly a Faustian deal with the devil. Which raises another trait for all the roads to riches! Folks making $20 million a picture aren't interested in making one picture and retiring. They don't quit—they're tenacious and driven. You must be too. I'm not trying to dissuade you—merely warn you. While on the talent road, you may want to cultivate other functional skills so transitioning to a more reliable road is less painful.

Not So Rich Or Famous

This is also far from the richest road—even for those making it huge. No *Forbes* 400 member is a talent-only richie. Oprah is more of a mogul. The top-earning pure talent is Tiger Woods—taking home a reported $100 million in 2006.[15] Tiger should be *Forbes* 400 material someday. But take Madonna—something is materially wrong with the Material Girl. She made $72 million in 2006 and big bucks for decades, yet her net worth is only $325 million.[16] Given her huge earning tenure, she's lagging. She's been huge for over 25 years—if she saved a mere $10 million a year, invested wisely, she'd have *at least* $1 billion by now. How much can rhinestone-encrusted bustiers cost?

Few actors accumulate astronomical wealth. **Brad Pitt** reportedly made $35 million in 2006, beating his buddy **George Clooney** by $10 million. Brad's ex, everybody's favorite Friend **Jennifer Aniston**, took home $14 million in 2006.[17] These folks are about as big as you get. But if Madonna can't reach the highest wealth echelons, they won't either.

A Short, Unsteady, No-Privacy Road

Then, too, talent life is fickle—an easy road to fall from. You're only as good as your last movie, hit song, or home run—but also the lifestyle tends toward self-destruction. I needn't dwell here as it's obvious from the news. Peer pressure, drugs, divorce; these all fuel self-destruction and don't aid wealth-building. And—no privacy. The stars simply can't go out in public or they get mobbed, putting them in physical danger. Don't believe it? A friend of mine tried going with Whoopi Goldberg to the local 7-Eleven at 3:00 AM. They had to flee from the paparazzi for safety. And Whoopi's no tabloid fixture.

If you don't do yourself in, your allies may. Boxer **Mike Tyson** accused his manager, **Don King**, of mismanaging his assets, and ultimately won a $14 million settlement.[18] While Mr. King probably wasn't the wisest custodian of Tyson's assets, Tyson famously lived an excessive lifestyle, throwing money away with both gloves.

For a lasting rich and famous career, don't do stupid, self-destructive things.

Child stars are ultra vulnerable since they need scrupulous parents and ethical management. **Gary Coleman** (from the 1980s sitcom *Diff'rent Strokes*) earned at least $8 million as a kiddie star, much of which his parents paid themselves in management fees.[19] He later sued and won. But his settlement couldn't protect him from bankruptcy. **Corey Feldman** (in a string of 1980s hits including *Stand by Me*) fell prey similarly—his folks left him with only about $40,000.[20] Rip-off management isn't all. Once-upon-a-time massive talents often don't remain on top for long. Where is **Macaulay Caulkin** now? On this road, you start early, must star early, and then stay persistent.

Hollywood demands youth and beauty. Pro sports require healthy joints. Even the music industry doesn't favor the old. **Springsteen**, **U2**, the **Stones**, and **Madonna** are still making hits and touring. **Van Halen**, led by a somewhat rickety Eddie, took in nearly $100 million touring in 2007.[21] All still huge, but that's about it. Older acts are notable, though few, compared with the endless roster of young bucks on the radio. **Barry Bonds** is a baseball superstar elder-statesman, yet his career is likely all but done. Few pro athletes are on top in their 40s. Actors have it easier than actresses. **Harrison Ford** and **Sean Connery** are still considered sexy. But not older actresses! Even though **Dame Judi Dench** is probably more age-appropriate for Mr. Connery, she's unlikely to be cast as his

If you can't make wise money decisions, hire someone who can.

romantic interest. Maybe **Michelle Pfeiffer,** but even she's probably deemed too old for a romantic lead. Starlets, like athletes, are usually done by their mid-40s. Their earlier earnings are their life savings.

With ridiculously low odds on the far-from-the-richest of the roads, and lots of ways to do yourself in (or have your supposed allies do you in), are you sure you want to continue down this road? If you do, there's probably no one but you that will ever stop you.

Pop Quiz

Who's the most financially successful pro athlete ever? Answer: *Matt White!* Who? White still pitches for Japan's Yokohama BayStars. Nine seasons and 254 games in, his financial success came from buying raw land from a cash-strapped aunt who needed nursing home money. On the land, Matt then discovered over 24 million tons of Goshen stone—used for landscaping and prized for its beauty. At $100 per ton, he owns property worth about $2.4 billion dollars.* Matt is a perfect example of talent not being how you make big money. The world's richest professional athlete didn't make his money in athletics. Cute. Despite his windfall, Matt claims he'll keep playing baseball. Everyone needs a hobby.

*Michael Farber, "The Billionaire in Triple A," *Sports Illustrated* (April 3, 2007).

MOGUL MEANDERING

A more reliable way to wealth and celebrity is becoming a media mogul. Moguls straddle the breadth of media and entertainment. They own studios, cable companies, networks, record labels, magazines, and maybe sports teams. Moguls even produce movies and music. As opposed to talents, moguls are far richer. The *Forbes* 400 is littered with moguls like:

- **Michael Bloomberg**, Bloomberg founder and current New York mayor ($11.5 billion)
- **Charles Ergen**, founder of EchoStar ($10.2 billion)
- **Rupert Murdoch**, News Corp CEO, just bought the *Wall Street Journal* ($8.8 billion)
- **Sumner Redstone**, owns major stakes in Viacom and CBS, gave Tom Cruise a public upbraiding (which Cruise likely deserved) ($7.6 billion)
- **James C. Kennedy** and **Blair Parry-Okeden**, brother and sister, Cox Cable heirs. He's the CEO ($6.3 billion a piece)
- **David Geffen**, founded Geffen records and co-founded DreamWorks, college drop-out and former mailroom clerk, erstwhile friend of the Clintons ($6 billion)[22]

It goes on and on—through **George Lucas** ($3.9 billion), **Steven Spielberg** ($3 billion) and beyond. You get the point. Not a single pure "talent" amongst the richest of the rich, yet plenty of moguls. Bigger bucks and longer-lasting opportunity! Murdoch is 77, Geffen's a spry 65—both in their prime. It requires grit, determination, business savvy, but not Cameron Diaz's looks or youth.

Though I've listed the biggest of the big, there are obviously myriad minor moguls too. Consider my friend **Jim Cramer** (estimated net worth $50 million to $100 million)[23]—a somewhat older guy (i.e., older than Cameron Diaz) who parlayed OPM success (see Chapter 7) into founding TheStreet.com and then moguling into celebrity.

There's no escaping Jim—on TV, in books, everywhere. His high-energy, eclectic TV show makes him a legitimate talent. But Jim didn't start there. Before TheStreet.com, before his hedge fund, before Goldman Sachs, before Harvard Law, he was a journalist on one of California's more unsavory beats—carrying a hatchet and gun for protection.[24] Multitalented, Jim had big but not super-mondo successes on multiple roads before settling in as a mogul and talent. The point: You needn't make it huge to make it here.

You can start small and build. Look at what's available on cable today—500 channels or more! And with Americans increasingly fleeing high-tax states for less punitive ones, there's increasing need for regional radio, news, and entertainment. But be warned: To mogul well, you need business skills. Read Chapter 2 on how to run a business and Chapter 7 on private equity. Buy enough little regional media businesses, and you become the force to reckon with.

Mistakes to Mogul-ness

There's really only one major mistake here—not diversifying. A perfect example is how those who concentrated in newspaper-based media have run aground. Newspapers, once hot, today are not. Yes, Rupert Murdoch may have just bought the *Wall Street Journal* as a toy. But scour the *Forbes* 400 and you'll learn lots of lessons. One: Newspapers are now a way to *lose* money.

It wasn't always so. **William Randolph Hearst's** fortune spawned generations of wealthy Hearsts—and made young Patty Hearst a kidnapping celebrity in 1974 (like Eddie Lampert in Chapter 7, but Lampert handled it better). **Joe Pulitzer,** of the Pulitzer prize, built an empire. So did **Si Newhouse,** whose fortune continues after his death because he had the foresight to diversify outside papers.

Newhouse was and remains such a New York City institution—a Staten Island ferry bears his name.[25] He became his family's main provider at age 13 and took over his first newspaper, the *Bayonne Times*, at 16. (Even though moguls don't need to, he started young.

Like Cameron Diaz!) In 1922 at age 27, Newhouse bought his first entire newspaper, the *Staten Island Advance*, for $98,000, which he owned his entire life.[26]

For all his success, Newhouse only founded one wholly new newspaper. He was an acquirer of down-and-out papers he could turn around in an area soon to boom. Newhouse was a bootstrapper—a wise decision for any founder-CEO. (See Chapter 1.) He plowed everything back in, was ever cost conscious, and fought off unions as costly and contributing to poor quality. At one point, Newhouse's media empire was America's third largest, behind only Hearst's and Scripps-Howard's. Then he diversified—into TV, cable, radio, and magazines. When papers started declining they didn't take him down, too.

When he died in 1979, he left his two sons his firm, Advance Publications Inc., with six TV stations, 15 cable stations, a handful of radio stations, seven magazines under the Conde Nast banner, and 31 newspapers—and the *Staten Island Advance*. Plus cash.

Side note: Successful wealth builders tend to have kids who aren't. Maybe life is too easy for them. But not with Newhouse's sons. Samuel and Donald kept building, adding high-profile magazines including *The New Yorker, Vogue, Vanity Fair,* and *Gourmet*.[27] They are among the few who've been on the *Forbes* 400 every year it's been published (since 1982)—a very tough feat. They're now each worth $8.5 billion.[28]

> *To build a lasting mogul empire, you must diversify.*

The Newhouse empire thrived only because it diversified away from newspapers. You can't find big, new newspaper fortunes today. Big papers have withered from free Internet news. Small city papers withered further from losing classified advertising to the likes of eBay and Craigslist. The lesson: Don't concentrate within one media area—diversify and be all media.

A Hipper Mogul Road

Much better than newspapers today? Hip-hop—it spawns boodles of cash. And hip-hop fortunes all seem well diversified. (Note: Like our pure talent friends, hip-hop mogul is a highly unlikely road. Start young and get a college degree in case it doesn't pan out.)

Sean Combs (aka "Diddy") founded Bad Boy—a media empire including a record label, clothing lines, a movie production firm, and restaurants. He's been a performer, music and TV producer, writer, and even appeared on Broadway. In 2006, his business ventures earned him $23 million and he's worth approximately $346 million.[29] **Russell Simmons,** another diversified hip-hopreneur like Combs, is worth an estimated $340 million. Simmons built his fortune with two record labels and a clothing line.[30] (Hip-hop moguls all seem to have clothing lines.)

Topping them all is **Shawn Corey Carter,** (once accused of stabbing a rival in the stomach for which he got three-years probation), also known as rapper **Jay-Z.**[31] When launching his career, Carter wisely took a stab at cutting out all middle men—the record label, distributor, manager, producer—to keep more himself. And it worked and paid off—huge. As a relative unknown, he launched his own record label, "Roc-A-Fella Records," with friends. In 1996 they released the first Jay-Z album. In this way he was a classic founder-CEO bootstrapper. He then started a riotously popular clothing line, Rocawear, which he sold in 2007 for $204 million. Though he sold the rights to the brand, Carter kept his stake in the firm and still directs marketing, product development, and licensing.[32]

Like any good media mogul, his income sources are diverse. He was formerly CEO of both Def Jam and Roc-A-Fella Records. He has a successful music career and his gig designing clothes. He owns the expanding sports club chain 40/40 Club. He has a film career, a bevy of hefty endorsements, royalties, publishing rights, and he manages other artists. (They're called *artists* even if you can't see what they do as very arty.) He's been a spokesperson for Budweiser and serves as a marketing consultant for Anheuser-Busch. Like any true mogul, he bought a sports team—he co-owns the New Jersey Nets. *Forbes* estimates his 2006 income at $83 million,[33] and his net worth is $504 million.[34] Movie stars, eat your hearts out.

At the rate he produces, manages, acquires, designs, and creates—as long as he doesn't allegedly stab anyone else (unlikely—his new wife **Beyonce** should keep him in check—she seems sweet), he should be *Forbes* 400 material in no time. Like my Mark Cuban comments, my editor winced at the stabbing comments, seeing them as demeaning and mean-spirited on my part and likely to trouble you, my reader. Jay-Z would be actually offended if I covered him and didn't mention the stabbing as he has promoted it himself as part of his bonafides in hip-hop-reality. If you want to take a stab down this road, you need sharkskin.

Read Your Way to Fame

As a media mogul, you should flip to Chapters 1 or 2 on being a CEO and read the books listed there—the same lessons apply. For riches on the strictly "entertainment" road, try the books mentioned earlier in this chapter, as well as these:

- *Audition* by Michael Shurtleff. This is *the* book for working actors, written by a guy who actually casts shows and films and knows what he's seeking. Your first stop on the acting road is here.

- *An Agent Tells All* by Tony Martinez. To act or be in any "entertainment" field, you need an agent. This book gives you valuable shortcuts from someone who knows.

- *Swimming With Sharks* directed by George Huang. You got me, this isn't a book. It's a must-see movie for anyone considering a Hollywood career. This just may cure you of your obsession if you aren't sufficiently and deeply motivated enough.

- *It's Not About the Bike: My Journey Back to Life* by Lance Armstrong and Sally Jenkins. Think you've had it rough? Try being told you're as good as dead at 25. If you seriously want to be a professional athlete, read Armstrong's tale to see if you have the grit.

The Rich and Famous Guide

This is the toughest road. For all who successfully navigate it, there are thousands (or millions) who fall off and flame out. The rewards of being rich and famous remain enticing, so folks keep trying. It's a sort of American Dream—one culminating in a house in Malibu and security guards protecting the privacy you spent decades desperately trying to abdicate.

But there are steps to increase the odds of being either a rich and famous talent or mogul. It's not easy. Otherwise, we'd all be Cameron Diaz.

How to Be a Rich Talent

1. *Start early.* Nearly universally, talents of all stripes start very young and stick to it. The few "discovered" late in life (in their late 20s or beyond) almost all toiled from a young age.

2. *Have responsible parents and/or management.* Talents who don't have a mid-20s meltdown all seem to have fairly responsible parents and/or ethical, responsible management. Talents lacking guidance from a parent or elder tend to end up in rehab repeatedly.

   Talents may also find themselves toiling with little to show for it if their management pockets the profits. As with hiring any professional, your manager must have a demonstrated history and transparent fees. (Creative Artists Agency and William Morris Agency are two of the largest and most respected artist agents.)

3. *Be responsible yourself.* Garnering huge paychecks for movies or records doesn't matter much if they're all blown on stupidity and rehab. I needn't list the near infinite examples of talents who've blown ungodly amounts on not only the tacky and tasteless, but also on drugs, lawyers, and more.

4. *Understand how much you'll need.* Talents likely wouldn't waste as much money on diamond jewelry and lawyers if they prepared a budget. Just because you make $10 million a movie doesn't mean you can spend $15 million a year. The rules of math apply even if you've won a Superbowl.

   Because the talent road is short-lived, talents must understand how much they must amass to support themselves, families, first few wives,

(*Continued*)

(*Continued*)

kids from the first few, and a bevy of girlfriends. If you need a driver, bodyguards, cook, masseuse, and yoga instructor as part of your regular staff, make sure your annual costs don't exceed about 4 percent of your total amassed liquid assets. More than that and you'll likely have to make do on less.

5. *Get a big contract.* If you can.

6. *Repeat over and over.* Repetition pays. "One-hit wonders" have a nice payday for their 15 limelight minutes, but unless they annuitize their fame (see Chapter 8), one hit won't support them their entire lives. One-hit wonders should think about reading the other chapters in this book.

HOW TO BE A RICH MOGUL

1. *Understand the market.* You may think you have the newest technology, best product and programming, and hottest content, but if your target audience is disinterested, then newest, best, and hottest = flop. Successful moguls "get" what their market wants and guess well at how that will evolve.

2. *Buy low, sell high.* Think like a private-equity firm. Si Newhouse didn't care about buying the high-profile properties, and you shouldn't either. Identify growth opportunities and invest there. But remember, sometimes emerging markets never emerge, they just submerge. High-profile doesn't necessarily translate into big profits—just ask *The New York Times.*

3. *Diversify.* Media is fickle and technology is ever-changing. It's tough to know where media might be in two years, let alone ten. Broadly and widely diversified moguls are best positioned to profit from changing trends. You can go deep, as long as you also go broad.

   The most successful moguls today have exposure to TV, cable and satellite, radio, movies, online, as well as traditional print media.

4. *Buy a sports team.* No idea why this is important, but it must be since it's a unifying factor for moguls.

5

MARRY WELL.
REALLY
WELL

Was Marilyn Monroe right when she said in Gentlemen Prefer Blondes, *"Don't you know that a man being rich is like a girl being pretty?*
You wouldn't marry a girl just because she's pretty, but my goodness, doesn't it help?"

Seem ridiculous? Then this isn't your road. See it like this: You wouldn't marry someone physically repulsive to you, so why marry someone fiscally repulsive? If money moves you, shop among the rich. If you don't like the notion, fine. Leave the rich to those who care.

Today, marrying for money is often decried. But marrying well is not new; it's archetypal in literature and mythology—the beautiful peasant girl marrying the earnest prince. In Europe most marriages used to be arranged among people of comparable wealth.

Marrying up was applauded! Marrying down was failure. Because of finances and technology, folks moved in limited circles. They chose mates from their circle or one was chosen by family from outside.

Only more recently has it been common for lovers to choose for themselves—paving another road to riches. Right or wrong, it's taken an unseemly connotation. Whereas in *Pride and Prejudice* we cheer when the heroine bags rich Mr. Darcy, now she might be called a "gold-digger." She shouldn't.

Warning: Marrying money can be rough whether done by a man or woman. We had a young female family friend of considerable inheritance. She married a handsome, energetic young man. All seemed peachy—kids and all. Did he marry for money? Hard to know! We do know he borrowed from her to start his own firm with modest success—it eventually sold for $5 million—which would make him his own man. On the very evening the deal closed, at a celebratory dinner she announced she was leaving him for her kayak instructor. What a slap! She liked being boss. His success annoyed her. She got revenge and a new boy-toy. To show her, he took up with *his* kayak instructor. True story. This can be a bumpy road when money skips love.

Yes, marrying money doesn't always work—but marrying in general doesn't always work either. Divorce rates are high everywhere. Still, there's zero evidence the divorce rate among those who marry up in wealth is any higher than for the general population. If you go about it right, there's a lot you can do to stack the odds in your favor. Most basic advice: Marrying rich is marvelous but you must make sure it's someone you will be good to and who will be good to you. Money can't ever be a replacement for love. But it can make a nice addition—icing on a cake.

You may laugh, but this road is legitimate. In a 2007 *Wall Street Journal* survey, two-thirds of women said they'd be "very" or "extremely willing" to marry for money. It's not just women—half of men surveyed said they'd marry for money too. Interestingly, women in their 20s had both the highest expectations of divorce (71 percent) and the highest asking prices ($2.5 million).[1]

I re-emphasize, marrying rich doesn't mean marrying badly. My paternal great-grandfather, Philip I. Fisher, worked his whole life for Levi Strauss—the person and the firm. My grandfather, Dr. Arthur L. Fisher (whom I wrote about at length in my last book), was a direct beneficiary of marrying for money and so am I. His eldest sister Caroline openly married for money in the nineteenth century when courted—through my great-grandfather's introduction—by a wealthy Levi Strauss relative, Henry Sahlein. Typical of nineteenth-century marriages, she came to love him during marriage. This was just the way it was done back then. He provided for her generously. She in turn provided for her many family members, including putting her brother (my grandfather) through medical school and my father through college. If she hadn't married for money, I'm certain my youth would have been tougher. I benefited through three generations. Even now, there's an annual Thanksgiving dinner Caroline started in the 1920s for the family. Now it's run by her granddaughters all in their 70s and 80s. I go almost every year and give thanks for Caroline marrying for money. Today, the only difference is you want to establish love before the wedding vows. Otherwise the same principles apply.

HOW TO MARRY A ~~MILLIONAIRE~~ BILLIONAIRE

First, how do you find an appropriate rich amour? Fret the other stuff later—falling in love, convincing them to marry you, you to marry them, prenups, etc. First, find the rich folks. They aren't everywhere—as of 2007, only the top 1 percent of Americans had incomes over $364,000.[2] That may not be enough for you. The top-earning 0.1 percent earn over $5.6 million[3]—now we're talking. Still, that's only about 300,000 people. Many are already married (though that may pose no problem for some on this road, since many may soon divorce anyway).

Another story, to emphasize the importance of just finding an eligible, potential rich amour. I knew a guy with about $300 million liquid—a founder-CEO who sold his business. He was 55, footloose, a bachelor—never married, no kids, no worries. He had modest desires, simple clothes, drove a VW—didn't really care for luxuries. He owned stocks and bonds. Whenever stocks wiggled, it drove him nuts so he finally put everything in bonds. I used to cite him in client seminars to show why some people needed stocks and others did not. He had more money than he ever needed, didn't need the higher returns from stocks, and their volatility bothered him. Bonds made him comfy. I finally stopped telling the story because every time I did, a few single ladies remained afterward or phoned later to ask for his contact information. True story! They were at the seminar, going where the money was. They were thinking well. They weren't committed to marrying him, stalking him, or anything else—just to finding him. So how do you find him/her?

Location, Location, Location

Like real estate, the three most strategic aspects in moneyed-mate hunting are location, location, and location. There are places you're more likely to bump elbows with the wealthy. If this is your road, go there. Where? Look at the *Forbes* 400. You needn't set your heights so high, but it's a good geo-wealthical map. On *Forbes'* website (www.forbes.com) is a country map showing where the richest live—an almost perfect visual of where the more modestly rich live. If a state has a high percentage of billionaires, it's safe to assume there will also be similar concentrations of folks with $5 million, $20 million, even $200 million. They flock together because they come from the same basic wealth-generating sources.

As of 2007, California had the most *Forbes* 400 members—88, or 22 percent. New York was next with 73—mostly New York

City (64). Texas (37) and Florida (25) also had lots. Those states are big, so it makes sense they'd have lots of rich folks. Per capita, the place to be is Alaska—with one member for every 220,000 people. (Of course, there are only about 660,000 Alaskans—few to choose from.) Next? Wyoming! One billionaire for every 255,000. Alabama is bad—only one out of 4.6 million. Still, that beats Arkansas, Delaware, Hawaii, Iowa, Kentucky, Maine, New Mexico, North Dakota, South Carolina, and West Virginia—all with none.[4] No mega-wealthy probably translates to fewer plain-old wealthy folks. So leave the poorer places and move to the richer—that's where they'll be! Simple first step.

Best and Worst Places to Hunt for the Richest Americans

Want to know where America's wealthy live? The following is a list of where you'll find the most and least *Forbes* 400 members.

Best Places

1. Alaska (1 for every 220,000)
2. Wyoming (1 for every 255,000)
3. New York (1 for every 264,000)
4. Washington, D.C. (1 for every 275,000)
5. California (1 for every 410,000)
6. Montana (1 for every 468,000)
7. Nebraska (1 for every 586,000)
8. Kansas (1 for every 549,000)
9. Connecticut (1 for every 585,000)
10. Nebraska (1 for every 586,000)

Worst Places

1. Arkansas (none)
2. Delaware (none)
3. Hawaii (none)
4. Iowa (none)
5. Kentucky (none)
6. Maine (none)
7. New Mexico (none)
8. North Dakota (none)
9. South Carolina (none)
10. West Virginia (none)

Source: US Bureau of the Census, www.census.gov; Matthew Miller, "The Forbes 400," *Forbes* (September 20, 2007).

Check Local Laws

Because divorce runs high everywhere, you may be safer marrying in a *community property* versus a *common law* state. Most are common law—41 in all—meaning each spouse has completely separate legal and property rights. Sounds grand, unless you aim to marry well—you always run the risk of being dumped! While I'm not advocating you marry expecting to divorce, you should marry with full awareness that high divorce rates do not escape the wealthy, and you should be prepared for that risk.

In a common law state, if the time comes to divvy assets, you're usually subject to what's known as "equitable distribution of the assets." Equitable? Sounds fair, right? Except "equitable" is in the eye of the judge. What you get becomes a court case, and for that you must review Chapter 6 and how court cases can sometimes become popularity contests—both sides vying for the judge's favor. If the judge decides you're the bad guy (like **Heather Mills McCartney** later this chapter), you may end up with less. And if you married for money, your wealthier mate might be able to buy better legal advice. That's too much uncertainty. You can battle uncertainty with an ironclad prenup or by finding a moneyed mate elsewhere.

For example Arizona, California, Idaho, Louisiana, Nevada, New Mexico, Texas, Washington, and Wisconsin are community property states. There, each spouse typically owns 50 percent of all income and assets acquired during marriage—even if one spouse earns big and the other nothing. Spouses also share equally in debt, but that shouldn't impact you if you travel this road properly. (Laws vary by state, so check with the IRS in your state: http:// www.irs .gov/irm/part25/ch13s01.html.)

A general rule (with many exceptions, of course) is community property states are better for the poorer partner in marriage, worse for the richer. Warning: When a recently married richer spouse wants to move from California to Georgia, he may be anticipating divorce. But moving to another community state is safe. I've been trying to get my wife of 38 years to move from California to Washington—community property to community property—so she knows it isn't for divorce planning. Think about it.

Follow the Money

Next, your odds rise by focusing your career and social activities around the wealthy folks. If you're in finance (52 billionaires) or investments (51), you're more likely to meet a rich mate than in the auto industry (zero). The service industry is fine (42)—maybe get a job in management consulting. Head to New York or Hollywood to swim in the media and mogul pools (33). If you're into environmental causes, you're out of luck—they have none—but oil and gas have 30 billionaires.[5] The mega-wealthy do lots of charity, but they may not like you if you attack the source of their wealth, so Greenpeace meetings aren't a likely meeting spot. But you could volunteer for causes like free trade, malaria-fighting mosquito nets, or vaccinating children globally (very uncontroversial).

Only Marry in Community Property States

Most states are common law—each spouse is separate, meaning their income belongs to them. Community property states consider income and assets gained in a marriage as shared equally by both spouses. To marry well, these community property states may be safest:

- Arizona
- California
- Idaho
- Louisiana
- Nevada
- New Mexico
- Texas
- Washington
- Wisconsin

Source: Kaye Thomas, "Community Property States,"Fairmark.com (May 12, 2002).

If you can stomach it, Republican or Democratic Party activities are a great way to meet rich party donors. Both parties have an ongoing multitude of events to entice and maintain their wealthy donor bases. (Both parties are about comparable in size and wealth, but typically come from different and somewhat conflicting industry slices. The oil guys, for example, are more likely to be Republican. Plaintiff's lawyers are more likely Democrats.) If you become a fund-raising volunteer, you'll naturally meet donors.

These activities tend to work best centered around larger cities and state capitals for obvious reasons. Community charities are a similar approach without the political edge and are everywhere. Just as you're more likely to find a rich mate in rich community property states like California or Nevada than poor states like West Virginia or South Carolina, you're more likely to meet them if you volunteer for the right social or political forums.

Location is key. Search in the ideal geography.

It really is about right place, right time. **Melinda Gates** would never have met **Bill Gates** had she not been in Washington working for Microsoft. Since he was always a workaholic, it would have been weird for him to find love anywhere else. Most of the ultra-rich are like that. They are very obsessed with what they do. You must be where they are.

Another perfect place is free investment seminars. Pick those aimed at high-net-worth investors as opposed to ones for people trying to get rich. Brokerage firms do these in every major community every week, trying to sell attendees commission-based investing products. The audience is a mixture of money, and they usually allow walk-ins—which is good if this is your road. My firm hasn't done these kinds of prospecting seminars in years, but we used to and there were always—always—single people with money in the crowd. New York is great for this—maybe the best.

One night in the 1990s we were doing one of these in Manhattan at the Plaza Hotel. Regis Philbin attended and people gawked—his presence lent the audience a sense of glamour. He ducked out fast before the crowd could maul him. A smattering of attendees hung around after, chatting with me and a coterie from my firm. Among them was a striking young brunette, chatting up one of our reps. Our employees were headed for drinks afterward. Her story was so interesting, our rep brought her to tell her story.

She was a young, practicing dentist who sought marriage but heeded Marilyn Monroe's credo—that you don't marry purely for money, but why not money too? She had a lot going for her and expected much back.

Every evening, Monday through Thursday, after drilling and filling, she sought a seminar hotel. Her two favorites were the Plaza and the Grand Hyatt since they held multiple seminars every night. She picked seminars that looked like they might have the most money and a not-too-old crowd. That's how she got to us. Then she approached the gate-keepers and showed them her dentist business card. She said she could almost always talk herself in. If she couldn't, she'd go down the hall to another seminar and get in there. Inside, there was always free food. Four nights a week she ate free—very frugal. She mingled pre-seminar, seeking targets. She was very direct—asked what they were doing there, told them her career, asked about theirs, and generally flirted—all with men picked at her discretion. In that first conversation she always asked if they wanted children—right then, right there—because the children topic was to her both critical and a gateway as to whether they might be appropriate marriage material or not.

With ones she liked she exchanged business cards and offered one free dental exam—that offer made them remember her. In a week she would call men she liked. If they didn't recall her vividly she knew she hadn't made a great impression and backed off. If they did, she asked to meet for drinks on the weekend. She said she'd been doing it a bit over a year and had dates every single weekend, taking every Sunday off. She received several marriage proposals, but never yet from quite the right guy.

But she said she had every confidence that within a year she would find Mr. Right. I'm sure she did. Marilyn would have been proud. We never heard from her again (we stopped doing that kind of seminar), but I believe she succeeded since she built a machine for it. She seemed way out on the bell curve in her method. But there is someone for everyone and I'm sure one night, the right moneyed man met her and had his light lit. Few are as disciplined and dedicated to this road as this young woman was. But if you're disciplined, you can do exactly what she did and it will work for you too. I'm certain of it.

LIKE A FINE WINE—WELL MAINTAINED

You probably must marry someone older. Few richies are very young. And many are married. However, **Daniel Ziff,** who inherited his $3.5 billion from his publisher father **William Ziff, Jr.,** is a mere 36 and still unattached.[6] Donald Trump's 27-year-old daughter Ivanka may inherit a bundle of dad's $3 billion.[7] And there is **Mark Zuckerberg**, CEO of Facebook—age 24, maybe worth a billion, and still single.[8] But most are older. This isn't just the older guy, younger wife—older rich women like younger men, too. Examples: The younger-man marriages of **Demi Moore** and **Susan Sarandon.** Think of people like a fine wine, improved with age, and in their prime. If you find this assessment lacking romance, remember love is vital on this road, but romance is somewhat optional.

While discounting romance, a fine wine must be well maintained. And like a good bottle of wine, a marriage must be packaged well, with a good prenuptial agreement, particularly outside community property states. The prenup will keep you contained in case of any breakage.

Even in community property states a prenup is vital—assets acquired before marriage can be in play. You need a deal for who gets what, how, and when. Prenuptials are unpopular among young folk these days. They feel too contractual—overwhelming romance. But to marry money, you must. If that's distasteful, consider: You wouldn't enter another arrangement without a contract. You don't adopt a child, buy a home or car, start a job, hire a money manager, even join a gym without a contract. Why is marriage different? Since marriage is arguably the most serious partnership, a prenup is even more vital.

> *Do the math. Know what you're worth and demand it up front.*

Sometimes wine goes bad! You can't control the other person in a marriage. Hence, the matter of divorce. It's never a goal but always a risk. What happens then? How much should you get? Put another way: How much is your life worth? What should your return be per year married? Your time and affection are valuable. It's up to you to value it. If you don't, no one else will.

Consider **Ron Perelman,** a private equity OPMer (Chapter 7) worth $10 billion.[9] And single! Ironically, some say he married wife number one, **Faith Golding,** for money. Shortly after their 1965 marriage (no prenup),[10] Ron borrowed money from Faith to buy his first business. But Ron was super successful. They divorced 20 years later. She got $8 million[11]—less than half a million for each married year. That seems light from a guy like Perelman.

Wife number two, **Claudia Cohen,** a high-society gossip columnist and television personality, fared better. When they quit, Claudia got $80 million for her nine years and one daughter— $8.9 million a year![12] Wife three, **Patricia Duff,** was a political fund-raiser (great way to meet richies, as said before) and sometimes-TV personality. If you want some juicy soap opera-like divorce she-nanigans, Google their divorce. She had one child by him and got $30 million after 18 months of marriage.[13] That's $20 million a year just to bicker in Le Cirque with a guy who couldn't stay married!

Finally came **Ellen Barkin.** I really loved her in 1991's *Switch* and 1992's *Man Trouble.* Later her career slowed, but she used celebrity for money through marriage. (See Chapter 4 on using celebrity to get money and acting being a young and rough road.) She married Perelman in 2000; it ended by 2006. Reports vary on what she got. Her friends claim $20 million, his claim $60 million. Say it's $40 million—$6.66 million a year for entertaining the guy that owns Revlon. In preparing this book and reading her side of the saga, I believe she thought her marriage would last and was shocked it ended. Divorce, again, is never a goal, but always a risk. Still, as Chapter 4 shows, precious few actresses make $6 million a year. And I bet none as old as Barkin (54) do.

But $6.66 million a year is far from $20 million. Where did Barkin go wrong? All his other wives had at least one child—she didn't. Maybe that was it. Also, she had a prenup, but she just didn't demand enough. Looking at Perelman's history she should have known there was the risk he couldn't stay married and demanded pay for early failure. After all, if the marriage endured, the prenuptial terms would never get applied and cost him nothing. My point: Always demand a lot up front. What is "a lot"? In Perelman's case, you use his history, as in, "at least as much as your best-paid former got—inflation-adjusted."

If you don't do this right at the start, it costs at the end. Perelman has more experience and better lawyers than you do, so a great lawyer is essential. For example, **Heather Mills McCartney** got more out of **Paul McCartney** than Perelman's financially most successful wife, Claudia Cohen, did—both with one child each. And that despite Perelman being vastly richer than Paul McCartney, and Heather Mills being a more obvious problem in front of a judge than Cohen. Even the judge said Mills was a pest![14] And judges rarely talk, much less squawk.

You need a good prenup because the list of moneyed marriages ending in divorced is long, like all marriages. A few examples? **Neil Diamond's** ex, **Marcia Murphey,** got $150 million for her 25-year marriage.[15] **Diane Richie, Lionel Richie's** former wife, got $20 million for eight years. **Wendy McCaw,** wife of telecom magnate and

Forbes 400 member **Craig McCaw,** got $460 million—$23 million a year for 20 years! The McCaws did it right and remain amicable.[16] If you do it, do it right with a prenup, and remain amicable after.

Anna Nicole Smith is perhaps the most infamous. I won't delve into it here (anything you want to know and more is in the blogosphere). But the moral of Ms. Smith's tale is always do it right:

1. Get it in writing with a good divorce attorney up front.
2. Don't do anything that looks stupid. In this, stupid is as stupid looks.
3. If you marry a good lawyer, you lose. They know; you don't.
4. Get a grip. You can't win on any road to riches without basic life control.

MEN CAN PLAY TOO!

The stereotype of "marrying money" is the young woman, older man. But this isn't just a female's game! Plenty of men marry successful, wealthy women—older or younger. Fewer, yes, because men otherwise control more wealth. That's not sexist. Just look at the *Forbes* 400—it's mostly men for whatever reason. But that doesn't mean this isn't as legitimate a road for men as women.

For example, if **John McCain** has had successes in life qualifying him to be president, surely his biggest, as near as I can tell, is marrying well. Great-looking, long-lasting, graceful, and mega-rich Cindy! (You've heard the jokes. She even came with her own beer supply!) Ditto for **Senator John Kerry** (net worth $314 million)[17] who married his wealth—twice! Wife one, **Julia Thorne,** was an American blueblood with a fortune to match. But she couldn't stomach political life (who can blame her?) and suffered from depression.[18] Kerry divorced and did it again with **Teresa Heinz.** Ironically, she married her money too! Working as a UN translator, she met and married *Republican* Senator Heinz—the ketchup Heinz.

When he died in a 1991 plane crash, she got about a billion, maybe more.[19] By 1995 she'd changed parties and remarried. Kerry proves you can marry money that came from marrying money. I would describe Kerry as someone who used celebrity to marry money, similar to what Ellen Barkin did.

Jane Fonda's first hubby, former politician **Tom Hayden,** got away with between $2 million to over $10 million, depending on which source you believe. For a third-tier politico that's not bad.

Marrying well works for men as well as women.

Then Fonda parlayed her aging fame into a richer marriage (like Ellen Barkin!) with *Forbes* 400-er **Ted Turner.** She must have known it couldn't last. She has claimed she never had a good relationship with any man. My guess is half those who marry money don't expect it to last, based on either divorce being so common or their own life experiences.

Marital Bliss

But they needn't end sadly. McCain and Kerry's marriages seem to work. Christopher McKown, president of a small health care consulting business, has been married to **Abigail Johnson** for 20 years. She came from Fidelity family money and now runs part of the firm and is worth $15 billion in her own right.[20] Meg Whitman, one-time eBay CEO worth $1.4 billion,[21] is still married to her brain surgeon husband—28 years and counting.[22] Brain surgery's pretty good money, but not as good as being married to a former CEO.

Brain surgeons seem to have a sixth sense about marrying well. Just ask Dr. Glen Nelson. He had the good fortune to marry current Carlson CEO, **Marilyn Carlson Nelson**—net worth $2.2 billion.[23] Did he marry her just for money? I'd guess decidedly not—they've been together for decades now, have four children, and suffered the tragic death of one daughter. Plus, for a period Marilyn left the family business to raise her kids and support her husband's medical career. Family money is nice, but CEO money makes it nicer—Marilyn returned to replace her founder father as

CEO. Dr. Nelson wasn't the only fellow clever enough to marry a wealthy Carlson girl. Edwin "Skip" Gage has been long, and by all accounts, happily married to Marilyn's equally wealthy sister, **Barbara Carlson Gage.**

Stedman Graham is interesting. He's Oprah's longtime companion, and though once engaged, they remain unmarried. He's CEO of his own company, S. Graham & Associates, a consulting firm that seems to primarily promote his books and speaking engagements.[24] He's a smart guy, very active in his community, but maybe wouldn't be so successful if not for his connection to Oprah. But why hasn't he married her? He won't see a dime of Oprah's $2.5 billion[25] since she's decided to not include him in her will.[26] But here's a guy who fell in with an insanely wealthy woman, and they've been together forever and seem very happy. He doesn't seem to care about locking up any of her wealth for himself, but he's benefited from her wealth and connections. Remember, marrying well doesn't mean cynically finding a rich target to dupe. Hopefully, it means finding someone you can love and respect, and my goodness, doesn't it help if she has money too?

He Said; She's Dead

Warning: Not everyone on this road means well—male or female. Another true story: Margaret Lesher married well and inherited a publishing fortune from her first husband—his family owned the *Contra Costa Times* and sister publications around San Francisco. When the 65-year-old widow married a 40-year-old professional cowboy, eyebrows raised. Soon, the two went camping in Arizona, alone, by a lake. What happened next is the ultimate "he said–she's dead"—she was found in the morning floating in eight feet of water. He claimed she must have gone for a midnight swim after they shared two bottles of champagne and some beers and drowned. Or did he get her soused, take her out in their canoe, and pitch her over? Her relatives alleged he drowned her but couldn't prove it. No prenup, but her will stipulated he got $5 million.[27] Some may just want your money, not you.

LOVE, MARRIAGE, AND MONEY

Love is in the eye of the beholder. What one man loves, another finds boring. By the time you're my age you've met a great many couples where it's impossible for you to see what one of them sees in the other. Yet that doesn't mean love isn't burning brightly there—and forever. It isn't for me to tell you what to find fascinating in a mate. But whatever it is that turns you on, there's no reason that person can't be wealthy as well. If you found wealth repugnant, which some do, you wouldn't be reading this book in the first place.

Many settle in marriage too easily. When romance strikes and endures for a relatively few months, folks start thinking "marriage" as if love can only be found with that one person in life. Wrong! There's an old saying, "There is someone for everyone." Well, if you work at it, there are really quite a lot of people you could fall permanently in love with. It's just a matter of working to find them and then picking the very best one for you. The most optimal. And that can include wealth.

Today there are so many wealthy people that if you set your sights solely among the wealthy you can find love there, just as likely as you could meet love at the local bookstore. Perhaps the most important step is accepting that it's ok to seek love among the wealthy—that there's nothing wrong with it.

Think it through, go where the money is, hone in locally, make a plan, and work the plan like our young dentist example, and there's simply no reason you can't find wealthy love and in no longer than it would take to find it among the non-wealthy. It's really all a mindset, and a fine one at that, if getting rich this way is your goal.

Do It by the Book

Like other roads, there's more you can read to help your journey. Most "marry rich" books are satires or take pot shots at both sides of mixed-wealth marriages and are a disservice. Ignore them. A few particularly good books that may help you include:

- *How to Marry the Rich* by Ginie Sayles. This is a good marriage and dating guide even if you don't want to marry wealthy. Good for anyone single who doesn't want to be.

- *How to Marry Money* by Kevin Doyle. Loaded with tips—at times tongue in cheek—it can seem satire-like but isn't. The author does satire on the same subject under the pen name "Ruth Leslee Greene."

- *How to Marry Money.* Same title, but this one is by Susan Wright. It never sold well but is a serious stab at the subject, with ideas you can deploy.

 ## The Guide to **Marrying Well**

Jane Austen told us it is a truth universally acknowledged that a single man in possession of a good fortune must be in want of a wife. Too true! And not just for fortune-hunting ladies. Today, when folks can freely choose mates, marrying well is a real road to riches. Scoff, but big bucks can be made capturing the right mate. So what would we tell Ellen Barkin to do better next time?

1. *Right place, right time.* Identify the right location and go where they are. It's easy. Also, check local laws and seek a community property state in case things go wrong.

2. *Be where they are.* Most richies are work-consumed. Go where they work. Proximity is critical. Charity work or political fundraising are great ways to meet the mega-rich, but only the right kind of causes work. Fundraising to save the piping plover probably just wastes your time. Investment seminars are also great for meeting targets (and for free food).

3. *Age matters.* Fact: Most wealthy people are older. You may meet a young heiress, but she's likely already surrounded by potential mates. Your odds improve with a more mature crowd.

(Continued)

(Continued)

4. *Get a prenuptial agreement.* Think long and hard about what you're worth and demand it up front. Failing to do so may mean you get nothing—particularly in a common law state. And get a great divorce lawyer. The better the lawyer, the bigger your payout.

5. *Don't do anything stupid.* The judge and the world are watching—particularly if you marry someone very wealthy. Learn from Heather Mills and Anna Nicole Smith and get your life together. It may mean getting a bigger payout earlier.

6

STEAL IT— LIKE A PIRATE, BUT LEGALLY

Ever wish you could just take the money?
Would you like some to see you as a hero?
And others fear you? This is your road.

n literature and mythology, thieves are often villain-heroes—
Robin Hood and Jesse James—stealing from the rich, giving to
the poor. Sounds romantic, even if it is fiction. But wait, you
can legally steal and be a hero as a plaintiff's lawyer (PL)—today's
Robin Hood.

Idolized by Hollywood, PLs posture themselves as crusaders
for the helpless—fighting big bad business to save the little guy—
winning huge awards in well-publicized show trials big on headlines
and emotion. My apologies to other lawyers and law students if this
sounds harsh, but it's true: Most plaintiffs' law is a perfectly legal
twist of thievery and thuggery.

Other lawyers do ok financially. Most work too hard for ok (or even very good) hourly pay on fairly dull but necessary functions, like estate planning, contract or transaction law, regulatory law, or labor law. A lifetime of hard work, some frugality, ok investment returns (Chapter 10)—they may end up with $2 million to $30 million dollars. But at what cost? Family life can suffer since most lawyers bill by the hour, so many work endlessly. The big money is in legal stealing—plaintiff's work.

CRUSADER OR PIRATE?

Question: Are these guys crusaders or pirates? The original crusaders left comfy European castles to reclaim Holy Lands from those they saw as godless and evil. Are PLs bringing evildoers to justice—fighting the big and mean to help the little and poor? No, they're pirates seeking booty. And if they had their way, they'd rarely step foot in court.

What they really want is to bring an action and settle out of court—be paid to go away—basic thug-like extortion with huge payouts and little work. If you sport a bit of the dark side and part of you likes playing the heavy, this is the best possible road for you. And you needn't think of yourself as bad. PLs always, *always* convince themselves they're crusaders and feel great about themselves. Go down this road and you will too.

But if PLs were really crusaders they wouldn't blackmail. They wouldn't set up cases just to get paid to go away. Real crusaders would take cases all the way through the conclusion of a trial, always, for justice. That PLs overwhelmingly seek to be paid to go away—and usually are thereby extorting their targets—demonstrates the fallacy in their crusader self-image. They're thieves. In their bones!

That's a great part about this road—that part of our society with a thieving bent can take this road, steal legally, make a boatload, and feel great about themselves at the same time. You can do it too. Be a hero! There's no other road linking all these qualities. Other roads are about voluntary transactions. Not this one.

Simply Swashbuckling!

If you've always had a childhood fantasy to be a pirate, but don't like the physical risk—or maybe just get seasick—this road has all the other benefits. You can scare the hell out of people. You can force folks to pay you the same basic way mafia protection rackets used to. You can swagger and loot. Huge chunks of society will see you as a crusading savior. And you will feel your victims deserved it— that is, if you go about this correctly, as I will describe. And it's exciting—simply swashbuckling! One of the most famous PLs of all time, Bill Lerach (now cooling his heels in jail—details later) openly bragged of scotch drinking being his prime exercise when he wasn't terrorizing CEOs.[1] He claimed a great scotch arm—just like a pirate at the wharf pub. Arg, matey!

Pirates could care less about pedigree. Forget fancy schools. Their success isn't about a degree; it's about who they are (pirates). Top PLs often went to mediocre colleges and lackluster law schools. Fact: You won't need a fancy school either. You needn't go to law school at all to pass the bar exam in California, Maine, New York, Vermont, Virginia, Washington DC, and Washington.[2] No law degree required to blackmail, extort, loot, pillage, and raid. And what is a pay-to-go-away class-action suit if not a raid?

RAIDER'S ROAD

Law school is a popular choice today, but many law school graduates don't become lawyers! Why? Again, most law requires grueling hours. Graduates ask, "Do I really want to do this?" Yet, despite so many choosing law school but not a law career, the number of lawyers has grown staggeringly. In 1972, we had one lawyer for every 572 Americans. In 2000, one for every 264.[3] Do we need so many?

Don't know, but there is endless competition now. I won't describe how to become a normal lawyer, pick law schools, apply, pass the state bar, or even get that first job. There are lots of books on all that. No, this chapter and road isn't about being a *normal* lawyer. It is about being a PL. But in contemplating that and why being a PL is a road to riches, it's worthwhile to see why normal lawyers don't normally get super rich.

You graduate law school and go work for a major law firm. It will be subdivided into practice areas like litigation, estate planning, securities law, and general business law. Different firms have different specialties. The biggest firms tend to cover the waterfront. Each practice area is managed by one or several partners, and the firm is managed relatively collegially by partners. Fresh out of law school you're what's called an *associate*. If you're really good, in seven to nine years they may make you a partner. If not, you probably leave.

Average 2006 associate pay at the 20 top-paying US law firms was in the $200,000 range.[4] That's for third-, fourth-, and fifth-year associates. Seem good? Remember, first you pay for law school and likely have huge school debt. You suffer *negative* cash flow and then endure the grueling first few years of legal work—infamous for 80-hour weeks. Only then might you make $200,000—*if* you're average at a top-paying firm. What if you're below average at a mid-tier firm? It's tough, competitive, and these folks work hard.

Being a normal lawyer is a good way to earn a nice income, but not necessarily a road to riches.

Worse, top firms are in the biggest, most expensive cities. And top lawyers aren't typically that frugal—but you must be and invest well to build a nest egg as a normal lawyer. Consider this: Median pay for all lawyers is $102,470 (as of May 2006).[5] Less than you'd think. Yes, this includes government lawyers, charity, and pro-bono lawyers doing social work (who often are real crusaders), self-employed lawyers who can't get clients, and first-year associates at lousy law firms in tiny towns. Many lawyers make not all that much. Even the better paid ones are still working by the hour. It's not poverty, but with these salaries you must save and invest well to retire with $2 million to $30 million. It's possible, but no more or less than anyone with an ok income on the "Road More Traveled" (Chapter 10).

Bigger bucks come from becoming a law firm partner—which is tough! It takes an average of seven to nine years, and few associates make it at all. Many firms have "up or out" cultures—if you haven't made partner by year nine, they can boot you. Yet 77 percent of associates don't make it past year five![6] Odds are worse at the top firms. But if you make it, the pay is good. Top partners might bill $500 an hour or more. Three New York firms' top partners now bill over $1,000 an hour, with fees growing 6 to 7 percent a year.[7]

I'm just showing you the clear demarcation among the bulk of the legal profession, which requires the Road More Traveled and doesn't get you mega-rich—versus the one area that does.

THE RICHEST LEGAL ROAD

For the biggest lawyer bucks, there's only one road—plaintiff's law—dealing only with civil cases or the "tort" system. It's huge—tort costs totaled $247 billion in 2007—2 percent of US GDP![8] (Double the percentage of other developed nations.[9] America is a PL's dream!) Of that, only 22 percent actually goes to reimburse victims. PLs get an additional 50 percent more than their clients—collecting 33 percent of the $247 billion![10] A piece of that can be yours.

Other lawyers bill by the hour. Example: You run over your neighbor's petunias. She sues. Your defense lawyer gets paid by the hour. Your neighbor's PL gets a percentage of any judgment received—20 to 40 percent typically, plus expenses. Suppose they convince the judge the petunias were so rare and the suffering sufficiently acute to merit a $10 million verdict. The PL might get $3.5 million, *plus* expenses. No one in law makes more than PLs when they do it right—nobody. (One potential exception is a legal counsel to a start-up firm that booms hugely, getting rich off options as a ride-along—see Chapter 3.)

Case in point: Joe Jamail (net worth $1.5 billion)[11] is fabled as the "King of Torts"—a legendary PL. He's won huge verdicts, including one for $3.3 billion—his fee there was about $400 million.[12] What case? Who cares! *Four hundred million!* (Ok—he represented Pennzoil against Texaco for screwing up its planned 1980s Getty Oil merger.)

Almost as impressive, Jamail won $6 million for a client paralyzed in a collision with a commercial truck. Sound easy? Maybe so, except Jamail admitted in court, on the record, his client *was drunk—completely plutoed*—his blood alcohol content fully triple the legal limit. Yet Jamail convinced the jury that, though sloshed, his client was otherwise driving responsibly, therefore not at fault.[13] That takes some serious skills. Arg, matey!

> There's no other profitable way to steal legally.

TORT US AND THE SCARE

So how can you steal in PL mode, make big bucks, strike fear in some folks hearts, while seeming like Robin Hood to others and having the media adore you? First, you need a client folks sympathize with. Kids, sick ones, are great. (Or kids with the *possibility* of being maybe exposed to something maybe dangerous. Maybe.) Deadly maladies are great—better if work-related or "created" by a big corporation. Clients needn't actually be sick. You can build a huge class action suit with one guy who died from possible exposure to Chemical X—though he was 89. But Chemical X may have added to his untimely death! From him you build a class of others who *may* have been exposed. Then extort Chemical X's maker for the possibility all those folks may die.

The extortion part comes in because the publicity and accusations of the chemical maker's culpability will damage the firm as it drives shareholders and customers away to other vendors. To stop the losses, the chemical maker settles—pays you to go away. It pays part of what it estimates you can do in damages from lost business—plus a piece of the not-insignificant legal costs it would spend defending itself. Even a small class action will cost at least $2 million to defend and will drag on for at least two years for the defendant—incurring opportunity cost on top! Usually they'll pay a piece of that just to have you sail away.

Your subject matter should also be confusing, murky, with little-tested, archaic laws applied in perhaps unintended ways. Gray areas are best. Complicated chemicals. Rare medical diseases of which scant is known about the definitive cause. Big, complex, multisyllabic technical terms jurors can't quite fathom. The more obscure and complex, the more the trial ends up about who the jury likes more. Possibilities are endless. Work-related suits are good because big business always has a bad image and employment laws across America are often foggy, gray, and vary by state. And workers are about as all-American and sympathetic as you can get!

Exploiting Kids for Fun and Profit!

Using sick kids is tried and true—and immortalized in **Julia Roberts'** Oscar-winning role in *Erin Brockovich*. If you saw the movie, you know Ms. Brockovich as a plucky non-lawyer, down on her luck, working at a two-bit law firm. She stumbles across a pattern of medical oddities in Hinkley, California, and investigates. That Erin! No legal background, no investigative training, but she's got grit, determination, and . . . well . . . if you've seen the movie you know.

She convinces her boss to take the case. Lo and behold, evil Pacific Gas & Electric (PG&E) had been intentionally dumping hexavalent chromium (multisyllabic, complicated chemical compound) in Hinkley's drinking water. Some kids there had cancer.

(Sick kids!) Why would PG&E do it? (In movies, businesses are always evil.) In this film, it was because they knew Hinkleyans were too poor and powerless to fight back. Powerless—until they met Ms. Brockovich and boss—real crusaders—who win them a big boodle in court. Then Ms. Brockovich got a big raise, a new car, and endless hot pants. Hooray! Roll credits.

In reality, this case settled in private arbitration and never saw the inside of a courtroom. Were they real crusaders, Brockovich and boss would have tried the case. PG&E admitted no guilt. I'm not saying PG&E was guiltless and kids didn't get sick. I don't know. Most scientists say hexavalent chromium, when ingested as alleged, is not toxic to humans. Just passes through.[14] But "facts" and "science" aren't the issue. A trial takes years, generates huge negative publicity for the stock, and drives away customers and general good will. PG&E's side of the story doesn't make a sexy movie.

PG&E paid $333 million to make them go away. Ironically, damage to their reputation from Steven Soderbergh's fictional movie must have been massively bigger—but it would have been bigger still with a trial. Note: This is a $14 billion market valuation stock with $13 billion in annual sales. The settlement seems big, but not settling likely would have hurt more. To prevail in a trial

Confusing subject matter. Sympathetic client. You're halfway there.

like that would have taken years and years. En route they would have been dragged through the mud publicly. People recall accusations more than when a court finally, quietly, rules for the defendant. There's no news then. Nothing happening is not news.

But for Brockovich and boss, you, or another PL, that's a fine payday. According to their contract, they got 40 percent plus $10 million for expenses—$143.2 million in all. And there were sick kids, whether hexavalent chromium caused it or not. What did they get? Class members with documented medical complaints reported getting only $50,000 or $60,000—not much when you're suffering from cancer.[15] Where did the rest go? Class members seem confused about that.[16] But you can bet Julia Roberts isn't concerned about having deceived the public. She played a classic Robin Hood role. America loves her for it.

Legal Scapegoats

Folks like finger-pointing when something goes awry—it's human nature—whether in medicine, in investing, in love, anything. Scapegoats help us cope. Behaviorists call this *regret shunning*. PLs succeed by pointing at scapegoats for otherwise random or non-random tragedies (or non-tragedies). Scapegoats pay PLs to make the finger-pointing stop.

Former senator, vice presidential and presidential candidate **John Edwards** is legendary for actually taking cases to trial. He repeatedly claimed cerebral palsy is entirely avoidable—caused by physician error during birth. In one famous case he "channeled" his young client, addressing the jury *as if he were the young girl in her mother's womb* begging them to do the right thing—that is, find for his client. They did. Edwards' client walked with $2.75 million from the hospital and $1.5 million from the doctor—$4.25 million in all.[17] Edwards' success spawned a mini-industry. You've seen the commercials: "If your child has cerebral palsy, it may be medical malpractice. You can sue! Call Dewey, Cheatem & Howe."

Cerebral palsy cases are perfect. They involve afflicted kids and a little-understood disease. One Florida couple sued the Jacksonville Naval Hospital for $150 million.[18] But according to the American College of Obstetrics and Gynecologists, cerebral palsy is in all likelihood linked to genes, prenatal infection, or other issues beyond doctor control more than anything else.[19] Try telling that to a jury or the media when they're witnessing tear-jerking theater.

Tort Is Just Part of *Extort*

Our tort system is extra tough on small firms. Legal defense costs and public relations damages may overwhelm relative to their size—making extortion threats more successful for you. Small corporate defendants are always scared to death and prone to caving in. Many PLs seek targets they suspect can't afford *not* to cave. As the case starts, they privately demand to be paid to go away. Usually, the defendant settles. Settlements are usually covered by the firm's insurance, making it easier for the defendant to do it. It's so much easier to pay PLs to go away than fight that this becomes your opportunity.

Even better, in this process these settlement discussions aren't admissible at all in court. The defendant can't scream at the judge, "But he told me if we would just pay $1.5 million he would drop everything—this is so bogus." Isn't that cute? Protects you as a PL.

So ideally, you want targets that are either big and visible—so the suit hurts their reputation with customers and shareholders like with Erin Brockovich—or you want many small firms that frighten easily.

There's a step in normal court proceedings where the defendant routinely asks for dismissal. Judges almost never grant these. This is good for you as a PL. You get more extortion time. Judges believe they should be judicious and hear the matter to ensure they don't dismiss something real with real damages. The judge, by acting judiciously, decreases the odds his or her decision gets overturned later on appeal. Getting overturned is maybe what judges hate most. So the case runs and you can keep scaring and damaging the defendant into settling.

Once started, defendant damage grows daily whether the defendant ultimately prevails or not. Here, there is no such thing as *innocent until proven guilty*. Defendants never really "win." Trials take two to four years if the defendant prevails through the end. Defendant costs easily exceed $2 million—bigger cases, much more.

But you as a PL have minimal costs—your time, minor travel, expert witnesses, copying, clerical—not that much. This stacks the odds in your favor. Every month costs them much more than you. The actual payout may be covered by insurance, but defendants' defense costs aren't unless they allow their insurance firm to run their defense, which means giving up control—usually meaning lousy legal work. So simply by moving forward every month, you put increased pressure on the defendant, motivating them to pay you to go away since they didn't get that message at first. You want to ask to be paid to go away immediately, then again after the judge refuses the defendant's request for dismissal, and then about every four months right up until the end.

If the defendant does go all the way through the trial, it means they either are confident they did nothing, are tough, or, in ways you as PL may not understand, consider themselves simply unable to settle. (We'll get to that later.) But if they prevail all the way through the trial, you again ask for money, much less, or else you threaten to appeal. If they won't pay you, then appeal. That will be another year, easy, and you can keep asking to be paid to go away. From beginning to end, you want to keep hitting them with body blows. What kind of blows are best?

Playing to the Press

PLs pretend they don't seek media coverage—doing so irks judges. But they usually do, and on this road you need to milk the media as hard as you can, particularly if the defendant has brand value you can damage—like the Erin Brockovich case. A little-known, major dirty secret in our culture: PLs are one of journalists' most important sources. Most negative articles are pirate-initiated. Journalists will do anything to keep their "source," the PL, concealed (again, the judge would hate it). Under First Amendment protection they can.

The media is your partner on this road because you feed them good dirt, and dirt equals bad news, which sells best. Meanwhile, the media campaign scares away your defendant's customers and potential customers, making the defendant more settlement-prone. If, as PL, you contact a major business journalist offering an exclusive on your new suit filed against a high-profile corporate defendant, I promise you will receive a warm reception.

Our tort system is set up for this process to run to your advantage. The defendant has two choices. Fight to the end, enduring damages and costs to prevail, which they'll never recover. Or pay you to go away. Most will pay.

As a defendant (all business owners become a defendant, multiple times, once they get over a certain size—and it's smaller than you think), I try to be rational about this as a business cost. My legal team considers each case individually. But sometimes as a defendant, we see things in ways you as a PL may not quite fathom. Example: Some years ago we were attacked by a San Diego–based PL attempting to bring a class action against my firm, claiming misleading advertising via a slimy law provision the judge said didn't apply for such suits. The suit sought a return of fees to all our clients. I not only knew they were dead wrong and hence we should be able to prevail in court, but also believed that if I paid them to go away to save the costs and media nightmare, my firm's clients would never believe we hadn't done something wrong. If we hadn't done anything wrong, why would we settle?

In an integrity matter like that—claiming we misled clients when we knew otherwise—my stance hardened to no settlement, at any price, at any time. Our client reputation was on the line. In my field, that is critically important. And by our standards, the PL wasn't overly frightening. So we fought—all the way. We prevailed. But the whole way through, the PL kept asking to be paid and couldn't fathom we simply wouldn't. My lawyers kept bringing me their latest offer and I kept returning them with a simple message: Go to hell, PL.

To me it was worth the millions we spent and the time our senior people, me included, diverted from our primary functions to conclude and prevail. I wasn't going to have our clients see us paying for something we hadn't done and have that hang over our heads forever. That would have damaged our integrity! At first, the PL wanted big bucks to go away, and at the end asked almost nothing—the amount stair-stepped down as the years ran. But the PL never got that we wouldn't pay under any circumstances. If you go down this road, you will run into these kinds of cases and you're better served to figure them out quickly. When the defendant simply won't pay, make sure you really have a case. You probably don't and should stop wasting your time immediately.

More Stacked in Your Favor

Another great feature for you as a PL is when you run a really rancid suit and screw up terribly—maybe you sue the Pope for child molestation and embezzlement with no evidence at all, pushing it all the way through trial, losing huge, and in the process breaking basic procedural rules like lying to the judge—it's still very hard for the defendant to collect damages against you. When they do, it's piteously small. You just don't have that much to lose. In the aforementioned case, we won right down the line and the PL made some egregious errors. We did win the almost impossible standard of being awarded costs—beyond rare. Still, all we got was a measly $13,000. You, as a PL, have a tough time losing more than your time. Great for you!

I've paid PLs to go away twice, totaling $5 million. Both involved class-action complaints against my firm, alleging we violated California employee wage and hour laws. These suits are routine and don't justify a trial defense. We did nothing wrong. But employment laws on this are murky. And it would've cost more to defend ourselves than to pay these guys to leave. And these suits aren't about something like fraud impacting clients' perceptions. They were about how we treat our employees—who already know exactly what we are and aren't—so their views of us couldn't possibly be hurt by these silly claims.

Pretty much all California firms have these once they hit a certain size. It's just a cost of business in some states (see Chapter 8). The PL doesn't want to go to court—just the booty. It's cheaper to settle than fight. Fighting wins nothing. It's great and easy PL booty with scant work. There's a whole industry doing this—*your* industry on this road. You can hit a group of employees at a firm once—then you need a different employee group. The key is figuring out which firm has just become big enough to merit going after. It happens at about 500 employees. It's like finding an undefended treasure ship at sea. Just be there first and do it before another pirate finds it.

TARGET PRACTICE

Beyond socially sympathetic clients (workers, kids), you want a corporate target that can pay and wants to settle early before you work much. Big business is easy to demonize.

Pharma

Pharmaceutical firms are great targets. The big ones are massive—huge market caps, hence big settlements. And big profits make them unsympathetic to our society. Pharma is a perfect marriage of sympathetic clients, complicated, technical subjects, and easy-to-villainize targets. Recall Merck's Vioxx hoopla? Vioxx is a COX-2 inhibitor (complicated), intended as a pain reliever for folks with osteoarthritis and sensitive stomachs—meant to be taken for brief periods. Further testing (done by Merck) showed increased cardiovascular problems if taken beyond 18 months. So Merck yanked it from shelves.[20] But Vioxx wasn't meant for long-term usage—so no worries, right? Wrong. When the news hit, Merck's stock tanked. Soon its credit rating was cut by rating's agencies fearing litigation and payouts.[21]

By October 2007, Merck was named in approximately 26,600 lawsuits. *26,600!* Some could be yours. And the fate? Juries can't decide. Of course they can't! How many average jurors understand the atomic makeup: $C_{17}H_{14}O_4S$? It's got a hepatic metabolism and a 17-year half-life (super complicated). So far, only 19 cases have gone to trial. Merck won 12, plaintiffs 5. Two ended in mistrial. Another 5,500 claims were dismissed—likely lacking evidence. Another 20 were dismissed or withdrawn before jury selection.[22] Still, by the time all this shakes out, PLs will have received nearly $2 billion in fees.[23] Can you make your client sympathetic enough to collect huge fees from a "villainous" target?

Tobacco

When I was young my father taught me to look both ways when crossing the street and never smoke. Forget there's been a surgeon general's warning since 1965 that cigarettes cause cancer. Anyone habituated since then was duly warned. But PLs keep finding new angles. You can too. Tobacco firms look bad, always.

Other Targets

Asbestos is a great target. Asbestos may eventually outshine tobacco as a cash cow. There are 50,000 to 75,000 new asbestos lawsuits filed yearly. Most of them—over 600,000 by year-end 2000—were filed by defendants who didn't have any asbestos-related disease and may never get one.[24] Great pirate's work!

A hot new target is vaccine manufacturers for an alleged link to autism from thimerosal—a mercury-based preservative. (Complicated chemical—sick kids—big pharma!) Probably the increase in autism diagnoses is because they actually diagnose it now—10 and 20 years ago, these kids would just be called "slow" or "off." But maybe I'm wrong. Either way, it's hot for suing.

You can get in early on the phthalate craze! This chemical makes plastic bendy and near-indestructible. It's used in children's toys,

With targets the media loves skewering—big business, pharma, tobacco—your odds improve.

and also IV bags and other hospital gadgets. Greenpeace decided it's "bad" and California issued a state-wide ban. Greenpeace prefers a replacement compound that makes plastic more brittle—meaning your kids' toys break more easily into handy, choking-size pieces. We'll likely soon be phthalate-free and choking-suit rich! Never mind the *founder of Greenpeace himself* thinks phthalates are fine and perfectly safe.[25] It's complicated and near unpronounceable!

Securities Litigation

A classic is suing public stocks whose prices plummet. Pirates find one shareholder and sue, alleging the firm should have disclosed something earlier or somehow otherwise avoided the drop (through magic?). These never made sense, but they're ubiquitous. The media loves them—painting firms as evil and intentionally defrauding the shareholder proletariat.

It works like this: Firm X trades at $50 a share—worth $10 billion. Earnings turn sour. When news hits, the stock drops 20 percent to $40—down $2 billion. A PL sues on behalf of shareholders for the full $2 billion. Firm X settles for $60 million. The PL gets $20 million. Note: Corporate payments *to* shareholders come *from* shareholders—it's zero sum. The only difference is some past shareholders may no longer be shareholders and new shareholders may have bought in. All current holders pay and suffer for the benefit of a few prior shareholders, so now current shares are worth even less. This is like stealing from Peter to punch Paul in the face. If you were and remain a shareholder, it's like getting a small dividend and paying the PL a 30 percent finder's fee. These suits are common.

WHEN A PIRATE BECOMES A VILLAIN

So when does legal piracy become illegal? When you break the law. Ask **Melvyn Weiss** and **Bill Lerach** (of the well-toned scotch arm). For decades, no two words struck more terror in CEO hearts than "Milberg Weiss." (Well, maybe the word "Lerach" did.) Founded in 1965 by Melvyn Weiss, Milberg Weiss claimed to fight for blue-collar workers duped by evil corporations into losing life savings on crummy stocks. As the workers' savior, Milberg Weiss collected over $45 billion from firms for "cheated investors." *$45 billion!* In 1976, Bill Lerach joined in the fun, opening Milberg West in San Diego, and was as feared as Weiss (if not more so).

They eventually had over 200 lawyers nationally—bigger than any rival—a machine, bringing in a case a week at their peak. Lead partners made hundreds of millions. They took on everyone! Some firms multiple times. Ninety percent of cases settled—they weren't interested in trying cases.[26] Lerach was famous for personally threatening CEOs with poverty and worse.[27] Pirate talk. Arg!

To get these cases, you must file in court before another PL does. This is called the *race to the courthouse steps*. He who files first gets the case. How can you make sure you're first? Weiss and Lerach knew. Every class action needs a lead plaintiff—a normal person who represents typical damages. Finding one takes time—slowing you in the courthouse race. So Weiss and Lerach built a stable of potentials with *pre-drafted* complaints.

How can you have a plaintiff and complaint beforehand? Milberg and Lerach drafted folks to buy tiny positions in thousands of stocks and wait. When one tanked they went straight to court. For this, that draftee got a cut—say, 7 to 15 percent of the lawyers' take—leading to a $1 million-plus payout one time. They reused plaintiffs—40 times for one man. This is illegal—a felony. Lawyers are routinely asked if they made additional payments to plaintiffs. For decades, Weiss and Lerach lied under oath. As did these star plaintiffs.

News flash! Stocks are volatile. Sometimes they drop. Them's the risks. Punishing firms for normal volatility just redistributes profits, hurts shareholders and stock prices. This doesn't help the little guy. This is simple extortion. But firms settle just to make PLs go away.[28]

A formal investigation started in 2001. You might think Milberg and Lerach would slow down. No! Their scheme continued—at least until 2005. In all, prosecutors claimed they paid kickbacks in over 150 class action cases.[29] Lerach pled guilty and got two years and a $7.75 million fine.[30] Weiss pled guilty too, to racketeering (like a mafia Don!), and got 33 months and paid $10 million.[31] The firm settled for $75 million to avoid a criminal trial (interesting a law firm is so anxious to avoid court).[32] Despite guilty pleas and fines, Bill "Scotch Arm" Lerach still insists, from jail, that what they did "was merely standard industry practice."[33] Yikes.

Don't Lerach yourself.

On this road or any other, never, ever break the law. You don't want to end up in the big house with Lerach and Weiss. As I detail in the next chapter on "Other People's Money," breaking the law is always bad business. On any road, orange prison jumpsuits are just ugly. Be a PL. Steal it . . . but do it legally, never illegally. Don't Lerach yourself.

Then again, these two felons will serve only part of their sentences, as happens with almost all felonies. An imperfect rule of thumb is that convicts serve about a third of the stated sentence. So maybe Lerach and Weiss do a year or so behind bars. They're banned from legal practice forever, but they're rich. No one knows how rich but them. Recall from Chapter 4 that entertainers don't end up as wealthy as folks commonly think. I'll bet Weiss and Lerach are both wealthier than any TV or movie personality except Oprah. For having screwed it up so badly, they won't end up so bad off. See it another way: America has tens of thousands of petty pirate-like criminals who would love to trade a year or so in the big house if they could sail quietly away afterward into the sunset, a fraction as wealthy as Lerach or Weiss. This form of pirate's life is lined with booty.

THE INSIDE TRACK

PLs won't openly admit this (but will in private): Success is rarely about the law. In civil trials, arbitrations, or even non-binding mediations, the key is your ability to convince the jury, judge, arbitrator, or mediator that you're the good guy. Judges won't admit it, but pretty much once he or she, or the jury, decides who are the good and bad guys, the rest is detail and degree of judgment. The law slides in around that character judgment. Once you convince the judge you're the good guy and the other the bad guy, it's basically over. This is why top PLs don't need top law schools. It's investigation, theatrics, and street-savvy reading of the judge and players—not legal nuance. Winning is strategizing—then creating the image convincing the judge or jury somehow, some way, you're good and your opponent's bad. Pretty ironic in a world of pirates!

There is an inside track. Many top PLs belong to the Inner Circle of Advocates. Join—if you can! It's an honor. (Visit them at www.innercircle.org.) They only let in the top-earning PLs. Membership is limited to just 100. Can you qualify?

To qualify, members must have tried at least 50 personal injury jury trials and at least 3 verdicts in excess of one million-dollars or 1 verdict in excess of ten million-dollars. Most of our members have won many multi-million dollar verdicts for their clients.[34]

There are obviously many more than just 100 top PLs. Lots of famous ones aren't on the list. And yes, John Edwards is a member. And actually, only five are women. This road definitely has a male bent at the top. Yet these 100 have taken down some serious bucks. Maybe some of that can be yours.

Legal Reading

Because these books teach you to persuade and negotiate, they're actually useful for anyone—not just those on the pirate road.

1. *Rules of the Road: A Plaintiff Lawyer's Guide to Proving Liability* by Rick Friedman and Patrick Malone. These authors are successful been-there-done-that PLs telling you how—better than law school. Friedman is one of the infamous Inner Circle of Advocates.

2. *Theater Tips and Strategies for Jury Trials* by David Ball. Professor Ball has turned a background in theater arts into a career as a leading courtroom consultant. He teaches trial lawyers the art of storytelling to evoke trial-winning emotions from the jury.

3. *David Ball on Damages* by David Ball. More from Professor Ball. See the inside of jurors' minds—how they think, what you must do to manipulate them. It's about convincing them you're good and the other guy is bad. A must-read on this road.

4. *Legal Blame: How Jurors Think and Talk About Accidents* by Neal Feigenson. This covers the same subject as *David Ball* but from a more psychological perspective.

 ## The Guide to **Stealing It, Legally**

You generally should graduate college and law school (though it's not an absolute). You must pass the state bar exam where you reside and/or practice. You find far fewer college drop-out lawyers than CEOs. But for those who graduate from even dreadful law schools, this road rocks. The big riches aren't about pedigree. Loneliness warning! Some people will fear and dislike you and shy away—like from any pirate.

1. *Be the right kind.* Just being a lawyer won't do. For big bucks, become a plaintiff's lawyer—a proud pirate.

2. *Think client and target.* All you need are:

   a. Sympathetic clients: Those perceived as poor and downtrodden make good clients: the sick, kids, low-level workers, Joe Six-pack.

   b. Villainous looking targets: Targets must be easily painted villainous. Big business is good—big oil, tobacco, or pharma. Finance, too—areas perceived as having deep pockets. Small firms can also be easy hits because they can't afford to fight back, so they settle easily. Think volume.

   c. Complex subjects: Sue on grounds that can easily confuse juries so you can control the image of good and bad. Then, it's more about who they like than facts.

3. *For the biggest bucks, focus on class-action lawsuits.* Collecting a percentage of these settlements is huge with a big class. Same rules—helpless clients, deep-pocketed corporate villains, complex subjects. Be a good storyteller.

4. *Get a dog.* Being a pirate can be lonely. Some people may dislike you. You will make enemies. A big dog provides protection and love.

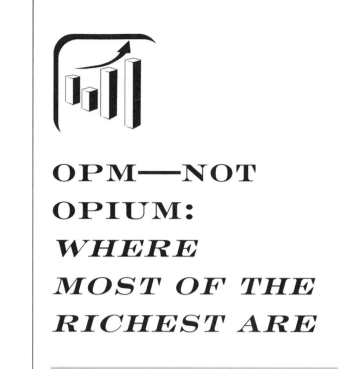

7

OPM—NOT OPIUM: *WHERE MOST OF THE RICHEST ARE*

Like telling folks what to do?
Have nerves of steel?
OPM may fit you fine.

This road is paved with fees from *Other People's Money* (OPM)—money management, private equity, brokerage, banking, insurance, etc. It's easy entry. You don't need a PhD or a brain surgeon's brain. There are lots of crossovers here too. OPMers frequently found big firms (Chapter 1) and generate very rich ride-alongs (Chapter 3). Some OPMers end up heroes, some in prison—there's ample room for conflict of interest. But a good OPM richie efficiently and ethically makes his (or her) clients rich at the same time. Getting rich while making others rich—what's more blessed than that?

117

OPM is the commonest road for the ultra-wealthy. It isn't how you get to be the very richest, but it's how most of the mega-rich get there. Eighty-six of 2007's *Forbes* 400 members got there on this road—the most of any category. And more modest piles of $2 million to $50 million are commonly made, often over just a few years.

BASIC OPM CAREER RULES

Folks often think they must first know technical aspects of finance or they can't succeed here. No! It's just as good to learn to sell first and learn finance later—maybe better. One counterintuitive rule I learned from watching others navigate this road is:

Young people learn to sell and communicate better than older people, and somewhat older folks learn finance better than younger ones.

Start by learning to sell. There's time later to learn finance and investments. Learning selling is like skiing—the younger you start, the faster and better you learn. But learning to analyze investments is like learning to hire people well—years of real-world experience make discernment easier. Time helps.

Learn to Sell. The Rest Follows.

Often young people want to start as hotshot research and investment analysts or portfolio managers—certain they'll be the next Warren Buffett or Peter Lynch—often naively disdaining anything sales-related. They almost never get their desired outcome. My advice to the young: Start by learning telephone sales—even if not investment-related. Here your youthful appearance won't hurt you. Then, move to in-person sales, first with simple, then more complicated products or services. Sales competence comes fast when young. But the ease of learning to sell drops steadily with age. People in their 40s who've never sold can learn, but it's harder, takes longer, and feels unnatural (like skiing!).

Product knowledge is less critical—can be learned fast as needed. Thirty years ago Ken Koskella, who originally built sales and marketing at Franklin Resources (he retired rich and now does stand-up comedy for fun—the old business guy in a suit joking about how old business guys are funny), taught me if you really know how to sell, you could be dropped into America's most remote town and make a living by the end of the week. Maybe not the living you'd want later, but you could get by—without knowing anything else beforehand.

Many think they don't need to sell—they'll start a firm and hire salespeople. On this road you simply can't hire and manage sales people well if you can't sell yourself. Won't work. This isn't a book on how to sell or manage sales (I offer a list of those books later), but one reason to learn sales is so you can hire and manage a sales force—key to many roads. Fact: Firms need salespeople more than they need 23-year-old ambitious but skill-less know-it-alls. Young folks on this road should learn to sell—anything—in their 20s, then sell finance products. You'll learn some finance naturally en route. In your early 30s, reposture yourself to plumb finance's analytical and technical depths. By then your extra real-world experience aids in learning finance.

Learn to sell. It's the most important OPM skill.

Find the Right Firm

Any firm is the right firm if they teach you to sell. Big firms hire in volume. It doesn't matter much if it's Merrill Lynch, JP Morgan, or New York Life. Visit, interview, talk, and decide which one doesn't make you want to jump out a window before you've learned to sell. Or go with a boutique firm—every major town has them. Neither is inherently better or worse. Big finance firms regularly hire folks straight from college or with no real experience—in volume with a "throw spaghetti at the wall" mentality. If newbies flame out fast, no skin off the firm's nose. (This won't be you if you focus only on learning to sell.) For a more touchy-feely start, try a boutique. But *learning to sell is key*. For that, buy or borrow these books and keep practicing what they teach repeatedly:

- *How to Win Friends and Influence People* by Dale Carnegie
- *You'll See It When You Believe It* by Wayne Dyer
- *The Psychology of Selling* by Brian Tracy
- *The Difference Maker* by John Maxwell
- *Confidence* by Rosabeth Kanter
- *See You at the Top* by Zig Ziglar
- *Spin Selling* by Neil Rackham

Then you must pass licensing tests before engaging clients. The tests are customized—based on what you'll sell. They aren't hard—if you study—and you don't need a degree to take them. But beware: At many firms, if you don't pass the first time—sayonara.

Then it's selling time. And if you don't sell you'll soon be shown the door. Most firms have periodic quotas—you must bring in maybe $500,000 or so in new client assets monthly. Fail to do so, and you're history. This isn't to discourage you but to emphasize the importance of learning to sell. You may be a super market forecaster, but if you can't get clients to hire you, take a different road. Your firm should help with lists of names to call, but then it's up to you.

STEPS TO OPM WEALTH

Next, what type of OPMer will you be? Consider two camps— *commission-based* and *fee-based*—defined by how you charge fees and maybe what you sell.

Commission-based OPMers—like stock and insurance brokers—sell *products* (e.g., stocks, bonds, mutual funds, even insurance) for commissions. What you earn all hinges on the sale. A client has $1 million. You sell him stocks paying you a 1 percent commish. You make $10,000. Keep finding clients and selling products—income keeps coming. The basic commission-based business model is:

1. Get the client.
2. Sell the client product(s).
3. Get a commission.

You make what you sell. Want a $250,000 salary? With a 1 percent commission you must sell $25 million of products. How? Find 100 clients with $250,000 each, or 50 with $500,000! Your call. The drawback? Unless you get them to sell what you sold them and buy something new, you need another slew of clients next year. Your time is spent hunting for clients. If you're a great hunter, no problem! That's *commission-based*.

Fee-based OPMers—like investment advisers, money managers, or hedge funds—provide *services* for some percent of assets involved. Say you have 100 clients. Each invests $250,000 with you. You charge 1.25 percent per year (a typical fee for fee-based advisers). That's $312,500 in annual revenue as long as the clients remain. The more their assets grow, the more your fee does. If you keep your clients and the market helps out, you make even more next year! But you get paid less if their assets shrink. The basic fee-based business model is:

1. Get the client.
2. Keep the client.
3. Do well for them.

Your income depends on how much in client assets you gather, how well you do keeping clients, and what returns you (or your firm) makes for them.

Fee-based is where I started decades ago. It was simple and compelling. I knew if I could gain clients, net of terminations, at

Choose your business model—fee-based or commission-based.

rate X percent, and grow their assets at rate Y percent, then my firm would grow at the rate of X percent + Y percent. So gain new net assets at 15 percent a year and grow assets at 15 percent a year—the firm grows

30 percent a year. That's hot. It's the Y in the X + Y formula that makes this OPM model so compelling. And my firm has grown at just above 30 percent a year for the last 25-plus years. If you can grow any business at 30 percent a year for 25 years without selling stock to outsiders, you end up very rich by anyone's standards.

Value the Business

So is it commission- or fee-based for you? To decide, think like a business owner. This is an exercise you can use many ways to figure what's worth what:

1. Go to Morningstar.com.
2. Search for any stock—a mutual fund like Janus Capital (fee-based) or a wire house broker like Merrill Lynch (commission-based).
3. Click on the "snapshot" button in the left-hand column.
4. Click on "industry peers" (across the top). Note: Whether a company is listed as a peer is up to Morningstar—sometimes the results seem wonky. For example, Merrill Lynch's industry peers include Goldman Sachs and Morgan Stanley (other brokers), but also NYSE Euronext and Nasdaq Stock Market (exchanges). Ignore the exchanges.
5. Make a list of similar companies.
6. Divide each firm's total value (market cap) by sales to create a ratio.
7. See who has higher or lower ratios.

Table 7.1 Mutual Fund Market Cap Versus Sales

Firm	Market Cap (Mil)	Sales (Mil)	Ratio
Franklin Resources	$28,258	$6,206	4.6
BlackRock	$25,641	$4,419	5.8
T. Rowe Price	$16,635	$2,120	7.8
Invesco	$13,148	$2,936	4.5
Legg Mason	$ 9,827	$4,653	2.1
Janus Capital	$ 5,746	$1,138	5.0
Eaton Vance	$ 5,889	$1,018	5.8
Waddell & Reed	$ 3,116	$787	4.0
Cohen & Steers	$ 1,195	$273	4.4

Source: Morningstar.com as of December 24, 2007.[1]

I've done this for you as an example. You can do it for any stock. Table 7.1 shows results for mutual funds—fee-based firms. Most fund families have ratios from four to nearly six. Legg Mason and T. Rowe Price are outliers. So the market says these kinds of firms are worth four to six times their annual sales.

Table 7.2 lists brokerage firms—commission-based. Note lower ratios—most under 2! Outliers are Charles Schwab and TD Ameritrade. (Schwab has a huge mutual fund business and is hybrid fee-based/commission-based.) The market values a buck of commissioned-based sales half as much as fee-based sales. The upside? Even medium-sized brokers are bigger than almost all money managers. The biggest brokers are almost 10 times bigger than the biggest money managers. There is vastly more business in the commission-based world, but it isn't as valuable. That's your trade-off—more versus more valuable. (Note: Even before Bear Stearns imploded in 2008, it was still about as profitable as its peers.)

Ditto for insurance (Table 7.3)—even more commission-based than brokers. With lower ratios they're less valuable than brokers,

Table 7.2 Brokerage Firm Market Cap Versus Sales

Firm	Market Cap (Mil)	Sales (Mil)	Ratio
Goldman Sachs Group	$85,230	$44,653	1.9
Morgan Stanley	$58,336	$40,344	1.4
Merrill Lynch	$46,000	$28,835	1.6
Lehman Brothers	$34,797	$19,400	1.8
Charles Schwab	$29,246	$ 4,745	6.2
TD Ameritrade	$11,848	$ 2,177	5.4
Bear Stearns	$10,253	$ 8,738	1.2
Raymond James	$ 4,084	$ 2,610	1.6
Lazard	$ 2,159	$ 1,805	1.2
E*Trade	$ 1,538	$ 2,259	0.7

Source: Morningstar.com as of December 24, 2007.[2]

Table 7.3 Insurance Market Cap Versus Sales

Firm	Market Cap (Mil)	Sales (Mil)	Ratio
AXA	$82,439	$139,351	0.6
Metropolitan Life	$46,991	$52,171	0.9
Prudential Corporation	$35,015	$65,901	0.5
Sun Life Financial	$32,138	$21,385	1.5
Aflac	$30,498	$15,063	2.0
Principal Financial Group	$18,500	$10,901	1.7
Lincoln National	$16,135	$10,750	1.5
Genworth Financial	$11,427	$11,751	1.0
Nationwide	$ 6,544	$ 4,472	1.5

Source: Morningstar.com as of December 24, 2007.[3]

but the potential business is huge. Smaller players in Table 7.3 have more total business than the biggest mutual fund families do.

Note: Huge insurers are older than most brokers and older still than money managers. So the trade-offs are size of opportunity versus value of revenue versus maturity. Think like an OPM founder-CEO. If a law dictated firms could have only up to $1 billion in revenue, no more, then hands down you'd want to be fee-based—the enterprise value would be so much higher. A small success in fee-based goes a long, long way.

This isn't to disparage insurance and brokerage—which have created lots of mega-wealth. Some see **Warren Buffett** (worth $52 billion)[4] as an investor. He's really an insurance CEO. Berkshire Hathaway's profits come overwhelmingly from insurance. Buffett's unusual—the next-wealthiest insurance OPMer is **Hank Greenberg**, former CEO of AIG, net worth a big step down at $2.8 billion.[5] **Arthur Williams** founded and sold an insurer to Primerica and is worth $1.8 billion.[6] **Ernest Stempel**, a Hank Greenberg ride-along (Chapter 3), started AIG's life insurance division (worth $1.7 billion).[7] **Patrick Ryan** ($1.4 billion) started a firm that became AON, America's largest re-insurance broker.[8] But beyond Buffett, they don't compare to fee-based wealth—the top 15 listed below.

Wealthiest Fee-Based OPMers

Name	Famous for	Net worth
Edward Johnson III	Fidelity	$10 billion
George Soros	Slew of hedge funds and tanking the British Pound	$8.8 billion
Charles Johnson	Franklin Resources	$6 billion
Charles Schwab	Eponymous firm	$5.5 billion
James Simons	Hedge funds	$5.5 billion
Rupert Johnson	Franklin Resources	$5.2 billion
Edward Lampert	ESL hedge fund and being kidnapped	$4.5 billion
Leon Black	Apollo Management	$4 billion
		(Continued)

Wealthiest Fee-Based OPMers (*Continued*)

Name	Famous for	Net worth
Ray Dalio	Money management and hedge funds	$4 billion
Stanley Druckenmiller	Tanked the British pound with Soros	$3.5 billion
Bruce Kovner	Hedge funds and a harpsichord	$3.5 billion
Paul Tudor Jones III	Hedge funds	$3.3 billion
Kenneth Griffin	Hedge funds	$3 billion
Charles Brandes	Brandes money management	$2.5 billion
David Shaw	Hedge funds	$2.5 billion

Source: Matthew Miller, "The Forbes 400," *Forbes* (October 8, 2007).

Beyond Charles Schwab, the only current *Forbes* 400 member coming from commission-based brokerage is **Sandy Weill** ($1.8 billion). But even he evolved out of it. Originally a straight-up brokerage firm CEO, and a dynamite one at that, Weill made his fortune parlaying that into Travelers, an insurer, which later merged with Citicorp to become Citigroup. His big wealth came at Citi on the CEO road (Chapter 2), not really from insurance or brokerage.

As a fee-based OPM founder-CEO, I'm not even successful enough to be among the 15 wealthiest fee-based OPMers. But worth $1.8 billion with my little firm, I'm just where Sandy Weill is and as high as anyone from insurance but Warren Buffett and Hank Greenberg. That's one attraction of fee-based OPM. You needn't be as big overall to be more wealthy.

Still, brokerage is lucrative. **Joseph Moglia**, TD Ameritrade's CEO, earned $62.3 million in 2007 compensation. **Richard Fuld** of Lehman Brothers got $51.7 million. And Bear Stearns' **James Cayne** got $38.3 million (before it blew up in 2008). Even Morgan Stanley's **John Mack's** $7.5 million is nothing to sneeze at.[9] For huge wealth, fee-based is best. But to accumulate $2 million to $50 million, any form of OPM is fine.

HEDGE YOUR BETS

Do you like huge risks and returns? Are you a maverick? Fond of big fees? Start a hedge fund. Hedge funds are known as the *2 and 20* model because they charge 2 percent of managed assets annually (i.e., give them $1 million, they take $20,000 yearly)—but also get *20 percent of annual gains!* If you're good, lucky, or both, that adds up quick.

Say you make one bet—some stock category will beat the market in the next five years—maybe big stocks, energy, or drugs. You bet big on that. You manage $100 million with a 2 and 20 contract. Assume your bet averages 20 percent per year for five years.

■ End of year one, your $100 million becomes $120 million. You take 2 percent ($2.4 million) plus 20 percent of the $20 million gain ($4 million)—*$6.4 million profit.*

■ Year two starts and, minus your fee, assets are now $113.6 million. Tack on another 20 percent, take your 2 and 20 fee—*$7.27 million profit.*

■ In year five, your profit is *over $10.6 million!*

Over five years, you get nearly $42 million in total fees! That's just on the assets you started with. Generate high returns and you'll get more clients with more assets.

Now, suppose you're a regular fee-based manager making the same bet—the assets still grow 20 percent a year for five years, but you charge only 1.25 percent a year.

■ First year, your $100 million becomes $120 million. You get 1.25 percent—$1.5 million. Not bad, but not $6.4 million.

■ Year two starts and, minus your fee, assets are now $118.5 million. Tack on another 20 percent, take your 1.25 percent fee—$1.78 million.

■ In year five, your profit is $2.96 million.

After five years, you've made $10.8 million in total fees—good, but far from $42 million. Of course your clients came out ahead because you took less of their money in fees. But a hedge fund manager thinks, "Why *not* bet big for extra return?" If you're right, that 20 percent "carried interest" is huge. If you're wrong, you *still* collect 2 percent of the assets, annually. Amazingly, if you bet wrong you don't pay back 20 percent of losses! Of course, if you're wrong, it's your clients who suffer. To get big reward as a hedge fund manager you must take big risk. Smaller risk means smaller reward.

Hedge funds aren't new—they're just newly popular! Before 1940, swindlers would create two funds. With one, they'd convince half their clients XYZ stock would rise and buy XYZ. In the other fund, they'd convince clients XYZ would fall and *sell* XYZ *short* (borrow it, sell it, hope it falls, then buy it back lower, pocketing the spread and repaying the borrowed stock). Neither client group knew about the other. As long as XYZ was volatile, the two funds got 10 percent of that volatility. Clients who lost fired the swindlers and disappeared. Clients who won didn't understand it was a swindle and would actually give the crooks more money for another bet. This con was put out of business by the combined Investment Company and Investment Advisers Acts of 1940.

But you can take one side of a big bet on blind luck and hit big or go home. If you're unlucky, you end up on a different road soon. If you're lucky, I promise: Few observers will think it's just luck. You won't either. The best hedge funders aren't just lucky—they're skilled. But few hedge funds hit big. Most go home. This arena is sprinkled with spectacular successes, yet most hedge funds flame out fast. Few survive two years before all their investors redeem and disappear. I've known dozens of folks who started hedge funds— only two survived over the long-term. It's treacherous. Taking monster bets your career rides on is nerve-racking. Jim Cramer quit for just that reason. I've seen folks get a run for a few years and then everything blows up on them in no time—ending with nothing.

Bet on Hedges

Hedge funds typically operate in specific categories like convertible arbitrage, distressed securities, long/short equity, market neutral, and more. Investors can buy them in multiple categories and diversify (although investors who do this invariably get poor returns because you can't diversify widely, pay huge fees, and still end up ahead—see Chapter 10 on this relative to being frugal).

Hedgers also have varied hiring practices. To go this route, just apply everywhere—shotgun style! You can find endless names by doing a Google search—thousands. Most don't hire. Most are one person, with maybe $10 million to $40 million, operating by him- or herself out of the bedroom. But if you keep looking you'll find those that hire—they'll invariably be the bigger ones.

There's no security—a fund can blow up fast. I'm not suggesting this for a long-term career unless as a founder-CEO or ride-along. But it's a great place to learn and launch. Work there a few years. Learn what they do. Get the lay of the land. Then you can start your own.

Hedge funds are lightly regulated, so they're very easy entry. A law firm like San Francisco's Shartsis Friese with a hedge fund specialty can get you set up legally and take you through the rules like they're spitting out popcorn. (Follow this URL for more law firm hedge fund practices: http://www.hedgeworld.com/sp_directory/search.cgi?category_name=3)

Then—and you may hate this—it's all about selling to get clients for your fund. The tactics of running a hedge fund are pretty generic. Pay attention to your law firm's do-and-don't rules and then find something you believe the heck out of in terms of doing well looking forward and bet the house on it.

Often people find one big anchor investor before they start their fund. Say you've been a Merrill Lynch broker with a client list totaling $100 million in assets. Among them you've got one big $40 million elephant you've served well and put tons of time into. People often decide they can make as much off the elephant in a hedge fund as everything else otherwise. So you quit, start your hedge fund with the one client as an anchor, and then try to build from there.

This whole process isn't much more complicated than:

1. Betting big.
2. Finding clients who will back you in the bets.
3. Adhering to the applicable laws . . .
4. . . . while you collect 2 plus 20.

Maybe the most successful recent young hedge fund manager has been **Ken Griffin**. Only 38, worth $3 billion,[10] he started Citadel Investment Group in 1990 in a classic hedge fund format. Today he has teams in multiple categories taking big bets on tiny profit potentials, which he leverages heavily for big returns. He's a phenomenon because most who try what he's done don't just fail—they splat.

Even if you succeed, your future is uncertain. I've known Alex Brockman through his father since he was a boy—one of the nicest guys you could ever meet and very smart. Alex trades Latin American sovereign debt for Ken Griffin and gets paid super well for succeeding. But Alex knows he lives and dies by the sword. He made monster money in 2007—what he did worked—and Griffin happily paid for that. Alex knows he might not be there at all in 2009 if 2008 fares badly. The guy who introduced Alex to Griffin, Alex's original Citadel boss, is now gone—died by the sword.

My first example assumed no skill—just blind luck. Ken Griffin obviously has skill. Look back at the list of fee-based OPMers—this is how famous hedge fund managers (Soros, Cohen, Kovner, Jones, Simons, Shaw) made it—by and large taking big risk for giant fees. This requires toughness, as **Eddie Lampert** knows better than anyone. Lampert's currently worth only $4.5 billion, but he's young and could become worth much more. Known for his keen-value eye, he bought K-Mart—America's third-largest discounter—in a 2002 fire sale that most thought was doomed to disaster. But K-Mart turned around, generating huge returns for Lampert's ESL fund.[11] (Again: One huge risk that worked.)

He almost didn't get the chance. One evening, just before then, Lampert left work. Heading to his car he was grabbed by four armed men, blindfolded, bound, and thrown into an SUV. He spent two days bound in a dingy motel bathtub. Lampert believed they would kill him, but remained calm. He noted they were disorganized. First they claimed they'd been hired to kill him for $5 million.[12] No, they were to hold him for $1 million ransom.[13] They were armed and terrifying—but also young and scared. Turns out there was no elaborate plan—the four thugs had merely Googled for local wealthy people and found Lampert.[14]

Lampert tried negotiating, offering to beat whatever they'd been offered. He claimed they should let him go—that only he could sign for a big ransom check. But his chance came when he overheard them ordering pizza—with Lampert's credit card! He pointed out the police would be alerted to his credit card being used—hadn't they thought of that? The only way to avoid prison was to let him go—now—and run. Lampert reminded them he couldn't ID them—he'd wisely averted his eyes when they removed his blindfold for the one meal they offered him.[15] Sunday morning they dropped Lampert off on a highway a few miles from his home. Until they left he still feared they might kill him. Lampert walked to a Greenwich, CT police station. They caught the thugs days later.[16] Lampert could have panicked or given up. But he remained cool and attentive, thinking creatively of ways to extricate himself. Tough, cool, and collected! Like you must be to succeed in the hedge fund world! Are you that tough?

PRIVATE EQUITY'S BIG BUCKS

Akin to hedge funds is *private equity*—also with a 2 and 20 fee scheme. They take over troubled publicly traded firms and fix them to later sell at a profit. These are often called *leveraged buyouts*. You do the takeover, maybe bring in new management, lop off losing divisions, fund winning ones, and maybe go public again later at higher prices. Done right, it's super profitable. Part of this is knowing how to borrow well. Another part is the skill to spot troubled firms that can be bought cheaply, because no one sees potential, but can be fixed and profits boosted to fat levels compared to interest costs incurred with the buyout.

Recent years have seen record buyout activity—making private equity firm partners huge bucks. Kravis, Kohlberg, and Roberts (KKR) had a busy 2007—offering to buy TXU Energy for $45 billion. Co-founder **Jerome Kohlberg** ($1.5 billion) is no longer with the firm, but both **Henry Kravis** and **George Roberts** are, with matching $5.5 billion net worths. Another group taking advantage of the times has been Carlyle Group founders—**William Conway Jr.** ($2.5 billion), **Daniel D'Aniello** ($2.5 billion), and **David Rubenstein** ($2.5 billion).[17]

Corporate Raiders Lead to a Better World

The media paints these OPMers as greedy scumbags, but why? The stock can get a nice price bump when deals are announced. This is capitalism's Darwinism. We all benefit from improved efficiency, productivity, and innovation. We don't always get a better company after these deals. Things can go wrong, but the acquirer better make a good go of it or they'll be history too. And CEOs of lackluster public companies not wanting to be acquired (and unemployed) know they'd best improve or be history too, adding incentive for corporate productivity, which benefits employees, shareholders, customers—everyone.

It's fashionable to skewer these OPMers for their super-sized incomes. (If the media's hot over some group's pay, you know you've found a righteous road to riches.) Mr. Kravis unexpectedly found himself starring in a mockumentary—*The War on Greed, Starring the Homes of Henry Kravis*—supposedly a "light-hearted" look at the "excesses" of private equity. It juxtaposes Mr. Kravis's homes against the modest abodes of "Average Joes" while detailing Kravis's earnings.

Mr. Kravis is mega-wealthy—no crime there. (If you see wealth as a crime, you need a different book. Try *Free to Choose* by Milton Friedman.) Robert Greenwald, the film's director, said "I saw the numbers of what the guys make, I truly did not believe it. I thought they were a mistake. I'm a New Yorker and this sort of egalitarianism is built into many of us."[18] Folks like Greenwald who object see big earnings as "unfair." If Mr. Greenwald wants "fair," he should check out Cuba or Venezuela to see how "fairness" really works. Just working at these firms isn't a bad career. There are lots of Alex Brockman equivalents—and lots of rich ride-alongs (Chapter 3)—and those just making fat salaries who take the Road More Traveled (Chapter 10).

DON'T BREAK THE LAW

With OPM it's crucial to get that you never break the law. OPMers sometimes forget. Cheaters may get rich, but they don't stay rich. Some OPMers may get wealthy legitimately, then cheat. Some cheat to get rich. Either way, they won't stay wealthy. It's not just illegal and immoral; it's also bad business.

Those stretching morality come in various flavors. **Dick Strong** comes to mind: former CEO of Strong Capital Management, a once thriving mutual fund firm started in 1973, now history. By 2003 he was number 318 on the *Forbes* 400, with an estimated $800 million net worth. By 2004 he was toast. Regulators honed in on

Strong, who had been short-term trading his own funds for his own account—not explicitly illegal. But a mutual fund CEO doing it on a non-disclosed basis at the expense of fund holders would irritate regulators. It moves to dead wrong when based on inside information—as Strong allegedly did.[19]

When the scandal broke, Strong stepped down—too late. The firm couldn't survive—Wells Fargo bought it at a huge discount and dropped the Strong name. Was his "stretching" worth it? Never is. His trading scheme netted him a reported $600,000.[20] This "gain" was probably the most costly gain in recent public record. Between the fines and decimated value of his firm when sold, Strong retained only a fraction of his prior wealth. And he was banned for life from the industry. Decimated, banished, name ruined, and a fraction of his worth. Ugh!

Then came **Alberto Vilar**, a villain who seemingly set out to cheat. He was capable but also twisted. I'd see him around in the early days when we were both first building our firms and would be in the same venues, seminars, conferences, competitions, etc. We'd chat. Something about him bristled. Too haughty, rigid, and regal! The women he dated were too young and pretty—showed too much skin. At least my wife thought so—said he gave her the "creeps."

He bragged of all the super-successful start-ups he helped fund—like Intel. It was unclear what was true versus not—it just sounded too much. He boasted of growing up privileged in pre-Castro Cuba, then being impoverished when Castro seized his family's assets. But his closest friends later recounted that as fiction—he grew up in New Jersey.[21]

His investing stories were stunning too, as were his late 1990s tech returns. In 2004 he ranked 327 on the *Forbes* 400, with an estimated $950 million net worth.[22] But his firm wasn't that big. At its peak in 2000, it managed only $7 billion. By 2004 it imploded to under $1 billion. Use the tables earlier in this chapter—at the peak you don't get near $950 million. He convinced folks (including *Forbes*) he owned lots of securities outside his firm—worth much more than his firm. Some people are. But an insider's rule about the *Forbes* 400 is the *Forbes* folks are skeptical of those trying to get on the list. They know they're usually worth less than they say—maybe lots less. That was Vilar. Still, he was convincing.

Vilar was a huge opera patron. Over the years, it's estimated he gave beyond $300 million to the arts.[23] (However, some, if not much of it, may not have been his to give.) When Vilar's tech-heavy funds lost over 80 percent during the tech crash, he delayed millions in pledged donations to the Metropolitan Opera House. (They'd already put his name on the building!) Investigators came looking. He was charged with mail fraud in 2005. He, who claimed to be mega-rich from investments outside his firm, couldn't make $10 million bail.[24] In my opinion, much of his net worth, like his background, was fiction—what he hadn't fabricated he'd given away to the opera.

And in a still-pending lawsuit, it's alleged Alberto embezzled those opera pledges from clients! It's hard to see that suit getting far since Vilar is penniless. No money to win. His performance may not have been up to opera standards, but for a long time it gave him a grand lifestyle. My wife of 38 years still wonders what his hot young women with excess skin showing think now. There are more Vilars. Don't be one.

True Villains

The occasional Vilar-like villain may hit the *Forbes* 400 briefly before blowing up, but most evildoers get caught long before then. Frank Gruttadauria was. He's doing time for copping maybe $300 million in client funds, plus perjury, obstruction, bribery, and racketeering—even an escape charge!

Seriously. Don't break the law.

As a Lehman Brothers branch manager in Cleveland, Gruttadauria basically ran a Ponzi scheme, targeting mostly elderly clients. Clients deposited money that he transferred to accounts under fictitious names—for 15 years! Clients never knew because Frank doctored fake statements, inflating account values. Who complains when statements show huge growth and no losses? When clients wanted withdrawals, Frank wrote checks from other clients' accounts. Meanwhile, Frank enjoyed country clubs, a ski condo, a private jet, and a mistress.[25]

The Internet Age did Frank in. He told elderly clients Lehman had no online access. One relatively Web-savvy grandma wondered why her account wasn't being impacted by the tech crash.[26] She led clients in an online charge and they found their accounts empty—despite monthly statements showing, in some cases, millions. Because Frank had faked documents for so long it was hard to know how much he stole—investigators estimate at least $40 million from 50 different clients. But because of the doctored returns, clients believed they lost much more.[27] He's now serving seven years.[28] Orange ain't beautiful.

LOVE CAPITALISM, NOT SOCIAL ACCEPTANCE

Warning: This road can make you unpopular. Sensational stories like Vilar and Gruttadauria are fortunately exceptions—but their existence is a reason this road's big bucks make it a hot Hollywood target, proliferating the bad-guy image in our culture. Movie villains are often rich Wall Streeters, cruelly enriching themselves off the poor proletariat. OPMers aren't movie heroes. Hollywood and pop fiction are littered with villainous OPMers: *Boiler Room*, *American Psycho*, *Bonfire of the Vanities*, *Rogue Trader*, *Ghost*, and the granddaddy, *Wall Street*—all movies featuring Wall Street villains. Even *Trading Places*, an otherwise hilarious movie, implies rich OPMers are crooked. Precious few are.

If you succeed on this road, you subject yourself to being degraded by social stereotypes. Some folks may not like you. But successful OPMers don't place high value on social acceptance. They place high value on capitalism. They operate close to the heart of the capital markets pricing mechanism and live and die by competitive forces. This is a great road to mega-wealth. I know. I've lived it all my life. It's a wonderful world where you get rich by helping others get richer. It's a world you can be proud of. It's also a world where many will assume you shouldn't be proud. If you're tough like Eddie Lampert, but won't become a villain like Alberto Vilar, and you want to be rich pretty easily—or put yourself where most of the richest are—OPM is, in my view, as fine a road as you can choose.

 The Guide to **Other People's Money**

OPM wealth is a fairly reliable road to riches, if you follow this fairly easy guide.

1. *Love capitalism and free markets.* Many folks—even misguided Wall Streeters—think capitalism is wrong, bad, or cruel. No! There's no better system for generating and building societal wealth. Yes, there are losers and winners. But capitalism isn't a zero sum gain. Every dollar you earn isn't a dollar someone loses. Capitalism allows opportunity for all. What folks do with that is up to them. Without capitalism, you don't have free markets. And without free markets, you don't have an OPM road. So love it.

2. *Get the client.* You must sell. You can: (a) Get referrals, or (b) sell directly. Both work. You can do both together. Selling directly, you find a way to get in front of someone who makes up their own mind. Most people have seen my firm's advertising, whether direct mail, Internet ads, radio, newspapers, or on TV. Many folks assume that if you advertise a lot, your product can't be good. Anyone who says that hasn't thought it through very fully. Tell it to Procter & Gamble. The marketing channel you use and how you do what you do otherwise for clients have simply nothing to do with each other—ever.

(Continued)

(*Continued*)

Seeking referrals means calling on people to get them to refer friends and connections. Common approaches are calling on accountants and estate-planning attorneys who have clients that may need your services.

3. *Keep the client.* Keeping clients has two subcategories: Performance and Customer Service.

a. Performance. *Performance* doesn't mean blowing the market away each and every day, week, year. It means setting realistic client expectations and achieving them. Sound easy? No! Clients often have too-high expectations, like high returns without risk—a fairy tale. Setting expectations is basic to client education and falls into the mantra: "Underpromise, overperform."

Speaking of which, avoid overpromising. OPMers—particularly new ones—may overstate what clients can expect in an effort to get business. Doing so sets you up for failure and a high client termination rate.

Exceeding client expectations helps keep clients around and keeps clients from doing something potentially harmful to themselves—like chasing hot markets but getting cold ones.

b. Customer service. If you have great performance, but don't attend to your clients, you lose them to someone who will. After more than 36 years as an OPMer, I believe performance is important, but success is half performance and half customer service. (In a different way, the third "half" is sales and marketing.) Too many people think it's either performance or service, but neither alone is adequate. Customer service doesn't just mean answering the phone when they call. The better and more high-touch your service, the likelier your clients remain.

Know your clients and understand their needs. Do they want to be called quarterly? Monthly? Daily? Find out, agree to a service level, and exceed it. Keeping clients is better. Most OPMers suffer high turnover. Part of what has made my firm successful is unusually low client terminations.

4. *Don't break the law.* OPMers operate in a regulated industry. Breaking the law may land you in jail. But even if you don't get caught (or simply are a rule bender), you're likely not best serving your clients. Revisit the previous step, "Keep the Client."

5. *Focus on core competencies.* OPMers wear multiple hats. They're salespeople, servicers, and traders. They do marketing and research. They watch screens, people, and employees. They may be a manager or CEO! With all that, how well are you really doing staying abreast of global markets, economies and making accurate forecasts?

Salespeople shouldn't manage money. Marketers shouldn't sell. Service people shouldn't research. The best business model has segmentation of responsibility so everyone focuses on core competencies. To make it to the top in OPM you must have all those skills, at least have rotated through them, and be able to orchestrate others engaged in them. That's a tall order but also why this is the most common road among America's very richest people.

8

INVENTING INCOME

Have a wild imagination?
Or none at all?
This could be your road.

Can you invent an endless stream of future income? I don't mean by *inventing*—though that can work. Here you make an annuity-like future cash flow from something you create, own, or patent that just keeps spewing cash. A gadget, book, song, movie, or even experience.

Ever thought, "If only such-and-such existed, life would be better"? Then someone invents such-and-such, changes the world, and gets rich! Why them and not you? The big money is in getting rights, licensed or patented, for future reuse and generating reuse. This is how a very few writers get rich, or how successful song writers do it via publishing rights like our Chapter 4 hip-hop friends.

THE TRUE INVENTORS

Yes, there are true "inventors"—folks who create things so earth-shatteringly life-changing you can't imagine life without them, like the PC or polio vaccine. Or mundane, everyday things. The trick is patenting it, so you collect every time your gadget is used or sold.

Everyone wrongly cites the guys who invented Post-its (**Arthur Fry** and **Spencer Silver**) as classic successful inventors—striking it big with a mundane idea. Fry, a 3M chemist, wanted bookmarks to stay put in his choir hymnal. He used his buddy and coworker Silver's adhesive—sticky enough, but not so much as to tear the page when removed—voila! A pop-culture icon was born.[1] But they weren't income inventors. Being 3M employees, their creation was a "work product"—they couldn't own it. They probably got a nice bonus but didn't invent a future revenue stream for themselves. Just "inventing" may not hack it.

Invent? Market? Do Both!

Nor will a patent. Lots of people hold patents—tens of millions! To create future income, you must have broad adaptation like our Post-it friends, but you must also maintain control of the future. Successful income inventors have an entrepreneurial soul and can market their ideas. If you can't preach the benefit, you go unnoticed—marketing is key. You must have broad reach and a compelling story—or a compelling personality, like the father of inventors, **Ron Popeil**. Ron haunts late-night TV, still pitching products energetically to insomniac audiences.

Marketing your product—even if your product is you—is vital.

As a teen, Popeil frequented Chicago's West Side flea markets—not to shop, but to watch the hawkers. He built flea market skills to sell kitchen and household wares at Woolworth's, making $1,000 a week—huge for a 1950s teenager selling blenders (about $7,500 today—$390,000 per year!). Remember from Chapter 7—learning to sell is powerful.

Next, Popeil set out on his own to sell his own kitschy inventions at flea markets and carnivals, honing his midway barker style.

Then he turned to TV, still a new medium then. With $550, he made his first commercial. In 10 years, Ron was pure TV. He founded Ronco in 1964 and dedicated himself to inventing and selling. He created Veg-O-Matic—boasting it chopped onions perfectly with no tears. He did the Pocket Fisherman—a fully equipped fishing pole that folded down for those crucial moments you're driving past a trout pond and think, "Dang! If only I had a pole handy!" (My mother bought one and then another each for me and my brothers.)

Popeil invented slews of goofy products—an Inside-the-Shell Egg Scrambler, the Smokeless Ashtray, the Electric Food Dehydrator, and the Cap Snaffler. I have no clue what "snaffling" is, but apparently you do it to caps. As Ron would say, "It really really works!" He invented goofy products, but also invented or synthesized catch phrases now common to infomercials. He teased, "But wait! There's more!" He urged buyers to rush because "operators are standing by." He told housewives they could "set it and forget it." He touted his bargain prices by asking, "NOW how much would you pay?" He enticed shoppers with low installment payments. A Cap Snaffler may not seem worth $160, but who can't afford four easy payments of $39.95?

His real invention was the infomercial—Popeil is synonymous with long-form TV commercials, an insanely profitable marketing vehicle. His products, while cute, weren't world changing. Who really needs a big bulky onion-chopping gadget? Don't knives do that—and fit neatly in a drawer? But Ron's genius was in making the mundane exciting. His persona was famous enough for **Dan Aykroyd** to satirize him on *Saturday Night Live* when he put a fish in a blender and touted the vitamin-boosted benefits of liquefied bass. Ackroyd called it the "Bass-O-Matic." **Lorraine Newman** purred, "That's good bass."

His net worth exceeds $100 million.[2] The best way to emulate Ron's success is to focus on finding the next efficient way to market something—anything. You can even create your own catchphrase and be parodied on *Saturday Night Live*.

WRITING FOR DOLLARS

Most successful writers don't get rich. Few books sell many copies—most less than 10,000. At that, if it's a $20 book, royalties may be $2 per book. The author makes $20,000 for much of a year's work and remains poor. A tiny percent sell better. Take stock market books, which are mostly what I've written. A real monster stock market book may sell 200,000 copies in its life. There are maybe two of those a year at most and they will make the *New York Times* Best Seller list like my 2007 book did. But $400,000 in royalties isn't enough to get rich on. And that's before expenses associated with promoting it.

Writers who succeed keep cranking out best sellers to maintain income and then go down the Road More Traveled (Chapter 10). Broader category monsters like **James Michener** are statistically and simply way out on the bell curve of success. You're as apt to become the next Babe Ruth. Long-term top-10 selling romance novelists accumulate $5 million to $30 million in their lifetimes. I know because two of them are my clients. But that's it. Nice—but not mongo huge.

That is unless you morph otherwise. For example, **Stephen King** will collect endless cash from royalties on *The Shining*—the movie, not the book, and subsequent remakes, prequels, sequels, remakes of prequel/sequels, reissues, special-edition DVD box sets, etc. Ditto for *Christine*, *Stand by Me*, *Pet Sematary* (yes, it's spelled incorrectly intentionally), *Shawshank Redemption*, and *The Green Mile*—for a few. He could have quit writing 20 years ago and been excessively rich. His book royalties were ok, but he earns exponentially more on licensing rights whenever another of his macabre tales is used as movie or TV fodder and then endlessly rented from Netflix. Did he intend to write books that translate easily into 2-hour movies? Don't know. But he sure evolved to it.

King may be king, but **JK Rowling** is the queen (and, incidentally, is richer than Britain's Queen). JK "Jo" Rowling invented Harry Potter's magical world and a magical income stream. The film series alone has grossed $3.5 billion so far—and there are another two to come. Rowling's currently worth about $1 billion—ringing in as the world's 1,062nd wealthiest human.[3] Her books keep selling. But her bucks come from movies, DVDs, endless Harry Potter lunch boxes, sneakers, backpacks, action figures, skateboards, wallpaper, pencils, Halloween costumes, paper plates, pajamas, you name it. If it's inanimate and kid-oriented, it's been stamped with Harry Potter's mug—and Rowling collects every time. A plain lunch box retails for about $5. Embossed with Harry and pals, it's $25. *That's* monetizing your creation.

> *Figure how to monetize your creation.*

If you will write—and want riches—think lunch boxes. After this book I'm starting my next—a made-for-movie adventure novel based on 10-year-olds who embezzle money from their neighborhood bad guys, get caught, flee, and become international spy sensations, saving the world from crooks and having implied (but not depicted) sex with other kids who look sexy to prepubescents. Named *The Ten Roads to Recess*, I'll smack it on every lunch box in America with clip-on action heroes. Only kidding! But, seriously, your chance for big bucks skyrockets if you think "lunch box" and plan an ongoing after-market.

You needn't be a Rowling-scale success. **Helen Fielding** went big with a little book based on a book by another writer who never got rich in her lifetime—Jane Austen. Yet, Fielding will collect on Bridget Jones books, movies, and Netflix residuals for years. No Rowling, but she's rich by most folk's standards. For most authors, writing is a labor of love, not a road to riches. For me, I'm already rich. I love my day job, which is how I got rich. I write because

I like to. That's the right reason for most writers to write. (I'm brutally blunt to help direct you to a more lucrative road.) Simply no one but JK Rowling made the *Forbes* billionaire list by writing alone. That doesn't mean you can't write and get rich—but writing alone won't make you huge.

Money for a Song

Songwriting beats performing. Just cobble together some rhyming couplets and a catchy tune. Performers get paid once for an album and collect on ticket sales while touring. They need endless talent (see Chapter 4) and don't get future income. This is why even megastars like **Whitney Houston** can end up destitute (the drug habit doesn't help) and why **Barbara Streisand** dusts herself off every few years to tour. They lack future income.

Some performers write music too. But many wealthy songwriters don't perform at all (or not much), don't suffer the personal strain celebrities undergo, and have longer shelf lives than performers do—and may not even have any more talent than book writers who never make much money. For instance, **Denise Rich** née Eisenberg never performed. But Rich is rich and more so than almost all non-songwriting performing artists. Admittedly, she captured money from *two* roads—her songwriting career and her married-well divorce (Chapter 5) from mega-rich **Marc Rich** (net worth $1.5 billion).[4]

Aside from her former marriage to Mr. Rich (the Clintons' commodities trader friend who fled America to avoid tax evasion charges and one-time fugitive pardoned by Bill Clinton on his final day in office),[5] she has a huge career as a Grammy-nominated songwriter. She's written for Aretha Franklin, Mary J. Blige, Celine Dion, Diana Ross, Donna Summer, Luther Vandross, Marc Anthony, and Natalie Cole, to name a few.[6] She's still cranking out hits for young starlets like Mandy Moore and Jessica Simpson. Her songs get recorded, re-recorded, covered, sampled, and still get radio play every day. Every time, she gets paid. The singer gets paid once! It's better to write than sing.

What can you earn as a songwriter? Our government mandates songwriters get paid 9.1 cents per unit sold. So, write one song on an album selling a million copies, you get $91,000. If you write all the songs—maybe 12—that can be over $1 million. Songwriters also get paid when the song is played on radio, used on TV or in movies, or downloaded.[7] Every time! From Denise Rich's first number-one hit "Frankie," recorded by Sister Sledge, through awards at the American Song Festival, she evolved to be worth $125 million.[8] (Aspiring songwriters can find resources at MusesMuse.com and SongWriter101.com—they detail contests, festivals, and agents to whom you submit songs to win money, acclaim, or both.)

This doesn't require being a performer or other talent. It requires simple skills at creating simple melodies and poetry-like prose that's catchy. Then it requires the selling skills to sell to those who may record. Like on so many roads, the sticky point is the selling. Then, once a talent records it, you have to sell it over and over again for future residual usage. Songwriters that monetize income are as much sales agents as anything else.

They have long careers. Richard Rodgers and Oscar Hammerstein didn't perform but created some of the twentieth century's most memorable songs. Irving Berlin, Jerry Herman, Stephen Sondheim, and **Sir Andrew Lloyd Webber** (net worth $1.6 billion)[9] all built huge careers (and piles of dough) writing. Yes, **Neil Sedaka** performed some of his songs but was bigger and better paid for his decades-spanning songwriting career that included hits like, "Love Will Keep Us Together" by Captain & Tennille. **Carole King**, like Sedaka, performs some but writes more—huge hits for artists like Bobby Vee, Aretha Franklin, Dusty Springfield, and Barbara Streisand, and "You've Got a Friend" for James Taylor. She still writes in her mid-60s.

The songwriting career is more business-like, infinitely less self-destructive, more lucrative, longer lasting, and more predictable to plan and build. My editor thought this section should go with the talents in our Rich and Famous chapter. I disagreed. Few are so famous, yet often much richer. You needn't start so young and need no performing talents. This section had to go somewhere and to me, it's better here—these folks are perfect income creators.

Cloning Cash

On this road, no one tops the Jedi Master income-inventing skills of **George Lucas,** worth $3.9 billion.[10] Lucas also qualifies as a founder-CEO who bootstrapped his way up. After his Oscar-winning success with *American Graffiti*, Lucas did a switcheroo. Yes, he did *Star Wars*. But here he went down our road, something directors hadn't done before—he created an income stream. To get 20th Century Fox to do *Star Wars*, Lucas waived his director's fee for 40 percent of the box office and merchandising rights. For Fox, if Lucas's kiddie space film flopped, it wouldn't hurt much. And who cared about merchandising rights? No one made money merchandising. So Fox bit.

Lucas created Yoda, the Death Star, and the Wookie—but also something more valuable—movie merchandising. The toys, lunch boxes, action figures, and gimmicky tie-ins didn't exist before Lucas and *Star Wars*. Lucas (with buddy **Steven Spielberg,** net worth $3 billion) saw how to monetize characters no one fathomed before. They realized kids would want to reenact their movies with 4-inch plastic dolls. This is the essence of what income inventors do. It's what Rowling and King do, it's what Popeil did, what Denise Rich did—they create an experience folks will pay to own a piece of. If you're creative you can do this. Just figure what you can monetize that hasn't been yet.

You can go the conventional routes of inventing, songwriting, or book writing for movies. You do what many have done before, just slightly differently, and make sure you keep all future rights. Or you can go nonconventional and do what hasn't been done before like Lucas did, maybe on the Internet, cell phone, or next platform we haven't fathomed. That's for you to figure, not me.

The possibilities are endless. My advice: Aim for as broad an audience as possible—as wide an adaptation as possible. If not that, then something unique but vital to something else widely and broadly needed or desired. The narrower your scope, the narrower your road, and the smaller your riches.

> *To invent huge bucks, figure out what you can monetize that no one else has yet.*

POLITICAL PENSIONS—AND GOOD NEWS

Want a really wide audience? And invented income without any economic linkage? Try politics! Run this fork well and taxpayers hand you wealth . . . for nothing! Fact: In aggregate, politicians show no ability or competency for actually contributing to our economy. Most have never taken any road to riches (except marrying for money, and a few as pirates). Few have built, invented, created, led, generated, managed, improved, or innovated. Yet most end up wealthy—invented income.

I don't expect you to become president, but take the **Clintons**. I want you to see how it worked for them. They were flat broke leaving the White House but are now worth $34.9 million.[11] How? Their life pre-White House wasn't very lucrative. Bill never did anything economically remarkable. Hillary was a modestly successful backwater lawyer whose career was intermittent, tied to Bill's campaign schedule, and cut short by the White House. Her final law year saw income of only $200,000.[12] Bill's governor salary was just $35,000.[13] If they saved half their pre-tax income (a stretch) and invested wisely—at best they'd have only about $3.6 million entering the White House.

As president, Bill got $200,000 a year, plus benefits.[14] But they had legal fees stemming from Clinton's impeachment battle, his ongoing female troubles, the botched Whitewater land deal, Hillary's suspiciously profitable foray into cattle futures, Travelgate, Filegate, and about 127.72 other "gates." They left office with about $12 million in unpaid legal fees.[15] If they saved half Bill's salary and invested wisely, adding that to our previous stretch assumptions, at very best, after their legal bills, they'd *still* be over $3 million in the hole![16]

The answer is obvious—they saved some of the $109 million they earned on books and speaking fees since 2000.[17] There are few careers more profitable than "past president." You get paid $150,000 a pop just to talk![18] And taxpayers load you up.

Presidential Income—Follow the Money!

Congress passed the Former Presidents Act (FPA) in 1958, giving past presidents an inflation-adjusted lifetime pension—currently, $186,600 annually—tax free![19] Tax-adjusted, that's $311,000. To generate that, you need a well-managed portfolio close to $8 million. Then they get "protection" and lifetime "office allowances"—a staff and "suitable" space (i.e., posh). That's cash. For 2007, it was $2.9 million to cover all FPA-related costs.[20] Said otherwise, our three former presidents are paid $967,000 each! Tax free!!! That's over $1.6 million tax-adjusted, requiring a well-managed portfolio over $40 million—each!

In the 2008 budget, Clinton's take rises to $1.162 million ($1.9 million tax-adjusted and a $48 million portfolio).[21] Then, past presidents get "transition" expenses to ease reentry to "real" life. How much? In 2001, Congress approved $1.83 million (TAX FREE) *on top* of their usual haul for the Clintons.[22]

But former presidents have other income sources. You can be on paid boards of directors—as many that want you. **Gerald Ford** was huge at doing these (as well as paid speeches—it's amazing how someone who was voted out of office and no one much wanted to hear as president is suddenly in demand after). You can be a paid adviser with consulting contracts as Clinton did with billionaire **Ron Burkle** (net worth $3.5 billion).[23] Hiring a past president is a thinly veiled attempt to pay for lobbying links. No one has better connections than a past president. Let me summarize. The Clintons went from being at least $3 million (and probably more) in the hole in 2001 to being worth $35 million seven years later.

IF YOU CAN'T BE PRESIDENT . . .

But few have the chops to run for president and win. Still, you aren't precluded from a lifetime of invented political income—become a member of Congress! Starting pay is $169,300 a year (as of 2008).[24] Not huge, but you're in America's 96th percentile while building your real wealth.[25] And you don't need to do anything in Congress. Of course, for bigger bucks you hustle. Get a leadership role and income bumps to $183,500. The Speaker of the House collects $217,400.[26] Nice for **Nancy Pelosi**! (With a net worth of $86 million, Nancy's the ninth wealthiest House member!)[27] Also, they get an annual cost-of-living adjustment. And they receive health benefits and a rich retirement plan that currently you'd need at least $1.5 million to equal—to which they're entitled after only serving five years (just three elections).[28]

For fun, you can review any congressperson's financial disclosures at the Senate appropriations committee website (http://appropriations.senate.gov/senators.cfm). It's a hoot. They must only report "ranges." Some disclosures run 300-plus pages as they excuse and offload wealth to spouses, presumably to seem more populist.

Why can't they own up and not make wealth seem unseemly? To avoid mind-numbing obfuscation, visit another gem of a website, OpenSecrets.org. To see who's funding whom and who gets money where, this website follows the money for you. It summarizes personal financial disclosure forms for these politicians along with other titillating details.

Inexplicable Political Wealth

One ever-nagging question lingers—how did they get their money? Many never had any job outside politics, yet they amass fortunes. Most never directly contributed to GDP, but they're rich. There are exceptions. Take the second-wealthiest House member **Herb Kohl** (D-Wisconsin), worth about $225 million.[29] His came largely from Kohl grocery and department stores—businesses he helped build. Or **Mitt Romney** (R-Massachusetts), with $202 million.[30] He started and sold a successful consulting firm. We know how the Senate's wealthiest guy, **John Kerry** (D-Massachusetts, net worth $314 million[31]), got money. He married it—twice! It's common for them to marry wealth. The House of Representative's wealthiest member, **Jane Harman** (D-California, net worth $597 million)[32] also took the married-well road, as did **John McCain.**

But most are career politicians or former lawyers. Example: Senator **Jeff Bingaman** (D-New Mexico, net worth $24 million)[33] was a lawyer before becoming senator in 1983. It's unlikely he could have socked away much of that from his short legal career. He graduated Stanford Law in 1968. Ten years later he became New Mexico's attorney general—been in politics ever since.

Former GOP presidential hopeful **Rudy Giuliani** spent most of his adult life as a government employee. He had a brief career as a prosecutor before being appointed to the US Attorney's office at 26, and eventually Associate Attorney General—the number three spot in the US Department of Justice. He then became a US

Attorney for New York's Southern District and, of course, New York City mayor—with a salary of $195,000. Nice, but Manhattan's cost of living is killer. How on earth did he get a net worth of $52.2 million?[34] (Go re-read the previous again and believe it.)

Senator **Olympia Snowe** (R-Maine, net worth $28 million)[35] entered public office at age 26. Not only did she make an inexplicable fortune, but she married a fellow politician . . . twice! Or former Senator **Bob Graham** (D-Florida)—in public office since 1966. First the House of Representatives, state senator, governor, US senator, then US presidential candidate (failed). Never, ever contributed to GDP—yet his worth is $8 million.[36] Senator **Richard Shelby** (R-Alabama, net worth $36 million)[37] entered politics in 1963 and hasn't worked an honest day since. Congressman **Rodney Frelinghuysen** (R-New Jersey, net worth $76 million)[38] comes from a long line of folks slopping off the public trough. Most mind-boggling is former vice president **Al Gore**. He reportedly left office with $2 million. Somehow, between 2001 and 2008, he made enough to invest $35 million—liquid—in various hedge funds and other private investments. He's worth a reported $100 million![39] He's got the Clintons beat!

I begrudge no one money. By now you've figured I'm no fan of politicians of either party. My last book went over why, so I needn't retread that turf. I've known hundreds of congressmen and governors. They do well for themselves.

Even though it's lucrative, think carefully before becoming a politician.

I couldn't have built or run my firm if it weren't for capitalists like Bob Noyce and his creation of the integrated circuit or Bill Gates with Windows—or so many more. Even Jack Kahl with Duck Tape! But I can't think of any subset of the politicians I've known or read about in my lifetime that I couldn't have done without. They only foil each other in aggregate and suck off the public trough.

How to Succeed in Politics

But it is a lucrative road—no matter how inexplicable their wealth is. Beware: The key skill is lying well—to yourself and others. (It's easy to tell when politicians lie—when their mouths move. I wish that were a joke.)

So how to get elected? Like other roads, start small. Locate an area where political turnover is high. Move to a medium-sized city there—small enough not to be a backwater and big enough that most people don't know everyone else there. It's good if their senior politicians are old or if term limits are imposed. Study what they espouse and what the citizenry believe. It's easier in an area that leans heavily toward one party—doesn't matter which. Hence you need memorize and regurgitate only one set of lies at first. It helps to study what the opposition party says so you can tell lies that ridicule them, too. Your voters will love that.

Get your lies down cold, then run for city council. Tell them what they want to hear. Blame the opposition party for everything evil. Claim you are the future—that you can *see* the future. Claim you did something important where you came from that you didn't do, but they can't prove it. At this level of politics, the people you run against aren't skilled. They probably mean well and have their community's interests at heart. So it helps that you don't. In this book, it is only here where dishonesty pays.

Three years later run for county supervisor. Same game, same idiots, more incompetence, bigger venue. Six years later, run for Congress. The whole time you're working off memorized lines based on what you know they want to hear. This is far easier than succeeding as a legitimate actor because the audiences aren't as discerning. And they must elect someone. You may not believe this, but basically it's right. Follow these steps, and you don't have to do a useful thing the rest of your life. It is invented income and beats robbing banks!

THINK TANKS RUN AMOK—A SHAM-SCAM

An offshoot of political income is starting a think tank. It's a different way to invent income politically. Think tanks are those not-for-profit organizations starring one or two charismatic individuals—championing some "cause." The think tank takes "nonprofit" donations so the leader (or leaders) can think and write noble thoughts about their chosen crusade, and pay themselves huge salaries. Maybe they do "research," which consists of questioning other like-minded people about their views, and then concluding the think tankers were right all along. The key: It's a nonprofit but pays a future revenue stream—to you.

The think tank's purpose is to institutionalize a cause by like-minded people and build credibility by creating a corporate-like structure around it. Those funding think tanks think they're contributing to some greater cause—that their think tank will make a difference with pondering, research, and publishing. But really, they create an annuity for think-tank founders and selected partners.

Think tanks champion an infinite variety of causes like free markets or helping the oppressed, but at the root they're similar. Take, for example, Reverend **Jesse Jackson**. Though Jackson once claimed annual income of $430,000,[40] he keeps his financial status a closely guarded secret. Part of his mystery is because several of his nonprofit organizations are religious, so they don't file tax returns. It's his prerogative to be secretive—it's nobody's business! (Well, perhaps the IRS thinks it is.) But why should people be ashamed of big income?

Jackson's nonprofits include People United to Serve Humanity (PUSH) and the Citizenship Education Fund (CEF). And in 1996, he founded Rainbow/Push as a for-profit.[41] His foundations are meant to attract corporate capital for minority and women-owned businesses as well as provide various other services. Over the years, various groups (including the Department of Education) have griped Jackson's groups are lax in reporting how their funds are spent. Jackson's been in and out of legal strife on tax reporting.[42] The think tank structure, no matter how lofty its cause, is about money—inventing an income stream.

Nonprofits and think tanks come in all stripes. On the liberal side is **John Podesta,** former Bill Clinton chief of staff, and his Center for American Progress. Another Clinton staffer, **Bob Reich,** co-founded the Economic Policy Institute. Both promote a "progressive" agenda and "shared prosperity." Conservative, but similar, are **William Bennett** and **Jack Kemp** who, through their Empower America, long paid themselves more than a million a year each. The list is long. You can find all the think tanks you want on Google. You can tell I don't like this approach, but it makes money.

In closing, let me say my editor didn't think I should write about politicians because many readers have ones they love and hate and I'd likely offend some of you. Fact is: This book is about getting rich, not about what doesn't offend you. I admit political creation of future income streams isn't quite like the others in this chapter. But it can and does guarantee a lifetime of sometimes huge income for those willing and appropriately constructed to go after it. I had to put these guys somewhere, and the only other place I could think where they should go was to hell. So here they are.

So if you want to invent income while contributing to the world, invent a new vaccine for a disease, a new marketing phenomenon, or even write songs or books for movies. If you just want to suck the public trough, politics is always waiting for you. Either way, keep all the rights.

Monetized Reading

To set it and forget it—like Ron Popeil—and get guaranteed future income, do a bit of homework first. These books can help you build your own annuitized stream of forever money.

1. *Patent It Yourself* by David Pressman. If you have a surefire idea that could provide income the rest of your life, make sure no one steals it from you by reading this book and then getting patents.

2. *The Complete Guide to Direct Marketing* by Chet Meisner. A good how-to primer on how to be like Ron Popeil and take your message straight to the masses more cheaply and efficiently. This book shows you direct-marketing means and methods.

3. If you want to write, read *The Screenwriter's Bible* by David Trottier. Books are fine, but the money's in lunch boxes and action figures. So write or adapt your own movie script, then sell it. This book shows you how.

4. For political bucks, you must be able to convincingly lie. For that, read *How to Lie with Statistics* by Darrell Huff. A gem—it shows how easily statistics can be manipulated. Then take otherwise unalarming stats on the economy, for example, and twist them for your own perverted gain.

The Guide to **Inventing Income**

The way to make a million dollars on this road is to start with a million-dollar idea. This is all about imagination turned into growing future revenue stream.

1. *Pick a talent and stick with it.* If you can't sing, you likely won't be a Beatle. If you suffer intense writer's block, you probably won't be the next Jo Rowling. And if you have a shred of decency, you won't end up a rich senator. That's how it is. Getting rich on this road is as simple as getting one super cool, patentable idea. More likely, you'll have to keep at your craft for years before the big licensing fees kick in.

2. *Make sure it endures.* Star Wars and Harry Potter will be here forever— the themes contained are broad and perma-appealing. Post-its too. But whoever invented the 8-track tape got bowled over by the next new thing. We know we will always have politics, so it's an enduring path.

(Continued)

(Continued)

3. *Monetize it.* Lucas did it with *Star Wars* figurines. Find something you want to immortalize, ensure it's got a big enough following or figure out how to build a following like Popeil did, and guarantee your right to it. It needn't be physical—an experience can be monetized as well. Hearing a catchy tune, forgetting a horrendous spouse, and feeling like "your guy" is there for you.

4. *Patent it or otherwise protect it.* Once you've found your niche, made your discovery, penned the novel, or drawn plans for the next great gadget—protect it. Patent it, or otherwise copyright it. Own it. Never sell.

Filing a patent form isn't hard. Go to the US patent website (www.uspto.gov/). They walk you through it. There are forms you can print and submit, as well as a list of the fees. To copyright something written, go to the US Copyright Office (www.copyright.gov) to download the needed forms. Copyrighting is only $45 per entry.

5. *Market and merchandise it.* Your innovation or invention may be life-changing, but if no one knows about it, you won't profit. Take another tip from pioneer Ron Popeil and become your own spokesperson.

6. *Plan for the future.* Once you've acquired a source of income, learn how not to lose it. Understand the structure of your income—is it guaranteed? For how long? How might your contract be broken? Could something better supplant your creation and hence your income? Keeping your income steady may mean banking some cash flow for a later rainy day. And yes, even making and sticking to a budget.

9

TRUMPING THE LAND BARONS

Dream of building skyscrapers?
Collecting rent?
You could be a land baron.

merica is a land of real estate moguls—homeownership is near 70 percent! Don't let the recent residential hoopla dissuade you—there's huge money in being a land baron.

Like other roads, it's not easy. Successful land barons don't just have a knack for finding tasty, unappreciated land and willing investors. They have the strategic vision of successful firm founders. Essentially, they are founders. Fail to create a realistic and actionable business plan and you likely won't do well on this road.

The truth? Long-term real estate returns aren't great—just 5.8 percent since 1964.[1] Barely beats inflation! How do **Sheldon Adelson** ($28 billion), **Kirk Kerkorian** ($18 billion), **Donald Bren** ($13 billion), **Sam Zell** ($6 billion), and "the Donald" ($3 Trumpbillions)[2] do it? Leverage!

Learn to love leverage. It super juices return.

They borrow! Done right, leverage super juices profit. Done wrong, losses and humiliation are massive—beyond total. Isn't borrowing risky? Sure, if you do it wrong. But this road requires leverage. If you're debt-averse, stop now and flip to another road. Otherwise, overcome your debt fears. Learn to love leverage to achieve land baron success.

The Magic

Here's how the magic works: Suppose you put down 5 percent on a $100,000 property—$5,000. In five years, you sell for $125,000. Ho hum—a 25 percent gain, just 4.6 percent annualized. But no! You only tied up $5,000—that $25,000 gain is actually 500 percent and 43.1 percent annualized. Magic! Yes, you had interest payments on the debt—we'll get to that. And if the value fell you would lose your $5,000. Leverage goes both ways. The key is finding a good value you can monetize that others don't want. You must turn property into a money-rendering machine by monetizing it.

MONETIZE IT

Here's how. But first, a disclaimer: I'm no land baron. Yes, I own over $100 million of real estate, mostly buildings my firm uses. But it's my wife Sherri who's the family land baron.

In 1999 two men bought 1450 Fashion Island Boulevard, a then 15-year-old, 104,000 square foot Class A office building in San Mateo, California, at the intersection of freeways 101 and 92—the crossroads of the San Francisco Peninsula connecting San Francisco to Silicon Valley and the Peninsula to the East Bay. Prime location—almost no vacancies in 1999. They paid $31 million, borrowing $25.5 million via a note from Credit Suisse First Boston Mortgage Capital LLC. Silicon Valley was booming, rents were high, office buildings were full, and dot-coms, flush with cash, were leasing expansion space they'd eventually never need (but they didn't know that then).

My firm was growing. Five years earlier, Sherri had built what was and is our headquarters in midst nowhere on a Bay Area mountaintop, 2,000 feet high, in a spot you'd never suspect. A jewel in the forest, surrounded on three sides by thousands of acres of government-owned open space—clear air and miles of Pacific Ocean views. She expanded it twice, but by 2000 we'd filled the postage-stamp size flatland atop this spectacular mountain. We needed more space elsewhere. Sherri chose San Mateo—20 minutes away. Rents were high and space tight. She couldn't lease much. But as the tech bubble burst, sublease space became available. By 2002 she could get one-year leases for all the Class B office space she wanted at ok rates.

By 2004, 1450 Fashion Island Boulevard was in default, foreclosure proceedings had begun, and a new receiver appointed. The men who bought it owned other office buildings—all levered and on the ropes. They had nothing to plow back into 1450 to attract tenants, so 1450's vacancy rate kept rising. Their anchor tenant left, leaving them in a tough spot. The note holder decided to sell out in a closed auction, where bidders wouldn't know what other bidders bid. Potential buyers would submit initial indications of interest in broad terms, and from that group, the seller would determine a smaller group allowed to make one hard final bid. The seller needn't sell to the highest-priced bid. A somewhat lower price might be better if it had better terms.

Terms are as important as price. Terms mean how much of the price is cash, interest rate on any noncash offer, a deposit to go with the bid, whether or not the seller keeps the deposit if the bidder backs out, and what legitimate reasons might let you back out. (For example, usually bidders specify building inspections to their satisfaction, or they can back out.) Also, speed of closing—how fast you can close—because sellers prefer a fast close. (Faster means less risk to the seller.) Institutional buyers often have internal procedures they must follow that may limit their speed. The seller assesses all these terms.

By then we had 400 San Mateo employees on one-year leases and were growing fast. Short-term leases leave you vulnerable to rent hikes if the market tightens. Sherri wanted to buy 1450's note, then as note-holder, foreclose and take over the building. (Don't ever mess with my wife; it's painful.) She figured with my trading background—horse-trading if you will—I might negotiate the auction better than she. Our general counsel, Fred Harring oversaw the nuts and bolts, because he's hell on details in any transaction. I'm more of a big picture guy.

One lucky presumption turned out right—that all other bidders would be financial firms seeking a rate of return based on pricing the note at existing rents and vacancy rates that couldn't be improved much in that high-vacancy market. But I could fill the building— with my own employees. They couldn't. I could pay more because I could monetize that vacant space. It was a year after 2003's stock market bottom. The recession was recent. Tech was reeling. Based on rents, vacancy rate estimates, and interest rates, Sherri guessed financial bidders couldn't pay much more than $14 million.

To win, I needed an initial indication of interest motivating them to keep me in the game so I could make that final, hard bid. That may seem trivial, but institutional sellers prefer institutional buyers to individuals like me. They weed out individuals, seeing us as likely to be loose cannons, prone to go off in strange ways—like litigation. They hate that. I had to offer sweetheart terms.

So I did. My initial price was $13.5 million—ok, but unlikely the highest. I needn't be highest at first; just had to make it to round two. But for terms, I promised all cash and a deposit totaling a third of the price—all of which they kept if I won but didn't close. That's huge. Usually in a deal this size, institutions offer maybe a $500,000 to $1 million deposit. So if I won and backed out, they kept my $4.5 million and could resell the note—coming out way ahead for having tolerated me. Further, I required no inspections. Sherri figured the institutional lenders on the $25 million note five years earlier had almost certainly done every inspection known to man. And to her nose, nothing had changed. I also promised to close any time they wanted.

Having offered dream terms, we got to round two. Here I kept everything identical but notched my price to $15 million, just over that $14 million number. I don't know what others bid, but we won. Note in hand, Sherri threatened to foreclose on the building owners, something few note-holders do—way too messy. Because Sherri does messy for breakfast, usually washed down with nails and bolts, the owners instead gave her the deed in lieu of foreclosure.

Financial note buyers don't like owning buildings—they just want a good return on their note. They can't manage buildings or fill them with tenants. We could. That was our monetizing advantage. Sherri spent almost $3 million improving the inside and moving our people in—all in all, an $18 million investment. With leases between my firm as tenant and me as owner, I now received cash flow on a full building. Sherri turned around and got Goldman Sachs to lend us $25 million based on the leases. Sherri pulled $7 million net from the transaction—39 percent over her $18 million. That's a land baron's game. You can't do that unless you have cash and tenants. But you can find a building, find someone with tenants, find financing—then put together a deal that creates wealth. That's the game.

THE FOOL'S BARGAIN

Folks fool themselves. Soaring pre-2005 home prices led to widespread overconfidence. If you owned a home someplace hot, like California from 2000 to 2005, and prices doubled, that didn't make you smart—just lucky. A good land baron is daring, but doesn't self-delude.

Here's the fool's bargain. Consider a profitable decade and place—again, San Mateo County, where I was raised. On January 1, 1995, San Mateo's median home price was $305,083.[3] Say you bought with 20 percent down (before the zero-down craze) plus 1 percent closing costs. The going rate was 7.5 percent for a 30-year fixed-rate mortgage so your monthlies were about $1,700.[4] Fast forward 10 years. You sell for the median 2005 price of $763,100.[5] Pay the $184,091 mortgage balance (after amortization payments) for a $579,000 gain. Subtract out your down payment. You have an 849 percent return—25.2 percent annualized! That's how most folks figure real estate, but it's dead wrong.

First, in 10 years you paid over $60,000 in principal. We must subtract that—should figure time-weighted payments—but to be quick and dirty, take your gain, subtract the down payment *and* principal, divide, and you have 379 percent, 17 percent annualized. But that mortgage wasn't free. You paid over $247,000 in interest. Ooh! Subtract *that*, recalculate—it's 174 percent, down to 10.6 percent annualized.

Still too high. San Mateo's annual home upkeep averages $1,820 (gas, water, other niggly details).[6] Maybe you remodeled for $40,000 and added a patio for $15,000. Don't forget your 1995 closing costs and 2005 realtor fee (about 5 percent). And property tax! In San Mateo you pay 1.125 percent of your purchase price—boosted by 2 percent each year. Over 10 years, that's over $37,000.

Learn to properly calculate returns. There are costs few consider.

Our quick, dirty analysis shows a cumulative 59 percent return, 3.1 percent annualized. That's lousy. Folks see homes as their greatest asset. Truth is, it's all leverage. You can easily fool yourself. Folks say, "Yeah, but I'd pay rent if I didn't own. There's value there." True! But the greatest value of your home is the roof over your head and the satisfaction it gives you.

Flippin's for Friggin' Losers

Many want to buy and sell, flipping real estate for a fast profit. Don't. Fact is, real land barons don't flip. The transaction costs are just too high. They focus on an internal rate of return—providing monetized profits while the land appreciates.

Take **Timothy Blixseth** (net worth $1.2 billion).[7] He flipped. Though hugely successful now, he screwed up huge early on. (Recall, as my preface said, on these roads you can blow up a few times and still get there.) An 18-year-old Blixseth wanted a fast way out of his poverty-stricken youth. So he pledged his life's savings of $1,000 as a down payment for $90,000-worth of Oregon timberland he saw in a newspaper ad. Why timber? He came from a timber town—thought he knew timber. He figured he would find a buyer and flip it. Fast. He promised the seller the rest of the $89,000 in 30 days.

The seller knew Blixseth had no money or investors and figured to teach the kid a lesson—sell him the land, then foreclose. Blixseth needed a buyer, fast. Amazingly, his little plot abutted Roseburg Lumber Company, a large landowner. Blixseth marched in and offered to sell to Roseburg for $140,000—a relatively random amount but a seemingly fat, fast profit. They bit. Later, Blixseth learned Roseburg had long needed that land for an access road, but the seller hated Roseburg's owner and in that way acted in his own worst interest.[8] Blixseth was flippin' lucky—nothing more.

Smitten, he flipped more—mostly timberland. He bought remnants with minimal down payments, selling fast to lumber firms. Blixseth *Flipping's a loser's road.* might hold title for mere minutes.[9] He was undone by the 1980s' sky-high interest rates and went totally bankrupt. Lost everything. He learned his lesson and flipped no more. He started again, building another real estate portfolio, this time leveraging only assets he actually kept and monetized—not assets he owned for hours. And that put him on this road, which led him to become a rich land baron.

GETTING STARTED

You're ready. First, find an economically vibrant market. Vibrant doesn't mean pricey or affluent—you don't need Beverly Hills. The best places are business- and employee-friendly, where future growth continues. Jobs pay for everything. Land barons need tenants, renters, or buyers. People go where jobs are, and jobs are where prosperity is—where folks want to shop, work, live, lease, and rent. This isn't a tough notion to fathom. You don't need (or even want) a major city. Third-tier cities in employee- and employer-friendly areas are fine.

How do you find such places? Research state income and sales tax rates. A shortcut: *Fortune* magazine occasionally does features like "100 Best Places to Live." An April 2008 feature titled "100 Best Places to Live and Launch 2008" assessed business environments, tax conditions, and overall quality of life. They did your homework for you! You can Google it or follow this address: http://money.cnn.com/magazines/fsb/bestplaces/2008/.

Then, incorporate. Or create an LLC. You shouldn't bear risk personally—your business does that for you. Your business protects you when people sue. And they will! It's better they sue your business, which is insurable for litigation, than sue you.

Start Small and Unsexy

Start small and bootstrap. (Revisit Chapter 1 for why.) You won't have enough cash for a big project—yet. So buy a decrepit duplex, fix it up, live in half, rent the other. Then, leverage that cash flow and buy a rundown four-unit vacant apartment house. Same thing, only bigger! Fix it up a bit so you can rent it at higher rates.

Find an economically vibrant area with low taxes and start small.

The key is finding tenants. The success formula is buying based on vacancy and creating value by filling it. If done right, it covers costs plus some. Meanwhile your building increased in value because you filled it. It's a little business—with inputs exceeding outputs. Do this several times, and you'll have cash flow and a track record and can convince investors to give you capital infusions for bigger buildings—maybe condos or office buildings. Then lever that into something even bigger with greater cash flow potential. That's it. Each time, the key is monetizing empty space that isn't worth much until you make it more valuable.

The Perfect Pro Forma

Beyond your first duplex or two you won't get or use bank lending. Banks are pretty leery about land baron lending. You don't want bank lending anyway. Banks readily lend to individuals for homes. But they aren't big on what we have in mind. So how do you get financing? You convince outside investors to fund you with a stellar pro forma—a land baron financial model. The idea is to create a compelling but attainable plan to sell to investors.

Like Mina, the Mini Land Baron

Life has compromises—you can travel this road without everything being perfect. My future daughter-in-law knows. She is one hot chick—UCLA Med School MD, child psychiatrist. Mina is a Korean-born, second-generation, self-made, all-American dream. Her mother came straight from Korea—worked herself to the bone supporting Mina and her brother. Mina has work ethic, moxie, and the terrific taste to love my most-excellent middle son.

She's also going land baron all on her own by levering her medical income to buy a beat-up old house with 13 legal but slum-like rental units in rent-controlled Berkeley. Because it was in bankruptcy with lots of vacancies, she can remodel and raise rents. It's just off the subway line near where her mom still works herself to the bone. So now Mina can put her mom in the house's nicer, prime part (beautiful woodwork and windows in front), improving her mom's plight, and

(Continued)

her mom can help oversee tenants (no chic woodwork there).

Then, Mina fixes it up and fills it with more desirable tenants at higher rents. Mina's got the leverage part, the monetizing the empty part, the how to get the tenants part all figured. The only part not optimal is it's rent-controlled (not great) in Berkeley (communist stronghold). But Mina must start her medical career here for a few years and can't do this elsewhere. She's doing the best she can in a suboptimal spot, but she'll be ok. Even if you're stuck in a suboptimal place you can do this. But it's better to do it where the wind is at your back.

Buy software to build a pro forma for about $199 and up (at ZDNet.com, Download.com, or RealtyAnalytics.com). Or build one yourself on Excel if you know how to calculate amortization and depreciation. If this flummoxes you, you simply must buy the software or take a class or both—or find another road. Without a good pro forma this road is bumpy. Also, check out the Urban Land Institute (ULI; www.uli.org). ULI is a national networking support group for developers, providing classes and mentorship.

What's in your pro forma? Interest costs, construction, depreciation, permitting, and upkeep costs—everything homeowners forget. The water and electric bill. Property taxes. Every detail nicking your bottom line. Then make assumptions about appreciation and income. Maybe you assume 85 percent occupancy collecting X dollars each year. You envision rents rising Y percent over the decade. You depreciate the building, decreasing taxes. Run different scenarios. If X happens, occupancy increases Q percent. If Y happens, rents fall Z percent. (This is why the software helps.) Finally, distill everything to a likely internal rate of return on investor cash—this is the piece of the action you'll offer investors in exchange for the down payment and a safety net.

Now what? Sell sell sell! You're offering them that piece of the deal, but with a huge haircut for your management—because you make it all happen. This is like OPM (Chapter 7—check that chapter for a good

> *A compelling but reasonable business plan is vital.*

parallel). Good land barons are super salesmen like founder-CEOs (or pretty much every other road). Many investors will decide your pro forma is fantasy. So you figure out what's wrong and fix it—or what's wrong with the investors and change them.

BUY, BUILD, OR BOTH?

What kind of baron will you be? Do you want to build fancy new properties like the Donald, acquire existing ones, or some of both? (Actually, Trump's father started in non-fancy apartments, handing the Donald a big bundle. The Donald grew that in the mid-1970s by buying troubled Manhattan buildings when New York was flat on its back. His fancy-new phase came later.) Build or buy, there are distinct considerations. First, consider the following.

Location, Location, Location

Concentrate in communities friendly to you—a rule that's true and untrue all at once. If you don't have political clout you must be in a business-friendly place. If you have political clout someplace that is otherwise hostile, you can do there what most can't. Political clout is another way to say the community is friendly to you, but maybe not to everyone else.

Lots of people can do deals where they come from, but can't do them in other areas. As known "favorite sons" (or daughters), they're trusted by the local governmental authorities to do what they say they will. If you're any place but where they really trust you, you need a business-friendly place or you must build political clout to overcome the obstacles awaiting you.

Know Thy Code

Whether building or buying, you must know the building codes (find them on Google) and other rules. This isn't trivial. Rule changes can parse huge profits into total loss. You can see why **Harry Macklowe** (net worth $2 billion)[10] went dynamite. He owned four old dumps he wanted to demolish to build glitzy Manhattan condos. But then-Mayor Koch passed a law preventing changing this usage, believing occupants, mostly low-income renters, had no other options. At night, hours before the bill went into effect, Macklowe dynamited the buildings. He paid $4.7 million in fines and was banned from building for four years.

Two years later, Mayor Koch acknowledged his ban was maybe unconstitutional. Macklowe didn't wait—he broke ground.[11] The city council griped he had no right—the ban still stood—but he built anyway and paid fines, creating the Hotel Macklowe. Few aspirants have his chutzpah or lawyers. So as stupid as many local building codes may seem, you must know them.

Buying existing property can be easier—but still rules abound. True story. Since 1970, the San Francisco Armory stood empty—a whole city block in the colorful Mission district. Repeated and varied development attempts failed. Condos, apartments, stores, offices—you name it—the city refused. So it stayed empty doing no one any good.

Know zoning and building codes cold before starting.

Meanwhile, San Francisco hurts for new housing supply. And new property taxes would help their budget, but no!

What finally passed muster in 2007—after standing empty for 37 years? In the very city that first created America's modern "adult" industry, Kink.com was allowed to put in an online adult movie studio specializing in, ahem, dungeon scenes.[12] They'd film them right there—in the Armory! High-end condos—no. But a world-scale porn studio? Sure! You don't want to buy a building only allowed for porn. Or maybe you do! But know your options first.

WHERE TO BE AND NOT TO BE; THAT IS THE QUESTION

Environments worse for employees and employers are worse for you. The California I was raised in was the Golden State, the one that set the trends America followed. No more. It's losing population while losing wealthy and high-income citizens—but taking in no-income deadbeats. It may be today's worst state to start out as a wannabe land baron. It suffers America's most complex and often contradictory local regulations. Unlike decades ago, it now has the worst labor laws and worst judicial system for employers and employees—that's real, social-based, and won't go away.

First they constrict construction. Then—I kid you not—city commissioners write hypocritical, affronted letters to newspapers deploring how land baron's expensive real estate prevents "middle class" families from living in their communities! The solution? Raise income and sales taxes to get the money so they, the politicians, can fix everything. Amazing!

Right now, supply is exceedingly limited and demand unstoppable. Demand will fade as the wealthy and high-income flee. My general recommendation: If you're starting down this land baron road, don't do it in places like California unless you have super political clout.

A Pothole in the Road

I'm not in a big hurry, but I'd like to sell my California commercial real estate in the coming years. The state has become a pothole on the road to riches. Long-term prospects are poor—it won't be a future vibrant economy. The state's spending dependency seems intended specifically to drive top earners and businesses (and therefore, primary providers of tax revenue) away. Not only does

Go to a state friendly to economic prosperity (i.e., states with no or low state income tax).

California have the highest marginal state income tax of any state starting at the lowest income level (9.3 percent at $43,000—below the nationwide median income and rising from there) and among the very highest sales taxes—7.25 percent (with cities and counties adding surcharges on top)—it also has the most job-hostile regulations. In starting out, avoid places like this if you can.

Tireless Taxers

Ironically, California knows it's in trouble. The state chases down folks who flee! If you're a big taxpayer and leave, California usually follows, audits, and often *keeps sending you tax bills—long after you left!* In the state's view, if you left to avoid owing taxes, then you still owe them. State law was intentionally created to make it tough to flee. Successfully doing so involves mastering myriad minor details. If you're considering fleeing any state's taxes to land baron elsewhere, bone up on the rules. Engage a top tax lawyer.

Folks continually scream of continued tax demands from sunny Cali.[13] My friend, Grover Wickersham, himself a lawyer, who helped advise on and edit this and my previous book, left California eons ago for London. He and his wife became UK citizens and had a child, Lindsey, born there, now nine years old. Only in 2008 did California stop hassling him for income tax. He will never move back. Nor will others.

Economists Arthur Laffer and Stephen Moore noted that of California's over 25,000 seven-figure-income families "more than 5,000 left in the early 2000s."[14] Where to? The top 10 states with positive inflows from 1997 to 2006 included no-tax states Florida, Texas, Nevada, and Washington. That's where you want to go. Or Tennessee, which taxes only dividend and interest income. Arizona, Georgia, North Carolina, South Carolina, and Colorado fill out the top 10, all with fairly low tax rates (as shown in the Table 9.1).[15] And they came from where? Mainly from high-tax New York and California. In 10 years, New York lost 2 million people! And California over 1.3 million net.[16] But it's the higher-income people leaving, not the poorest. As a land baron, follow the money. Better yet, get there before the money does.

Best Land Baron States

For further guidance on where to baron, look at net domestic migration of productive people over 10 years. Go to the inflow states.

Table 9.1 Best Land Baron States

States with Highest Net Population Inflow, 1997–2006

State	Net inflow
Florida	+1,643,073
Arizona	+769,679
Texas	+667,810
Georgia	+650,941
North Carolina	+570,716
Nevada	+491,325
Tennessee	+258,838
South Carolina	+258,109
Colorado	+231,891
Washington	+218,304

States with Highest Net Population Outflow, 1997–2006

State	Net outflow
New York	−1,955,023
California	−1,318,266
Illinois	−727,150
New Jersey	−409,409
Louisiana	−402,745
Ohio	−362,601
Massachusetts	−330,657
Michigan	−317,389
Pennsylvania	−182,078
Connecticut	−109,930

Arthur B. Laffer and Stephen Moore, "Rich States, Poor States: ALEC-Laffer State Economic Competitiveness Index," American Legislative Exchange Council (2007), Washington, DC. Page 15.

But wait—as a new land baron, you're not building ritzy properties for the wealthy, right? True! But if top income earners flee, economic prosperity sags, as do property values, rental, and lease incomes. Said simply, the higher the proportion of rich people in an area, the better it will be for land barons. Follow the money.

In conclusion, veer from the places losing jobs and toward those gaining them. Seek properties no one wants that can be bought cheaply but you can monetize quickly. Lever and pull more money out than you put in and fast, but don't sell or flip. Hold on and use the increasing cash flow from your property to borrow and buy more, repeating the formula endlessly. Keep building cash flow and levering. Keep finding investors to fund down payments in exchange for a part of your action. You're a scout, an entrepreneur, a builder, a buyer, a borrower, a planner, a salesman, a monetizer—and all that makes you a land baron.

Baron Books

Those are the broad-stroke basics. Learn more from these books meant for folks wanting a strategic approach to a land baron career.

1. *Real Estate Investing for Dummies* by Eric Tyson and Robert Griswold. The *Dummies* books have silly titles but give good guidance for beginners—and lead to even more good reading. Eric Tyson is a friend, is trustworthy, and has your interests at heart. And Wiley publishes the *For Dummies* series! What more could you want? Read this one first.

2. *The Wall Street Journal Complete Real-Estate Investing Guidebook* by David Crook. The *Wall Street Journal* people put out easy, fast reference books. This is no exception.

3. *The Complete Guide to Financing Real Estate Developments* by Ira Nachem gives you the nuts and bolts for getting financing. It also walks you through creating a detailed pro forma so you can find investors and not anger them later. It's a textbook-style book and pricier, but you can buy it used most places online.

4. *Maverick Real Estate Investing* by Steve Bergsman. This one shows more about how the biggest names did it. It isn't great for folks wanting prescriptive advice, but with the right expectation, you'll enjoy it. Once you're done with it, move onto Bergman's *Maverick Real Estate Financing*— great for land barons ready to make bigger deals.

The Guide to **Being a Land Baron**

1. *Learn to love leverage.* Debt isn't bad. It's good! You can't make decent land baron returns unless you lever up. Get over your fear or get on another road.

2. *Monetize it.* Find a good value no one wants, and trump them by filling it with tenants. If you can see value no one else does, you get a good price. And by filling it with tenants, you immediately have cash flow and leverage for your next deal.

3. *Don't fool yourself.* Even experienced homebuyers fool themselves about returns. There's considerable cost in owning real estate, and it cuts into your return.

4. *Don't be a flipper.* I don't care how many people you know who made a "killing" buying foreclosed properties and flipping them. Don't do it. Bankruptcy and foreclosure are great, but flipping is inherently a short-term game and a dead-end road.

5. *Find a vibrant market.* You don't need to build/own in an affluent market—too expensive for beginners. You just need an area likely to remain or become prosperous. It's easy to know—look for business-friendly communities with low taxes.

6. *Create a pro forma.* You can't get investors without a business plan, and you can't do anything very big without investors. Your pro forma is the alpha and the omega. Take a class to learn how to create one or buy software online.

7. *Know thy code.* Before you build or buy, know what arcane building codes and zoning regulations you'll be hit with. Plan ahead for attacks by your town commies to cut down on costly delays.

10

THE ROAD MORE TRAVELED

Like boring, predictable paths?
The sure and steady way could be yours.

The least sensational, but most reliable, road to riches is saving linked to good investment returns. This is very American—the Calvinist catechism, rooted in Judeo-Christian values of virtue. Frugality and industriousness *do* pay. This road is wide enough for anyone with a paycheck. It has spawned thousands of how-to books over the decades ranging from Suze Orman to *The Millionaire Next Door*.

The first step is saving. Fact: Some folks just can't—regardless of income. Some make half a million a year and blow it all. Some are naturally frugal. Some folks can improve. Others never will. But saving is a must here.

Step two is getting ok, but not phenomenal, investment returns. The magical power of compound interest assures even the lowliest, part-time garbage collector can do this if he or she saves a few thousand a year. *Forbes* list? No. But anyone can be a multimillionaire.

Note: A million's not much anymore! A million invested well kicks off about $40,000 a year in cash flow (see why later)—not enough to feel rich. But it isn't a stretch to hit maybe $10 million-plus with an ok job and discipline. This road's not sexy. Frugal isn't known for sexy! But the good news: This road doesn't require degrees—or even high school (but education helps with better-paying jobs). This is the exact reverse of the road less traveled. It is the road more commonly traveled to riches.

INCOME MATTERS

Earn more to save more—easy as that. Garbage collectors can't save as much as a doctor may. That doesn't mean doctors save more—they're notoriously bad savers—but the possibility is there. Find a job in a well-paying, relevant field you like. If you're in a sinking industry, get a different job. If you live in a low-paying geography, move. Where? Preferably to Texas, Florida, or Washington! All have no state income taxes and in 10 years will have more better-paying jobs than high tax states. (Read more about why some states are just better, and others worse, in Chapter 9.)

In any career, consider the cost/benefit payoff. How long must you go to school and intern? Is it worth it? Review Chapters 1 and 7 on sectors likely to become or remain relevant. Some may bristle and say, "But you should do what you love!" Yes, but like Marilyn Monroe would say—my goodness, doesn't it help if what you love pays a lot too? If your passion is truly social work, teaching kindergarten, or quilting—fine. Then focus on frugality. It can be done! I have clients who were postal carriers, teachers, cops, etc. They did it. Frugal!

> *Do what you love—but it's better if what you love pays really well.*

The Job Hunt

Whether starting your career or farther along, read *What Color Is Your Parachute*, the classic by Richard Nelson Bolles. It helps determine what exactly you want/need from a career. Maybe you find you don't want riches at all! You may land a high-paying job, but if you're miserable, you won't stick with it.

Ok! You know what you want to do—now find a firm paying better than its peers. Ignore job-hunting online blogs and "chat rooms." They're patrolled by job hunters knowing nothing about the firm and disgruntled current and former employees with motivation to mislead. I know a guy whose son told me he gets all his job-seeking tips from chat rooms. I haven't figured a graceful way yet to tell the father his son is an idiot.

Instead, think like a private equity manager. Pick up the *Wall Street Journal* and read about your target industry. Find folks you know in the industry. Interview them. They'll have insight and likely help with interview material—and have the skinny on who pays what. An added benefit: When you ask someone for advice, you appeal to their ego. Now, they're invested and want to help. If they help you land a job, that's great for you and an ego boost for them!

Making the Pitch

A job hunt is just a sales pitch—you're the product. You must sell on every road! The better you sell, the faster you get a bigger paycheck. Get *Guerrilla Marketing for Job Hunters* by Jay Conrad Levinson and David Perry. Ignore its nonsense about "outsourcing" being a problem. Overall, it's a good job-hunter's book. Also *The Job Search Solution* by Tony Beshara has unique and helpful insights.

Post your resume on Monster, HotJobs—all those places. But that's not enough. You must sell. Network. Call firms that *aren't* hiring and request an informational interview. Have lunch with friends of friends and friends of friends of friends. Ask what they do. Find it fascinating. Ask them for help. Don't forget, you need a good, professional resume, so read *The Elements of Resume Style* by Scott Bennett.

Before you interview, practice with a friend. And don't volunteer personal information. Talking personal stuff is (a) creepy and (b) turns off your interviewer. To ace an interview leave your personal stuff at home.

Once you get the job you're not done. Keep selling yourself. See yourself as a ride-along or potential CEO (read those chapters for tips on being a well-compensated standout). You may need to choose—will you go deep as a specialist, or broad as a manager? Both can pay well, but in your field one may pay better. Never stop researching and selling yourself. Maybe you don't want to work this hard—your choice, but the more you earn, the more you can save. And the more you save, the more your money works for you and the richer you get on this road.

> *A job hunt is a sales pitch. Perfect yours to get more offers.*

SAVING GRACE

How much should you save, realistically? Pick a retirement age, then calculate what you need. A financial calculator or Excel helps. (If you're afraid of either, ask a teenager's help.) Figure how much do you want by date X. Is $2 million enough? $10 million? (Much above that and you need a really high-paying job or another road.) Will you need more or less income (inflation-adjusted) than you need now? Will your kids be done with school and life be cheaper? Can you skip the vacation home to save more? Or travel? What about other income sources? Some advisers suggest you assume 70 percent of your income post-retirement. No! It's all personal—some need more, some less. Pick a number in today's dollars—be a touch generous to be safe. Then, adjust for inflation for date X.

But how? Easy, even if the following formulas *look* scary. Basically, you assume an inflation rate. Then, pick a time in the future—say, 30 years. Then, calculate how much inflation increases the value of money today (i.e., *compounding interest*). To do it, use this formula:

$$FV = PV \times (1 + R)^n$$

For those who've forgotten their statistics, *FV* is the *future value*—how much a dollar today will be worth later after *compounding interest* does its trick. *PV* is *present value*—money today. *R* is the *interest rate*—what we're using for inflation. *n* is the number of years between now and then.

To live on $100,000 in today's dollars, figure how much that is in 30 years with inflation averaging 3 percent. Multiply $100,000

Four percent?

I've said you generally shouldn't take more than 4 percent from your portfolio annually if you want your money to last as long as you do. But don't stocks have a 10 percent long-term annual average? Maybe, depending on the period you check. Doesn't that mean you can take up to 10 percent yearly? Nope—not unless you want to run out of money really fast.

Stock returns are wildly variable year to year—and extreme returns are far more "normal" than average returns, as shown in Table 10.1. Big down years are more rare than you think, but you'll live through a few of them. If you take 10 percent during a big down year, you must make up not only the big downswing, but you've put yourself an additional 10 percent in the hole. Over time, that can add up.

By running a simple Monte Carlo simulation (find one at http://www.moneychimp.com/articles/volatility/montecarlo.htm), you'll find annual distributions of 4 percent or less give your portfolio the best chance of lasting at least as long as you do.

by 1 plus 3 percent, raised to the power of 30. Use Excel (it has an *FV* shortcut) or a calculator:

$$\$100,000 \times (1 + 3\%)^{30} = \$242,726.25$$

You need about $243,000 (more if you assume higher inflation). But how much must you save to get there? That's easier. For your portfolio to last as long as you do, you generally shouldn't take more than 4 percent in cash flow each year. So divide $243,000 by 4 percent to get $6,075,000. So go save $6 million.

Table 10.1 Average Returns Aren't Normal

S&P 500 Annual Return Range	Occurrences Since 1926	Frequency	
> 40%	5	6.1%	Big Returns 37.8% of the time
30% to 40%	13	15.9%	
20% to 30%	13	15.9%	
10% to 20%	16	19.5%	Average Returns 34.1% of the time
0% to 10%	12	14.6%	
−10% to 0%	12	14.6%	Negative Returns 28.0% of the time
−20% to −10%	6	7.3%	
−30% to −20%	3	3.7%	
−40% to −30%	1	1.2%	
< −40%	1	1.2%	
Total Occurrences	82		
Simple Average		12.2%	
Annualized Average		10.3%	

Source: Global Financial Data.

Saving $6 Million???

Seems too much. How can you save so much? That would be salting away $200,000 annually for 30 years. Few folks can do that. So you save less and invest en route. Over time, through the magic of compounding interest, you get to $6 million. So how much to really save each year?

$$(i \times FV)/([1 + i]^n - 1) = PMT$$

PMT is your payment—how much you must save each year. This is the number we're trying to figure out. The interest rate is *i*—your assumption of what rate of return you will get. The number of years between now and when you want to start taking money is *n*. And, again, *FV* is your desired future value—in this case $6 million. (If this terrifies you, Excel has a function you can use—just remember *future value*—or you can ask your teenager for help.)

For this exercise, assume *i* is 10 percent (about what I expect the long-term stock market average to be). *FV* is $6 million, and you retire in 30 years (*n*):

$$(10\% \times \$6 \text{ million})/([1 + 10\%]^{30} - 1) = \$36,475.49$$

So for $6 million, save $36,000 a year for 30 years—$3,000 a month. Still seem like a lot? That's why a high-paying job helps. But it's not hard to get to $36,000:

- Contribute the 2008 401(k) maximum—$15,500 (plus, that cuts your tax liability!).

- If your employer matches 50 percent as my firm does, that's another $7,750 (*free!*).

- Contribute the 2008 IRA maximum—$5,000.

That's already $28,250. Now save another $7,750 a year—$646 a month—in a taxable account. Easy! If married, get your spouse to save via 401(k) and/or IRA. Maybe you can save every dime tax deferred!

Maybe saving $36,000 per year is out of reach now. Should you give up? No! Use Excel and make assumptions about how you can increase savings each year, assume a rate of return, and tinker until you hit your end value. Stick to the plan. Remember the *time value* of money—earlier saving is simply worth more. Save as much as you can as early as possible and you'll have an easier time later. Can't say it any simpler!

Estimate a desired ending value and create a saving schedule. Stick to it.

What difference do a few years make? Tons. A 25-year-old saving $6 million by age 60 need only save $22,000 a year (assuming 10 percent returns). Max your 401(k) with a partial employer match, max your IRA, and you're done. But start at 40 and you must save $105,000 a year, or not retire at 60, or give up your $6 million dream. Your call.

The 3 percent inflation and 10 percent returns are just assumptions. Play with those a bit. For example, maybe you're a pessimist who thinks the stock market will only average 6 percent over the next 30 years. Then you must save more. I'm not saying saving $36,000 a year is easy. I'm saying know how much you need and create a plan to achieve it. Then stick to it.

How the Heck Should I Save?

A high-paying job helps. Being frugal helps, too. There are plenty of books preaching how to be frugal—I don't even need to name them. They're all variations on the same theme: Skip mocha-caramel-triple-lattes. Pay off credit card debt. Avoid designer labels. Buy used cars. Eat in more, out less. Total no-brainers. Some can't do this—just can't. If you can, great! If you can't, reprogram yourself (very difficult) or get a better-paying job.

Here's an eye-opener if you don't think you can save that much. Figure what you're saving and see where you'll be after 30 years. Suppose last year you saved $2,000. Solving for *future value* (you're a pro at these by now):

$$PMT \times ([(1 + i)^n - 1]/i) = FV$$

You promise yourself you'll save more next year. Will you? Use the previous assumptions for *i* and *n*. Your *PMT* (amount saved each year) is $2,000:

$$\$2000 \times ([(1 + 10\%)^{30} - 1]/10\%) = \$328,988.05$$

Saving $2,000 gets you to $329,000—kicking off about $13,000 a year in 30 years (about $6,150 in 2008 dollars). That's no road to riches.

GET A GOOD RATE OF RETURN (BUY STOCKS)

We keep using 10 percent as our assumed return. Fact is few folks do that well. Most *professionals* don't, even though it's not hard.

How can you? Easy—invest in stocks, pretty much all the time. Diversify globally, using something like the MSCI World Index or ACWI Index as your guide (www.mscibarra.com). While you must be sure of your goals, time horizon, and cash flow needs, I am a huge fan of stocks because they have superior long-term returns. An all-equity approach is wrong for people with short time horizons. But that's not you on this road. This chapter, by definition, means you have a long growth goal and need stocks. Almost always.

To get rich on this road, you must own stocks, pretty much always.

There may be times when, to sidestep an upcoming prolonged market downturn, you step into cash and bonds—that can help put serious spread against stocks. If your benchmark is the global MSCI

World Index, and it's down 20 percent one year, but you're down just 5 percent, you've beat stocks by 15 percent—that's awesome. But true bear markets are more rare than the media want you to think and if you really know how to time them you should go into OPM instead (see Chapter 7).

Most folks have a far longer time horizon than they think (we'll get to that in a bit) and if you weren't interested in growth, you wouldn't be reading a book about getting rich.

Life Expectancy Tango

Does being all in stocks scare you? It's less risky than most think because they envision their time horizon all wrong. People think, "I'm 50. I want to retire at 60. That's 10 years, so I've got a 10-year time horizon and should invest that way." Very wrong! Unless you want to run out of money, your time horizon is as long as you need your assets to last—usually your life or your spouse's (at least as long as both of you)—longer if you leave money to kids.

Even those who get that right usually err—they underestimate how long they'll live. Figure 10.1 shows median life expectancy as well as 75th and 95th percentile expectancies from IRS mortality tables. The X-axis shows current age. The Y-axis shows years past current age. The dashed line is median life expectancy—85 for a 65-year-old.

The average 65-year-old will live another 20 years—if you're average. Half live longer. If you're healthy and from a long-lived family, you may live much longer! Plus, you should assume on the long-lived side so you won't hit age 85 and run out of money. A healthy 65-year-old should plan on at least a 35-year time horizon. And life expectancy keeps rising. If you're young now, by the time you hit 65, median life expectancy will be much longer.

So? Longer means holding more stocks longer. Figure 10.2 shows how to think about equity exposure based on your time horizon. For time horizons greater than 15 years (like you), you want all-equity if this is your road to riches.

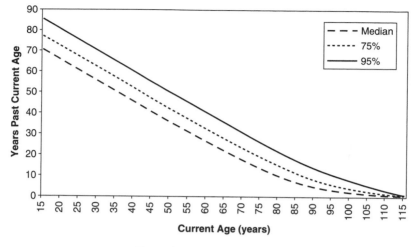

Figure 10.1 Life Expectancy

Source: IRS Revenue Ruling 2002 – 62 Mortality Table

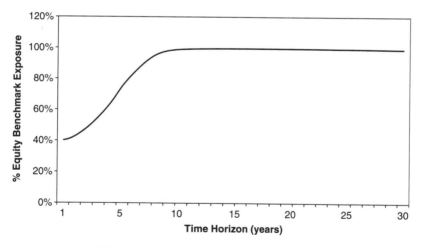

Figure 10.2 Benchmark and Time Horizon

Goal Confusion

Another factor where investors err is determining goals. Most can't articulate their goals in a few short words. We think we're unique (we are—just about like everybody else) and our goals must be too. No. The finance industry likes to confuse with complicated surveys and questionnaires—from which they can justify expensive services. There are only three prime investing goals:

1. *Growth*. You need your money to grow as much as possible to cover living expenses later, or stretch now to cover current cash flow needs. Or maybe you just want to leave a bundle to kids, grandkids, or albino snow leopards or whatever you're into.
2. *Income*. You need cash flow now or soon to cover living expenses, and you don't really care about growth so long as you get your cash flow.
3. *Growth and income*. Some combination of the first two.

One of these goals fits 99.993 percent of you. I didn't include *capital preservation*. It sounds nice! But it means you take no risk and get no growth—not helpful on this road. A true capital preservation strategy means losing money at inflation's pace. *Capital preservation and growth* is a finance industry fairytale. Not possible. Ever! For growth, you take risk, and capital preservation is total *absence* of risk. Someone selling you this strategy is conning you, whether he knows it or not. If you're on this road, the more equities you can stomach, the better.

THE RIGHT STRATEGY

So, you know you need stocks, preferably global, like the MSCI World. Now what? Invest like your benchmark, most of the time. Sounds simple, right? But I can't tell you how often I hear, "Yes, I need an equity benchmark, but stocks scare me *right now*. I'll be safer *for a while* with bonds and cash." People see being *safe* as having big allocations to cash or bonds. Bonds reduce volatility. That's safe—right?

Wrong! Cash and bonds when you need an all-equity benchmark is about as risky as can be! You are seriously deviating from your plan—increasing the odds you miss your goal, maybe by a lot. That's not safe, that's dangerous. If your benchmark is up 30 per-cent one year, but holding bonds you're up

Invest smarter by investing globally.

only 6 percent, you may be comfy but you lagged by 24 percent. You're behind now—huge. You need to *beat the market* by an average of 1 percent every year—tough to do—for the next 24 years to make up for that.

Go Global

Why the global emphasis? Isn't the S&P 500 enough? US stocks are only about 41 percent of the overall world if you include emerg-ing markets (and you generally should).[1] By not investing globally, you miss opportunities—and a chance to reduce volatility. Why? The broader your index, the smoother the ride.

Think of the super narrow and very volatile NASDAQ—it had a steep ride up in the late 1990s and a steep ride down since. Broader indexes are smoother, and nothing's broader than global. Plus, US and foreign stocks trade leadership, as shown in Figure 10.3—one leads

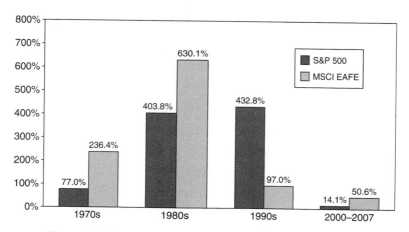

Figure 10.3 Domestic and Foreign Performance Are Cyclical
Source: Global Financial Data, Thomson Datastream, MSCI, Inc.[2] as of 12/31/2007

the other for years, by a bunch. You just don't know which will lead next. So own both by going global. If you *do* know which will be best; again, be an OPMer.

Passive or Active?

Now what? How much time do you want to spend on investing instead of focusing on your job to earn as much as you can so you save and then invest? If a lot, I'd say, "Really?" If you're on this road to get rich, you probably don't have the spare time to become expert at a very difficult activity where most folks fail. If you're determined, then read my 2007 *New York Times* best seller, *The Only Three Questions That Count*. It covers the turf.

Avoid anything suggesting a "magic formula" or "all you need is these types of stocks and not those." Most investing books lead you astray because they're largely based on faulty assumptions that one size, style, or type of stock is best forever. Untrue! (I give heavy detail why in my aforementioned book too.) Fact is, the only way to beat the market in the long term is knowing something others don't, repeatedly. And that is very hard to accomplish. Just a warning.

If time for you is scarce, as it should be on this road, what you do depends on how much money you have and whether you want to be passive or active. (*Passive* means getting market-like returns investing just like the market, *active* means trying to beat the market by varying from it somehow.) With less than $200,000, just be passive.

Many try to be active, but odds are 4-to-1 or more you lag markets—huge. Most who try fail. With under $200,000 you'd mostly use mutual funds. Many people do, but they're costly and tax inefficient. You can actually have a loss and receive a tax bill for *gains*—very perverse tax-wise. You own the fund but get taxed on realized gains inside the fund. Only in America! Overseas they don't do this.

Next, most funds lag the market. And there's no way to know which will and won't, so the odds are stacked heavily against you.

Diversify into a handful of active mutual funds and you are almost guaranteed to lag a passive strategy.

Doing Passive Right

You can do passive easily! As I write, the whole world market is about 41 percent US, 47 percent developed foreign, and 12 percent emerging markets.[3] Open a brokerage account somewhere cheap—I don't care where. A discount online broker is fine. Now, buy index funds or exchange traded funds (ETFs—pure passive slices of the market but taxed like a stock instead of a fund) to match the weights of the world. Buy about 41 percent of a cheap S&P 500 index fund or ETF; 47 percent Europe, Australasia, and Far East (EAFE); and 12 percent Emerging Markets. Buy more in the same percentages as you save. Then leave it alone. The idea is, like Chapter 8's Ron Popeil would say, "Set it and forget it." Hands off, for decades.

Make sure your funds have low expenses. For the S&P 500, you could buy the "Spider" ETF (stock symbol, SPY), an iShares ETF (IVV), or Vanguard's index fund (VFINX). Whatever you choose, make sure you buy a cheap, plain, vanilla ETF or index fund. Some fund families label pricier strategies as "index" funds. Don't be fooled. Be frugal. For EAFE, consider the iShares ETF (EFA), Vanguard's ETF (VEA), or their VDMIX. For Emerging Markets, you could buy the iShares ETF (EEM) or Vanguard's ETF (VWO). Your broker may have differing additional fees for these, or not. There's scant difference between ETFs and index funds except maybe 30 basis points of costs—pick the cheaper one.

Help or DIY?

Have much over $200,000? (Good for you! You're making the world a better place.) Now you belong in individual stocks. It's cheaper and more tax efficient—hands down. Folks rarely notice, but lump in expense ratios, broker fees, etc., and you can give away 2.5 to 3.5 percent *or more* on mutual funds.

If you're in the $200,000 to $500,000 range, you'll do less harm and be more efficient with an ETF strategy. (Remember, ETFs track indexes but act and trade like single stocks.) Under $500,000 you really can't diversify enough with individual stocks; but above $200,000, you can begin making country and sector decisions via ETFs that, done right, can add to your bottom line. And if you have over $500,000, you absolutely belong in individual stocks. No mutual funds! Too expensive for you.

But that question again: Passive or active? Passive beats most who try to manage money actively. To be passive, you want to own stocks best representing the world. To do this, you can go to www.tenroadstoriches.com and click on the Fisher 1500—this is a list of the world's 1,500 largest stocks by market cap, updated quarterly. You needn't own all 1,500—that would be very pricey—but you could buy the largest 100 or so and get good global coverage. To round out your portfolio, you could buy some percentage in a small cap, global ETF (like State Street's International Small Cap ETF—ticker GWX)—the cheapest way to go. That's passive. As you save more, keep buying in the same percentages. Otherwise, leave everything alone.

Whether you have a smaller asset pool in ETFs or have graduated to individual stocks, to be active and try to beat the market, you must hire a money manager. This isn't easy either. You must ask the right questions. You don't want anyone who suggests he "manage" a portfolio of mutual funds or "selects" a stable of discretionary money managers. All you're doing is layering cost on more cost, eating into return. Don't hire an intermediary—hire a decision maker who knows what he/she is doing. Few do. On the following page I list questions to ask the potential caretaker of your assets. Memorize them. Type them up. Take them with you.

Stick With Your Stocks, Unless . . .

Stocks sometimes fall a lot but most years they're up. For almost the entire bull market that started in 2003, folks griped about how

Great Questions to Ask a Money Manager

Don't have time or training to manage your own assets on this road to riches? You're not alone. But hiring money managers isn't trivial. These questions help assess whether you want to trust someone with your money.

Since asset allocation is the single most important decision made on my account . . .

- Who's responsible for making or recommending changes to my asset class mix? You? Someone else at your firm? Does the ultimate responsibility lie with me?
- Are my portfolio's reallocations primarily driven by your market views or my needs?
- How often is my portfolio allocation reviewed?
- How would my asset mix change if you forecast a bear market? A bull market?
- Who's responsible for making those forecasts? And how successful have they been?
- How has your recommended asset class mix changed over the last 10 years?
- What do you monitor, specifically, to forecast the market's direction?
- How does your market forecast affect your asset allocation recommendation?

Global market leadership has always and will continue to shift over time . . .

- Who makes changes to my portfolio's domestic versus foreign mix?
- How do you (or your firm) know when and how much to under- or overweight US stocks?
- How do you (or your firm) decide which countries to invest in and which to avoid?
- Who makes these decisions, and do they have a proven, verifiable track record?

Overallocating to the wrong equity style can seriously hamper performance . . .

- What is your firm's equity style? Large or small cap, growth or value? All?
- Will the style mix be static, or will there be ongoing changes?
- What makes you/your firm shift in or out of small or large stocks? Value? Growth?
- What makes you/your firm shift in or out of specific sectors?

The right manager's interests are fully aligned with mine . . .

- Are you a Registered Investment Adviser or a broker?
- Aside from what I pay directly, what other compensation do you receive (e.g., commissions

(Continued)

Great Questions to Ask a Money Manager (*Continued*)

from insurance products, incentives for selling stocks or bonds from your firm's inventory, spreads on the sale of bonds)?

■ Can you demonstrate your firm's money management capability? Can I see:

   ■ GIPS (accounting standard) compliant performance for your clients' accounts?

■ A public performance history of strategic market decisions?

■ How your decision making worked through the last bear market and recovery?

---

terrible stocks were and how bad they would do. Yet stocks rose each year: 2003, 2004, 2005, 2006, and 2007. Take most five-year periods and they'll be up too. The 1990s bull market ran nearly the entire decade, as did the 1980s. During all that time, you belonged in stocks. And you will in the future.

Believe me, staying in stocks is harder than it sounds. You will absolutely be tempted to bail when the market gets bumpy. Don't do it unless you're really, really, really darn sure stocks will fall a lot for a significant period. Ask yourself, what do you know about market timing that everyone else doesn't? My guess is nothing. Again, if you do you should start an OPM firm (see Chapter 7).

How can you know if it's a bear market? It's tough. It's certainly not when everyone expects one. Professionals are terrible at forecasting bear markets. The media's worse. So if folks are commonly predicting bad times, know you should own stocks. Again, to become a bear scholar, go read my 2007 book. If you won't do at least that much individual study, you shouldn't try to make these decisions yourself.

Bearing with Bears

Even if you suffer a bear market fully invested, it's ok. Stocks' long-term superior averages *include* bear markets. You needn't miss every bear market. True passive investors rigidly remain invested in good times and bad, no matter what! And they overwhelmingly beat those who time markets. To time markets you really must know what you're doing and precious few do. That's really hard.

One warning: Corrections are different from bear markets. They are short, sharp shocks—big, sudden drops designed to scare the pants off you. They can happen once or twice a year. Don't be fooled. Remain invested and it will be over in a few months. Real bear markets start slow and calm. People are optimistic after the peak. Anyone pessimistic then is seen as nuts. Stocks drop a little month-to-month, but nothing dramatic. Meanwhile, fundamentals unravel and few notice. Bear markets don't start violently—not even in 1929—if measured correctly. (See my 1987 book, revised in 2007, *The Wall Street Waltz*, on this.)

BONDS ARE RISKIER THAN STOCKS. SERIOUSLY

But wait! Can't stocks be down huge? Isn't it better to give up some return for a sleep-at-night factor? No. Remember, this is *The Ten Roads to Riches*, not *The Nine Roads to Riches and One Road to a Comfy Night's Sleep*. In the long-term, stocks aren't risky. In the short-term, they're volatile, which scares people. Ignore the caveman in you wanting to hide from scary things. Investors fail with long-term returns because they can't get this in their bones: The near term doesn't matter—hardly at all! The roads to riches are long. The following box shows the stock-versus-bond decision over 20 years. It's a no-brainer. Since 1926, there have been 63 20-year rolling periods. In 62, stocks beat bonds—927 percent to 243 percent! The one period bonds beat stocks, January 1, 1929 through December 31, 1948, saw the Great Depression and World War II. But bonds barely beat—1.4 to 1. So it's not worth the risk with bonds at all, long term.

The Stock-versus-Bond Decision

Stocks have outperformed bonds in 98 percent, or 62 of 63, 20-year rolling periods since 1926.

	Average Total Return Over 20-Year Rolling Periods
US Stocks	927%
US Bonds	243%

Stocks outperform bonds by a 3.8-to-1 margin.

In the one period bonds outperformed stocks—January 1, 1929 to December 31, 1948—it wasn't by much.

	Average Total Return in 20-Year Period When Bonds Outperformed Stocks
US Stocks	84%
US Bonds	115%

Bonds outperform stocks by a 1.4-to-1 margin.

Source: Ibbotson Analyst, Copyright 2008, Morningstar Inc.

Still unconvinced stocks are better? Most folks think bonds are safer. They are, if you just consider volatility risk over short periods. Fact: Given just a bit of time, stocks not only have far better returns, but more consistent ones. Figure 10.4 shows three-year trailing returns, adjusted for inflation and taxes, for bonds. Compare that with stock returns in Figure 10.5.

Given a bit of time, stocks have fewer negative periods than bonds. *Even supposedly safe US Treasuries have periods of multiple, consecutive negative returns.* And three-year returns over 10 percent are rare. Yes, stocks' negative periods are bigger, but they're blown away by the bigger, more consistently positive periods. If you have a longer time horizon (you do), stocks are less risky.

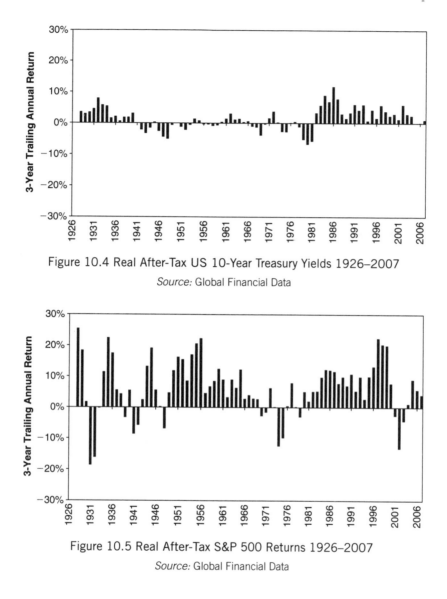

Figure 10.4 Real After-Tax US 10-Year Treasury Yields 1926–2007

Source: Global Financial Data

Figure 10.5 Real After-Tax S&P 500 Returns 1926–2007

Source: Global Financial Data

Maybe you're one of those nut jobs who believe "everything's different now" and the world's worse, and capitalism is horrible, and stocks are done. Forever! Nothing I can do for you but recommend you find a good therapist.

There are some people, who no matter what, won't ever hold 100 percent stocks. If this is you, that's fine! Just remember, when calculating for how much to save each year, use a lower return expectation. It will be tougher and slower to get rich on this road if you don't use the magical power of stocks' superior compounding returns. It can be done, though it takes longer. From our earlier example, to get $6 million over 30 years with less stocks, maybe you assume an average 7 percent return. That means saving $63,500 a year with a better-paying job. If you can, great! If not, maybe retire later, start saving earlier (you get to $6 million at 7 percent in 40 years saving only $30,000 a year). Or maybe die sooner. It's up to you.

Stocks, Stocks, and More Stocks . . .

I spend no time telling you how to pick winning stocks because, first, no one can teach you to do that in one chapter. For that, go to my first and fourth books (*Super Stocks* and *The Only Three Questions That Count*). Next, the decision whether to hold stocks, bonds, or cash, and in what percentage, *determines most of your portfolio return*. Stock-picking, done right, still doesn't add that much to your returns. My firm does that for a living. Trust me.

LIKE HETTY?

On this most common road there are few famous folks to learn from. One famous character and one of my favorites was too frugal—Hetty Green. Hetty didn't much do stocks. She rarely sought big returns—aiming for 6 percent (before income taxes existed) via mostly bonds. She only bought stocks at the height of panic when stocks were cheap. She had ice water for blood—she was sanguine during market crises that made somber men sob in fear.

In 1916 she died with about $100 million.[4] She saved every penny. Hetty didn't need higher returns. She was neurotically frugal. She didn't spend on clothes—she wore the same black dress endlessly. She sewed securities (before online trading!) into her dress and shawl for safekeeping—they kept her warmer.

She had her son resell her newspapers. She lived in a cold-water, unheated apartment. She could afford anything but ate mostly oatmeal and graham crackers. When her young son injured his leg sledding, she wouldn't pay for a doctor. She stood in line for a free clinic and used a homemade poultice. It didn't work. Her son's father (who divorced Hetty—her thrifty ways bugged him) stepped in to pay to have the gangrenous leg amputated. She wouldn't.

For a woman to build a portfolio over $100 million in those days wasn't rare—it was unheard of. Her financial prowess and shabby attire earned her the nickname "the Witch of Wall Street."

So no, you don't need stocks' superior returns on this road. But I bet you won't let your kid's leg get amputated. You can do it like Hetty, or you can ignore your fears and handle more stocks. Or you calculate what you'll need to save given a lower return expectation.

Reading for Dollars

There's thousands of books on saving and investing. Most aren't so good—it's the same advice over and over again. If the advice worked in the first place, you wouldn't need the same old advice regurgitated countless times—just the one book would suffice. But don't be discouraged. You can read the ones I recommended earlier or one of these.

- *The Ultimate Gift* by Jim Stovall. I gave a copy to each of my sons—a story with a key message—not only how to think about money, but how to be a better human being.
- *The Millionaire Next Door* by Thomas J. Stanley and William D. Danko. This one won't tell you how to save or invest, but it was pretty eye-opening for a lot of folks when it first came out. It's true: Most millionaires are Average Joes.

■ If you can't tell a stock from a bond from cattle futures, read *Investing for Dummies* by Eric Tyson. Here you'll learn how to open an account, navigate a broker, and start buying stocks.

■ *The Only Three Questions That Count: Investing by Knowing What Others Don't* by yours truly. Fact: Most investing books are bad for your health. They tell you to "only buy these stocks, not those" or imply there's some magic equation. Nonsense. You can't beat the market by doing some trick a million other people can read about. To beat the market, you must know something others don't. Tough to do! My book shows you how to figure out what most others don't know using just your noggin and some statistics. For that matter, try any of my other stock market books: *Super Stocks*, *The Wall Street Waltz*, or *100 Minds That Made the Market* (with a Hetty Green biography).

The Guide to **Saving and Investing**

This is the most commonly traveled road. Done right, it yields pretty consistent results. No, you won't be a mega-millionaire—unless you're neurotically frugal and live on oatmeal. But you can easily get to a few million and a pleasant retirement by following these steps:

1. *Get a decent job paying a good wage.* With a high-paying job, or one that will eventually pay well, you save more, more easily. Do what you love, but it's best if what you love pays above-average.

2. *Figure out how much you want/need.* Don't just save without a target. Think about what you want to live on. Don't forget to adjust for inflation.

3. *Calculate what you need to save each month.* Based on your goal, figure out what you must save. You don't have to save the same amount each month or year, particularly if you're young. You can create a plan to increase saving over time. But remember, money saved earlier is worth more later. Get started now.

4. *Now save.* How? Your choice: Be frugal. Earn more. Do whatever to keep up with your saving plan. Most books preach frugality—some folks can't do it. If that's you, get a raise.

5. *Make your money work.* On this road you must own stocks, pretty much always. Stocks have better long-term returns. If you're on this road, you have a long time to invest. If you just can't stomach volatility, plan accordingly. Reduce your return expectations. Save more. You can still get rich with less stocks if you plan well and are disciplined.

CONCLUSION

While I was writing this book, folks frequently said things like, "You shouldn't promote getting really rich. Not everyone can do that. Besides, that's like 'filthy' rich. It's still filthy."

First, it's simply false that *mega-rich* means *filthy* somehow. If you've read through to this conclusion, you've seen ample evidence of wealth being good. Believing it's not is a perverse social myth bred from ignorance and inadequate direct experience with the really rich, who are among the world's most fascinating and beneficent people. I firmly believe if we could make everyone really rich the world would be a far better place.

And maybe it's true everyone won't be rich, but it isn't clear that anyone can't be rich. You can. It's just up to you. There's no reason many more people can't reasonably try for a few or even many millions—without harming anyone. Problem is, the naysayers have less faith in you than I have. They think you shouldn't try, shouldn't reach. That you can't do it. I know you can. I know far more folks could be wealthy with a little planning and gumption, if they take the right road (or roads).

Maybe the wealth critics haven't seen as many people get rich as I have, so they don't know how possible and beneficent it is. Hard? Yes. Long hours? Skill? Toughness? Yes, yes, and yes! But impossible? No! I give you more credit than they do.

Forget the most famous rich! All 25,000 or so of my clients—all relatively wealthy people with money to invest—got rich on one of these roads. Most rode the Road More Traveled. But plenty others rode the different roads successfully. Some rode roads you may dislike—like marrying well or being a pirate—but folks who chose those roads know what they did and they feel just fine about it. I've seen them all build big wealth in ways the folks who think you shouldn't try can't fathom. So I know you can, too.

Now it's up to you. You've read the roads, seen examples, and learned what to do and lots of what not to do. Now choose. Remember, you needn't choose perfectly at first—you just need to try. Initial failure is common and doesn't imply a permanent dead end. Learn from failures, try again differently, fail, and try again. Your odds keep improving the more you try. And as you improve your odds in life, you become richer naturally. It just happens and it will for you. Thanks for your time reading and thinking about richness.

NOTES

PREFACE

1. The Associated Press, "Helmsley's Dog Gets $12 Million in Will," *Washington Post* (August 29, 2007), http://www.washingtonpost.com/wp-dyn/content/article/2007/08/29/AR2007082900491.html (accessed April 15, 2008).

2. Stephanie Strom, "Helmsley Left Dogs Billions in Her Will," *New York Times* (July 2, 2008), http://www.nytimes.com/2008/07/02/us/02gift.html?incamp=article_popular_3 (accessed July 21, 2008).

3. The Associated Press, "Two Arrested in Slaying of Illinois Lottery Winner," CBS2Chicago (July 29, 2005), http://cbs2chicago.com/topstories/local_story_210225424.html (accessed April 15, 2008).

4. Shaya Tayefe Mohajer, "Powerball Win: Fantasy or Nightmare?" *Washington Post* (September 14, 2007), http://www.washingtonpost.com/wp-dyn/content/article/2007/09/14/AR2007091400612.html (accessed May 20, 2008).

Chapter 1: The Richest Road

1. Matthew Miller, "The Forbes 400," *Forbes* (September 20, 2007), http://www.forbes.com/2007/09/19/richest-americans-forbes-lists-richlist07-cx_mm_0920rich_land.html (accessed April 21, 2008).

2. Ibid.

3. Small Business Association, "Frequently Asked Questions" (August 2007), http://www.sba.gov/advo/stats/sbfaq.pdf (accessed April 21, 2008).

4. Bureau of Economic Analysis.

5. See note 1.

6. George Raine, "LeapFrog Founder Steps Down," *San Francisco Chronicle* (September 2, 2004), http://www.sfgate.com/cgi-bin/article.cgi?file=/chronicle/archive/2004/09/02/BUG8M8I4K41.DTL&type=business (accessed April 21, 2008).

7. See note 1.

8. Ibid.

9. Bloomberg, as of 03/24/2008.

10. See note 1.

11. Ibid.

12. Samantha Critchell, "Resorts Recruit Top Designers to Outfit Ski Patrol," *USA Today* (December 20, 2006), http://www.usatoday.com/travel/destinations/ski/2006-11-28-ski-fashion_x.htm (accessed April 20, 2008).

13. Gwendolyn Bounds, Kelly K. Spors, and Raymund Flandez, "Psst! The Secrets of Serial Success," *Yahoo! Finance* (August 28, 2007), http://finance.yahoo.com/career-work/article/103425/Psst!-The-Secrets-Of-Serial-Success (accessed April 30, 2008).

14. "Franchising: New Power for 500,000 Small Businessmen," *Time* (April 18, 1969), http://www.time.com/time/magazine/article/0,9171,844780-1,00.html (accessed April 30, 2008).

15. H. Salt Fish & Chips locations found at http://www.hsalt.com/locations.htm.

16. See note 1.

17. Daniel Fisher, "Mr. Big," *Forbes* (March 13, 2006), http://www.forbes.com/global/2006/0313/024.html (accessed April 30, 2008).

18. See note 1.

19. See note 17.

20. Inflation calculator found at http://data.bls.gov/cgi-bin/cpicalc.pl.

21. Jackie Krentzman, "The Force Behind the Nike Empire," *Stanford Magazine* (January 1997), http://www.stanfordalumni.org/news/magazine/1997/janfeb/articles/knight.html (accessed April 30, 2008).

22. Ibid.

23. Benjamin Powell, "In Defense of 'Sweatshops,'" *The Library of Economics and Liberty* (June 2, 2008), http://www.econlib.org/library/Columns/y2008/Powellsweatshops.html (accessed June 3, 2008).

Chapter 2: Pardon Me, That's My Throne

1. Nancy Moran and Rodney Yap, "O'Neal Ranks No. 5 on Payout List, Group Says," *Bloomberg* (November 2, 2007), http://www.bloomberg.com/apps/news?pid=20601109&sid=aPxzn5U8zNBo&refer=home (accessed April 22, 2008).

2. Matthew Miller, "The Forbes 400," *Forbes* (September 20, 2007), http://www.forbes.com/2007/09/19/richest-americans-forbes-lists-richlist07-cx_mm_0920rich_land.html (accessed April 22, 2008).

3. Ibid.

4. Clive Horwood, "How Stan O'Neal Went from the Production Line to the Front Line of Investment Banking," *Euromoney* (July 2006), http://www.euromoney.com/article.asp?ArticleID=1042086 (accessed April 22, 2008).

5. Reuters, "Business Briefs," *New York Times* (March 11, 2006), http://query.nytimes.com/gst/fullpage.html?res=9902EED91331F932A25750C0A9609 C8B63 (accessed April 22, 2008).

6. About Duck Brand at http://www.duckproducts.com/about/.

7. See note 1.

8. "Oil: Exxon Chairman's $400 Million Parachute, Exxon Made Record Profits in 2005" *ABCNews* (April 14, 2006), http://abcnews.go.com/GMA/story?id=1841989 (accessed April 22, 2008).

9. Thomson Datastream. XOM return from December 31, 1993 to December 31, 2005.

10. Ibid.

11. Exxon Mobil Employment Data, http://www.exxonmobil.com/corporate/about_who_workforce_data.aspx (accessed April 22, 2008).

12. "The Not-So-Retired Jack Welch," *New York Times* (November 2, 2006), http://dealbook.blogs.nytimes.com/2006/11/02/the-not-so-retired-jack-welch/ (accessed April 22, 2008).

13. John A. Byrne, "How Jack Welch Runs GE," *BusinessWeek* (updated May 28, 1998), http://www.businessweek.com/1998/23/b3581001.htm (accessed April 22, 2008).

14. Thomson Datastream, December 31, 1980 through December 31, 2001.

15. Associated Press, "Fox News Hires Carly Fiornia, Ex-Chief of HP," *International Herald Tribune* (October 10, 2007), http://www.iht.com/articles/2007/10/10/business/fox.php (accessed May 20, 2008).

Chapter 3: Along for the Ride: Ride-Alongs

1. Matthew Miller, "The Forbes 400," *Forbes* (September 20, 2007), http://www.forbes.com/2007/09/19/richest-americans-forbes-lists-richlist07cx_mm_0920rich_land.html (accessed April 22, 2008).

2. Luisa Kroll, "The World's Billionaires," *Forbes* (March 5, 2008), http://www.forbes.com/lists/2008/10/billionaires08_Jeffrey-Skoll_PB9U.html (accessed May 20, 2008).

3. "Peter F. Chernin Profile," *Forbes* http://www.forbes.com/finance/mktguideapps/personinfo/FromPersonIdPersonTearsheet.jhtml?passedPersonId=935400 (accessed May 20, 2008).

4. News Corp, "The Best & Worst Managers of 2003: Peter Chernin," *BusinessWeek* (January 12, 2004), http://www.businessweek.com/magazine/content/04_02/b3865717.htm (accessed May 20, 2008).

5. See note 1.

6. Ibid.

7. David Weidner, "Pottruck Ousted from Schwab," *MarketWatch* (July 20, 2004), http://www.marketwatch.com/News/Story/Story .aspx?guid=%7B8F3F0844-2338-44F0-9209-9861036087D4%7D&siteid= mktw (accessed July 22, 2008).

8. J. P. Donlon, "Heavy Metal—Interview with Caterpillar CEO Donald Fites," *The Chief Executive* (September 1995), http://findarticles.com/p/ articles/mi_m4070/is_n106/ai_17536753 (accessed May 20, 2008).

9. "Moe S. Nozari Profile," *Forbes* http://www.forbes.com/finance/mktguide-apps/personinfo/FromPersonIdPersonTearsheet.jhtml?passedPersonId=87 8433 (accessed May 20, 2008).

10. "Dr. Joan E. Miller Profile," *Forbes* http://www.forbes.com/finance/mkt guideapps/personinfo/FromPersonIdPersonTearsheet.jhtml?passedPerson Id=1137833 (accessed May 20, 2008).

11. See note 1.

Chapter 4: Rich . . . And Famous

1. Matthew Miller, "The Forbes 400," *Forbes* (September 20, 2007), http:// www.forbes.com/lists/2007/54/richlist07_The-400-Richest-Americans_ Rank.html (accessed April 11, 2008).

2. Lea Goldman and Kiri Blakeley, "The Richest 20 Women in Entertainment," *Forbes* (January 18, 2007), http://www.forbes.com/digital-entertainment/2007/01/17/richest-women-entertainment-tech-media-cz_ lg_richwomen07_0118womenstars_lander.html (accessed April 11, 2008).

3. Ibid.

4. See note 1.

5. "Cuban Slammed with $25,000 Fine," *ABCNews* (June 20, 2006), http:// abcnews.go.com/Sports/story?id=2098577&page=1 (accessed April 11, 2008).

6. Associated Press, "Mavs Owner Serves Smiles and Ice Cream," *The Daily Texan* (January 17, 2002), http://media.www.dailytexanonline.com/media/ storage/paper410/news/2002/01/17/Sports/Mavs-Owner.Serves.Smiles .And.Ice.Cream-505789.shtml?norewrite200608240019&sourcedomain= www.dailytexanonline.com (accessed April 11, 2008).

7. Cathy Booth Thomas, "A Bigger Screen for Mark Cuban," *Time* (April 14, 2002), http://www.time.com/time/magazine/article/0,9171,230372-1,00 .html (accessed April 11, 2008).

8. Mike Morrison and Christine Frantz, *InfoPlease*, "Tiger Woods Timeline," http://www.infoplease.com/spot/tigertime1.html (accessed April 11, 2008).

9. Associated Press, "Madonna announces Huge Live Nation Deal," *MSNBC* (October 16, 2007), http://www.msnbc.msn.com/id/21324512/

(accessed June 9, 2008); Jeff Jeeds, "In Rapper's Deal, a New Model for Music Business," *New York Times* (April 3, 2008), http://www.nytimes.com/2008/04/03/arts/music/03jazy.html (accessed June 9, 2009).

10. U.S. Department of Labor, Bureau of Labor Statistics, "Actors, Producers, and Directors," (December 18, 2007), http://www.bls.gov/oco/ocos093.htm (accessed April 11, 2008).

11. "Dell Dude Now Tequila Dude at Tortilla Flats," *New York Magazine* (November 7, 2007), http://nymag.com/daily/food/2007/11/dell_dude_now_tequila_dude_at.html (accessed April 11, 2008).

12. Nicole Bracken, "Estimated Probability of Competing in Athletics Beyond the High School Interscholastic Level," *National Collegiate Athletic Association* (February 16, 2007), http://www.ncaa.org/research/prob_of_competing/probability_of_competing2.html (accessed April 11, 2008).

13. National Collegiate Athletic Association, "Major League Baseball General Information," http://www1.ncaa.org/membership/enforcement/amateurism/player_contacts/mlb_info/mlb_gen_info?ObjectID=25544&ViewMode=0&PreviewState=0 (accessed April 14, 2008).

14. See note 12.

15. Lea Goldman, Monte Burke, and Kiri Blakely, "The Celebrity 100," *Forbes* (June 14, 2007), http://www.forbes.com/2007/06/14/best-paid-celebrities-07celebrities_cz_lg_0614celeb_land.html (accessed April 14, 2008).

16. See note 2.

17. See note 15.

18. Jon Saraceno, "Tyson: 'My Whole Life Has Been a Waste,'" *USA Today* (June 2, 2005), http://www.usatoday.com/sports/boxing/2005-06-02-tyson-saraceno_x.htm (accessed April 14, 2008).

19. "Actor Gary Coleman Wins $1.3 Million in Suit Against His Parents and Ex-Advisor," *Jet* (March 15, 1993), http://findarticles.com/p/articles/mi_m1355/is_n20_v83/ai_13560059/pg_1 (accessed April 14, 2008).

20. Daniel Kreps, "Van Halen Reunion Tour Grosses $93 million," *Rolling Stone* (June 5, 2008), http://www.rollingstone.com/rockdaily/index.php/2008/06/05/van-halen-reunion-tour-grosses-93-million/ (accessed June 12, 2008).

21. Amy Fleitas and Paul Bannister, "Big Names, Big Debt: Stars with Money Woes," *Bankrate.com*, (January 30, 2004), http://www.bankrate.com/brm/news/debt/debt_manage_2004/big-names-big-debt.asp (accessed July 22, 2008).

22. See note 1.

23. "The Mad Man of Wall Street," *BusinessWeek* (October 31, 2005), http://www.businessweek.com/magazine/content/05_44/b3957001.htm (accessed April 11, 2008).

24. James J. Cramer, *Confessions of a Street Addict* (New York: Simon & Schuster, 2006).

25. New York City Department of Transportation, "Ferries & Buses," http://www.nyc.gov/html/dot/html/ferrybus/statfery.shtml (accessed April 14, 2008).

26. Advance Publications Corporate Timeline found at http://cjrarchives.org/tools/owners/advance-timeline.asp.

27. Geraldine Fabrikant, "Si Newhouse Tests his Magazine Magic," *New York Times* (September 25, 1988), http://query.nytimes.com/gst/fullpage.html?res=940DE0DE1439F936A1575AC0A96E948260 (accessed June 11, 2008).

28. See note 1.

29. Panache Report, "Three Richest Men in Hip-Hop For 2007," http://panachereport.com/channels/coverstories/jennifer.htm (accessed April 14, 2008).

30. Ibid.

31. Bill Johnson, Jr., "Jay-Z Stabbing Results in Three Years Probation," *Yahoo! News* (December 6, 2001), http://music.yahoo.com/read/news/12050127 (accessed April 14, 2008).

32. "Jay-Z Cashes in with Rocawear Deal," *New York Times* (March 6, 2007), http://dealbook.blogs.nytimes.com/2007/03/06/jay-z-cashes-in-with-200-million-rocawear-deal/ (accessed April 14, 2008).

33. See note 15.

34. See note 29.

Chapter 5: Marry Well—Really Well

1. Robert Frank, "Marrying for Love . . . of Money," *Wall Street Journal* (December 14, 2007), http://online.wsj.com/article/SB119760031991928727.html?mod=hps_us_inside_today (accessed April 14, 2008).

2. Internal Revenue Service.

3. Ibid.

4. U.S. Bureau of the Census at www.census.gov; Matthew Miller, "The Forbes 400," *Forbes* (September 20, 2007), http://www.forbes.com/lists/2007/54/richlist07_The-400-Richest-Americans_Rank.html (accessed April 14, 2008).

5. Marlys Harris, "How to Marry a Billionaire," *Money Magazine* (July 3, 2007), http://money.cnn.com/magazines/moneymag/moneymag_archive/2007/07/01/100116670/index.htm (accessed April 14, 2008).

6. Matthew Miller, "The Forbes 400," *Forbes* (September 20, 2007), http://www.forbes.com/lists/2007/54/richlist07_The-400-Richest-Americans_Rank.html (accessed April 14, 2008).

7. Ibid.

8. Fred Vogelstein, "How Mark Zuckerberg Turned Facebook into the Web's Hottest Platform," *Wired* (September 6, 2007), http://www.wired.com/techbiz/startups/news/2007/09/ff_facebook (accessed April 14, 2008).

9. See note 6.

10. Geoffrey Gray, "Tough Love," *New York Magazine* (March 19, 2006), http://nymag.com/relationships/features/16463/ (accessed April 14, 2008).

11. Geoffrey Gray, "The Ex-Wives Club," *New York Magazine* (March 19, 2006), http://nymag.com/relationships/features/16469/ (accessed April 14, 2008).

12. See note 10.

13. See note 11.

14. Catherine Mayer, "The Judge's Take on Heather Mills," *Time* (March 18, 2008), http://www.time.com/time/arts/article/0,8599,1723254,00.html (accessed April 14, 2008).

15. Forbes staff, "The 10 Most Expensive Celebrity Divorces," *Forbes* (April 12, 2007), http://www.forbes.com/2007/04/12/most-expensive-divorces-biz-cz_lg_0412celebdivorce.html (accessed April 14, 2008).

16. Davide Dukcevich, "Divorce and Dollars," *Forbes* (September 27, 2002), http://www.forbes.com/2002/09/27/0927divorce_2.html (accessed April 14, 2008).

17. OpenSecrets, "John Kerry (D-MA) Personal Financial Disclosures Summary: 2006," http://www.opensecrets.org/politicians/pfds.asp?CID=N00000245 (accessed April 14, 2008).

18. Mark Feeney, "Julia Thorne, at 61; Author, Activist was Ex-Wife of Senator Kerry," *Boston* Globe (April 28, 2006), http://www.boston.com/news/globe/obituaries/articles/2006/04/28/julia_thorne_at_61_author_activist_was_ex_wife_of_senator_kerry/ (accessed April 14, 2008).

19. Ralph Vartabedian, "Kerry's Spouse Worth $1 Billion," *San Francisco Chronicle* (June 27, 2004), http://www.sfgate.com/cgi-bin/article.cgi?file=/c/a/2004/06/27/MNG4T7CTRN1.DTL (accessed April 14, 2008).

20. See note 6.

21. Ibid.

22. Erika Brown, "What Would Meg Do," *Forbes* (May 21, 2007), http://www.forbes.com/business/global/2007/0521/058.html (accessed May 29, 2008).

23. See note 6.

24. S. Graham & Associates Website found at http://www.stedmangraham.com/about.html.

25. See note 6.

26. MSNBC staff, "Oprah Leaves Boyfriend Stedman Out of Her Will," *MSNBC* (January 9, 2008), http://www.msnbc.msn.com/id/22578526/ (accessed June 17, 2008).

27. Charles Kelly, "Drowning of Heiress Left Many Questions, Rumors," *The Arizona Republic* (May 23, 2002), http://www.azcentral.com/news/famous/articles/0523Unsolved-Buffalo23.html (accessed April 14, 2008).

Chapter 6: Steal It—Like a Pirate, But Legally

1. Peter Elkind, "Mortal Blow to a Once-Mighty Firm," *Fortune* (March 25, 2008), http://money.cnn.com/2008/03/24/news/companies/reeling_milberg.fortune/ (accessed April 23, 2008).

2. Jeffrey MacDonald, "The Self-Made Lawyer," *Christian Science Monitor* (accessed June 3, 2003), http://www.csmonitor.com/2003/0603/p13s01-lecs.html (accessed April 23, 2008).

3. American Bar Association.

4. "The Highest Pay per Hour for Associates," *AveryIndex* (2007), http://www.averyindex.com/2007_highest_paid_1.php (accessed April 18, 2008).

5. U.S. Department of Labor, Bureau of Labor Statistics, "Occupational Outlook Handbook," (December 18, 2007), http://www.bls.gov/oco/ocos053.htm (accessed April 23, 2008).

6. Saira Rao, "Lawyers, Fun & Money," *New York Post* (December 31, 2006), http://www.nypost.com/seven/12312006/business/lawyers__fun__money_business_saira_rao.htm?page=1 (accessed May 19, 2008).

7. Nathan Koppel, "Lawyers Gear up Grand New Fees: Hourly Rates Increasingly Hit $1,000, Breaching a Level Once Seen As Taboo," *Wall Street Journal* (August 22, 2007), http://online.wsj.com/article/SB118775188828405048.html?mod=hpp_us_whats_news (accessed April 23, 2008).

8. Towers Perrin, "Study Highlights First Decrease in US Tort Costs Since 1997," (December 2007), http://www.towersperrin.com/tp/showdctmdoc.jsp?url=Tillinghast/United_States/News/Spotlights/2007/2007_12_20_spotlight_tort_costs.htm (accessed June 11, 2008).

9. Michael A. Walters and Russel L. Sutter, "A Fresh Look at the Tort System," *Emphasis* (January 2003).

10. Ibid.

11. Matthew Miller, "The Forbes 400," *Forbes* (September 20, 2007), http://www.forbes.com/2007/09/19/richest-americans-forbes-lists-richlist07-cx_mm_0920rich_land.html (accessed April 23, 2008).

12. Steve Quinn, "High Profile: Joe Jamail," *Dallas Morning News* (November 30, 2003), http://www.joejamail.net/HighProfile.htm (accessed April 23, 2008).

13. Ibid.

14. Cheryl Pellerin & Susan M. Booker, "Reflections on Hexavalent Chromium: Health Hazards of an Industrial Heavyweight," *Environmental Health Perspectives* (vol. 108; September 2000), pp. A402 - A407 www.ehponline.org/docs/2000/108-9/focus.pdf (accessed April 23, 2008).

15. Walter Olson, "All About Erin," *Reason Magazine* (October 2000), http://www.reason.com/news/show/27816.html (accessed April 23, 2008).

16. Ibid.

17. Marc Morano, "Did 'Junk Science' Make John Edwards Rich?" *CNSNews* (January 20, 2004), http://www.cnsnews.com/ViewPolitics.asp?Page=%5C Politics%5Carchive%5C200401%5CPOL20040120a.html (accessed April 23, 2008).

18. "Parents File $150M Suit Against Naval Hospital," *News4Jax* (February 8, 2007), http://www.news4jax.com/news/10965449/detail.html (accessed April 23, 2008).

19. Jim Copland, "Primary Pass," *National Review* (January 26, 2004), http://www.nationalreview.com/comment/copland200401260836.asp (accessed April 23, 2008).

20. Robert Steyer, "The Murky History of Merck's Vioxx," *TheStreet.com* (November 18, 2004), http://www.thestreet.com/_more/stocks/biotech/10195104.html (accessed April 23, 2008).

21. Ibid.

22. Merck press release, "Merck Agreement to Resolve US VIOXX Product Liability Lawsuits," (November 9, 2007), http://www.merck.com/newsroom/press_releases/corporate/2007_1109.html (accessed April 23, 2008).

23. Peter Lattman, "Merck Vioxx By-the-Numbers," *The Wall Street Journal Law Blog* (November 9, 2007), http://blogs.wsj.com/law/2007/11/09/merck-expected-to-announce-485-billion-vioxx-settlement/ (accessed April 22, 2008).

24. American Bar Association, "Tort Law: Asbestos Litigation," http://www.abanet.org/poladv/priorities/asbestos.html (accessed March 6, 2008).

25. Patrick Moore, "Why I Left Greenpeace," *Wall Street Journal* (April 22, 2008), http://online.wsj.com/article/SB120882720657033391.html?mod=opinion_main_commentaries (accessed May 30, 2008).

26. Peter Elkind, "The Fall of America's Meanest Law Firm," *Fortune* (November 3, 2006), http://money.cnn.com/magazines/fortune/fortune_archive/2006/11/13/8393127/index.htm (accessed April 23, 2008).

27. Ibid.

28. Ibid.

29. Michael Parrish, "Leading Class-Action Lawyer Is Sentenced to Two Years in Kickback Scheme," *The New York Times* (February 12, 2008), http://www.nytimes.com/2008/02/12/business/12legal.html (accessed April 23, 2008).

30. Ibid.

31. Peter Elkind, "Mortal Blow to a Once-Mighty Firm," *Fortune* (March 25, 2008), http://money.cnn.com/2008/03/24/news/companies/reeling_milberg.fortune/ (accessed April 23, 2008).

32. Jonathan D. Glater, "Milberg to Settle Class-Action Case for $75 million," *International Herald Tribune*, June 18, 2008, http://www.iht.com/articles/2008/06/17/business/17legal.php (accessed June 17, 2008).

33. Editorial Staff, "The Firm," *Wall Street Journal*, June 18, 2008, http://online.wsj.com/article/SB121374898947282801.html?mod=opinion_main_review_and_outlooks (accessed June 19, 2008).

34. The Inner Circle of Advocates, http://www.innercircle.org/.

Chapter 7: OPM—Not Opium—Where Most of the Richest Are

1. © 2008 Morningstar, Inc. All Rights Reserved. The information contained herein: (1) is proprietary to Morningstar and/or its content providers; (2) may not be copied or distributed; (3) does not constitute investment advice offered by Morningstar; and (4) is not warranted to be accurate, complete, or timely. Neither Morningstar nor its content providers are responsible for any damages or losses arising from any use of this information. Past performance is no guarantee of future results. Use of information from Morningstar does not necessarily constitute agreement by Morningstar, Inc. of any investment philosophy or strategy presented in this publication.

2. Ibid.

3. Ibid.

4. Matthew Miller, "The Forbes 400," *Forbes* (September 20, 2007), http://www.forbes.com/2007/09/19/richest-americans-forbes-lists-richlist07-cx_mm_0920rich_land.html (accessed April 21, 2008).

5. Ibid.

6. Ibid.

7. See note 4.

8. Ibid.

9. "CEO Compensation," *Forbes* (May 3, 2007), http://www.forbes.com/lists/2007/12/lead_07ceos_CEO-Compensation-Diversified-Financials_9Rank.html (accessed April 16, 2008).

10. See note 4.

11. Robert Berner, "The Next Warren Buffet?" *BusinessWeek* (November 22, 2004), http://www.businessweek.com/magazine/content/04_47/b3909001_mz001.htm (accessed April 21, 2008).

12. Patricia Sellers, "Eddie Lampert: The Best Investor of His Generation," *Fortune* (February 6, 2006), http://money.cnn.com/2006/02/03/news/companies/investorsguide_lampert/index.htm (accessed April 16, 2008).

13. See note 11.

14. Ibid.

15. See note 12.

16. See note 11.

17. See note 4.

18. Andrew Ross Sorkin, "A Movie and Protesters Single Out Henry Kravis," *New York Times* (December 6, 2007), http://www.nytimes.com/2007/12/06/business/06equity.html?ex=1354597200&en=18531ee4bfaf9f2d&ei=5088&partner=rssnyt&emc=rss (accessed April 16, 2008).

19. Peter Carbonara, "Trouble at the Top," *CNN Money* (December 1, 2003), http://money.cnn.com/magazines/moneymag/moneymag_archive/2003/12/01/354980/index.htm (accessed April 16, 2008).

20. Andy Serwer, Joseph Nocera, Doris Burke, Ellen Florian, and Kate Bonamici, "Up Against the Wall," *Fortune* (November 24, 2003), http://money.cnn.com/magazines/fortune/fortune_archive/2003/11/24/353793/index.htm (accessed April 16, 2008).

21. James B. Stewart, "The Opera Lover," *New Yorker* (February 13, 2006), p. 108. http://www.newyorker.com/archive/2006/02/13/060213fa_fact_stewart (accessed April 16, 2008).

22. See note 4.

23. See note 21.

24. *Bloomberg News*, "Two Advisers Defrauded at Least 8 Clients, S.E.C. Says," (November 12, 2005).

25. Charles Gasparino and Susanne Craig, "A Lehman Brothers Broker Vanishes, Leaving Questions, and Losses, Behind," *Wall Street Journal* (February 8, 2002), http://online.wsj.com/article/SB1013123372605057920.html?mod=googlewsj (accessed May 19, 2008).

26. Ibid.

27. U.S. Securities and Exchange Commission, "Litigation Release No. 17590," (June 27, 2002), http://www.sec.gov/litigation/litreleases/lr17590.htm (accessed April 16, 2008).

28. U.S. Securities and Exchange Commission, "SEC To Recover about $4 Million in Settlements with the Girlfriend and Estranged Wife of Jailed Stockbroker Frank Gruttadauria," (January 21, 2004), http://www.sec.gov/litigation/litreleases/lr18549.htm (accessed April 16, 2008).

Chapter 8: Inventing Income

1. *3M History*, "The Evolution of the Post-It Note," http://www.3m.com/intl/hk/english/in_hongkong/postit/pastpresent/history_tl.html (accessed April 14, 2008).

2. Stacy Perman, "He Invents! Markets! Makes Millions!" *BusinessWeek* (October 3, 2005), http://www.businessweek.com/smallbiz/content/oct2005/sb20051003_862270.htm (accessed April 14, 2008).

3. "The World's Billionaires: JK Rowling," *Forbes* http://www.forbes.com/lists/2008/10/billionaires08_Joanne-(JK)-Rowling_CRTT.html (accessed April 14, 2008).

4. Matthew Miller, "The Forbes 400," *Forbes* (September 20, 2007), http://www.forbes.com/lists/2007/54/richlist07_The-400-Richest-Americans_Rank.html (accessed April 14, 2008).

5. The Staff, "Interview with Morris 'Sandy' Weinberg, Esq," *Jurist* (March 7, 2001), http://jurist.law.pitt.edu/pardonsex8.htm (accessed April 14, 2008).

6. Denise Rich, "Denise Rich Biography," http://www.deniserichsongs.com/bio.html (accessed April 14, 2008).

7. "Making Money with Your Music," *Taxi.com* http://www.taxi.com/faq/makemoney/index.html (accessed May 12, 2008).

8. Alison Leigh Cowan, "Ex-Advisor Sues Denise Rich, Claiming Breach of Contract," *New York Times* (August 17, 2002), http://query.nytimes.com/gst/fullpage.html?res=9502EED7153DF934A2575BC0A9649C8B63 (accessed May 12, 2008).

9. "Mr. Music, Back to His Old Haunts," *Sydney Morning Herald*, April 29, 2008.http://www.smh.com.au/news/arts/mr-music-back-to-his-old-haunts/2008/04/28/1209234762134.html (accessed June 23, 2008).

10. See note 4.

11. Marlys Harris, "Millionaires-in-Chief," *CNNMoney* http://money.cnn.com/galleries/2007/moneymag/0712/gallery.candidates.moneymag/index.html (accessed April 14, 2008).

12. Stephen Labaton, "Rose Law Firm, Arkansas Power, Slips As it Steps onto a Bigger Stage," *New York Times* (February 26, 1994), http://query.nytimes.com/gst/fullpage.html?res=9A05E2DB163AF935A15751C0A962958260&sec=&spon=&pagewanted=all (accessed April 14, 2008).

13. The Council of State Government's Survey January 2004 and January 2005.

14. Dan Ackman, "Bill Clinton: Good-Bye Power, Hello Glory," *Forbes* (June 25, 2002), http://www.forbes.com/2002/06/25/0625clinton.html (accessed May 19, 2008).

15. John Solomon and Matthew Mosk, "For Clinton, New Wealth in Speeches," *Washington Post* (February 23, 2007), http://www.washingtonpost.com/wp-dyn/content/article/2007/02/22/AR2007022202189.html (accessed April 14, 2008).

16. Assume half their income saved 1979 through 1992 ($117,500) then $100,000/year 1993–2000, assuming 10 percent ARR.

17. Ken Dilanian, "Clinton's Income: $109M since 2000," *USA Today* (April 4, 2008), http://www.usatoday.com/news/politics/election2008/2008-04-04-clinton-income_N.htm (accessed May 12, 2008).

18. See note 15.

19. Stephanie Smith, CRS Report for Congress, "Former Presidents: Federal Pension and Retirement Benefits," (March 18, 2008), www.senate.gov/reference/resources/pdf/98-249.pdf (accessed April 15, 2008).

20. Ibid.

21. Ibid.

22. Ibid.

23. See note 4.

24. Ida A. Brudnick, "Salaries of Members of Congress: A List of Payable Rates and Effective Dates, 1789–2008," *The Library of Congress* (February 21, 2008), http://www.senate.gov/reference/resources/pdf/97-1011.pdf (accessed May 19, 2008).

25. U.S. Census Bureau 2006.

26. "Salaries for Members of Congress, Supreme Court Justices, and the President," *National Taxpayers Union* (January 2008), http://www.ntu.org/main/page.php?PageID=23 (accessed May 19, 2008).

27. "Nancy Pelosi (D-Calif) Personal Financial Disclosures Summary: 2006," *OpenSecrets.org* http://www.opensecrets.org/pfds/CIDsummary.php?CID=N00007360&year=2006 (accessed May 14, 2008).

28. Patrick J. Purcell, "Retirement Benefits for Members of Congress," *Congressional Research Service* (February 9, 2007), http://www.senate.gov/reference/resources/pdf/RL30631.pdf (accessed May 19, 2008).

29. "Herb Kohl (D-Wis) Personal Financial Disclosures Summary: 2006," *OpenSecrets.org* http://www.opensecrets.org/pfds/CIDsummary.php?CID=N00004309&year=2006 (accessed May 14, 2008).

30. See note 11.

31. "John Kerry (D-MA) Personal Financial Disclosures Summary: 2006," *OpenSecrets.org* http://www.opensecrets.org/pfds/CIDsummary.php?CID=N00000245&year=2006 (accessed May 14, 2008).

32. "Jane Harman (D-Calif) Personal Financial Disclosures Summary: 2006," *OpenSecrets.org* http://www.opensecrets.org/pfds/CIDsummary.php?CID=N00006750&year=2006 (accessed May 14, 2008).

33. "Jeff Bingaman (D-NM) Personal Financial Disclosures Summary: 2006," *OpenSecrets.org* http://www.opensecrets.org/pfds/CIDsummary.php?CID=N00006518&year=2006 (accessed May 14, 2008).

34. See note 11.

35. "Olympia Snowe (R-Maine) Personal Financial Disclosures Summary: 2006," *OpenSecrets.org*, http://www.opensecrets.org/pfds/CIDsummary.php?CID=N00000480&year=2006 (accessed May 14, 2008).

36. Sean Loughlin and Robert Yoon, "Millionaires Populate US Senate," *CNN* (June 13, 2003), http://www.cnn.com/2003/ALLPOLITICS/06/13/senators.finances/ (accessed April 15, 2008).

37. "Richard C. Shelby (R-AL) Personal Financial Disclosures Summary: 2006," *OpenSecrets.org* http://www.opensecrets.org/pfds/CIDsummary.php ?CID=N00009920&year=2006 (accessed May 14, 2008).

38. "Rodney Frelinghuysen (R-NJ) Personal Financial Disclosures Summary: 2006," *OpenSecrets.org* http://www.opensecrets.org/pfds/CIDsummary.php ?CID=N00000684&year=2006 (accessed April 15, 2008).

39. Miles Weiss, "Gore Invests $35 Million for Hedge Funds with EBay Billionaire," *Bloomberg* (March 6, 2008), http://www.bloomberg.com/apps/ news?pid=20601070&sid=a7li9Nhmhvg0&refer=politics (accessed April 15, 2008).

40. Patrick J. Reilly, "Jesse Jackson's Empire," *Capital Research Center* http:// www.enterstageright.com/archive/articles/0401jackson.htm (accessed April 15, 2008).

41. Steve Miller and Jerry Seper, "Jackson's Income Triggers Questions," *The Washington Times*, February 26, 2001.

42. Walter Shapiro, "Taking Jackson Seriously," *Time* (April 11, 1988), http:// www.time.com/time/magazine/article/0,9171,967157-1,00.html (accessed May 22, 2008).

Chapter 9: Trumping the Land Barons

1. National Association of Realtors, Average Single Family Home Price.

2. Matthew Miller, "The Forbes 400," *Forbes* (September 20, 2007), http:// www.forbes.com/lists/2007/54/richlist07_Donald-Trump_U5WX.html (accessed May 20, 2008).

3. Department of Housing and Community Development, State of California, "Median and Average Home Prices and Rents for Selected California Counties," http://www.hcd.ca.gov/hpd/hrc/rtr/ex42.pdf (accessed May 20, 2008).

4. Federal Housing Finance Board, "National Average Contract Mortgage Rate," http://www.fhfb.gov/GetFile.aspx?FileID=4328 (accessed May 20, 2008).

5. City Data, "San Mateo County, California (CA)," http://www.city-data .com/county/San_Mateo_County-CA.html (accessed May 20, 2008).

6. Ibid.

7. See note 2.

8. Edward F. Pazdur,"An Interview with Tim Blixseth, Chief Executive Officer, The Blixseth Group," *Executive Golfer*, http://www.executivegolf-ermagazine.com/cupVII/article3.htm (accessed May 20, 2008).

9. Ibid.

10. See note 2.

11. Alan Finder, "Koch Disputed on a Benefit to Developer," *New York Times* (January 16, 1989), http://query.nytimes.com/gst/fullpage.html?res=950 DE5D9133FF935A25752C0A96F948260&sec=&spon=&pagewanted=all (accessed May 20, 2008).

12. Steve Rubenstein, "Ex-Armory Turns Into Porn Site," *San Francisco Chronicle* (January 13, 2007), http://www.sfgate.com/cgi-bin/article.cgi?f=/c/a/2007/01/13/BAG0INI8PD1.DTL (accessed May 20, 2008).

13. George Andres, "For Tech Billionaire, Move to Nevada Proves Very Taxing," *Wall Street Journal* (July 17, 2006).

14. Arthur B. Laffer and Stephen Moore, "Rich States, Poor States, ALEC-Laffer State Economic Competitive Index," American Legislative Exchange Council Washington, DC (2007), http://www.alec.org/am/pdf/ALEC_Competitiveness_Index.pdf?bcsi_scan_23323C003422378 C=0&bcsi_scan_filename=ALEC_Competitiveness_Index.pdf (accessed May 20, 2008).

15. Ibid.

16. Ibid.

Chapter 10: The Road More Traveled

1. Thomson Datastream, as of 05/31/2008.

2. MSCI. The MSCI information may only be used for your internal use, may not be reproduced or redisseminated in any form and may not be used to create any financial instruments or products or any indices. The MSCI information is provided on an "as is" basis and the user of this information assumes the entire risk of any use made of this information. MSCI, each of its affiliates and each other person involved in or related to compiling, computing or creating any MSCI information (collectively, the "MSCI Parties") expressly disclaims all warranties (including, without limitation, any warranties of originality, accuracy, completeness, timeliness, non-infringement, merchantability and fitness for a particular purpose) with respect to this information. Without limiting any of the foregoing, in no event shall any MSCI Party have any liability for any direct, indirect, special, incidental, punitive, consequential (including, without limitation, lost profits) or any other damages.

3. See note 1.

4. Almanac of American Wealth, "Wealthy Eccentrics," *Fortune* http://money .cnn.com/galleries/2007/fortune/0702/gallery.rich_eccentrics.fortune/2. html (accessed May 20, 2008).

INDEX